NORTHAMPTONSHIRE
IN THE
FIRST WORLD WAR

MIKESH MISTRY

Northamptonshire in the First World War

The Northampton War Book Publishing Ltd

First published in Great Britain in 2022 by
The Northampton War Book Publishing Ltd

A CIP record for this book is available from the British Library

ISBN: 978-1-7391345-5-6

Typesetting and design by Megan Daniels

Cover design by Megan Daniels (Bergamot Brown Illustrations)

Printed by Stephens & George Ltd

Dedicated to my mum and uncle.

It matters not how strait the gate,
How charged with punishments the scroll,
I am the master of my fate,
I am the captain of my soul.

Also to the men of the Northamptonshire Regiment who lived this
book & all those who suffered from the pain caused by this war.

CONTENTS

LIST OF ILLUSTRATIONS

ACKNOWLEDGEMENTS

This book is the culmination of over six fragmented years of research and writing. When the idea of writing this book first came to me, as a fresh graduate from the University of St Andrews exploring various possibilities for my next steps, I'll admit I didn't realise how hard it would be, and just how much work would be involved. Countless late nights, endless hours spent in dusty archives, the frustration at dead ends, organising masses of material, precisely selecting from said masses, writing chapters, rewriting chapters, proofing, agonising over book dimensions, interviewing relatives of soldiers ... the list is a long one.

I also didn't realise how rewarding this long journey would be. My initial plan was for this book to be a much smaller, focused project. I can't pinpoint the exact moment this changed, but after learning more about the men of the Northamptonshire Regiment, their stories and suffering, and of course the remarkable courage of those back in Northamptonshire in their determination to carry on, I knew if I was going to do this, I would have to do it right.

While this journey has been a long one, it has not been a lonely one. Looking back at everyone who has helped, I find it remarkable how long the list is.

First and foremost, I wish to express my deep gratitude to Megan Daniels, from London, for designing this book. Throughout this whole process, right from the beginning in 2014, Megan has always been there. Whether it was diligently putting in the hours meticulously designing this book, editing all the pictures, or scrutinising every detail to the millimetre, Megan has been rock solid. I first met Megan while a student at the University of St Andrews, and it is one of my greatest joys that she has brought her artistic talents to this book. I vividly remember the first serious draft Megan produced; the whole book became so real, and all those hours spent in the archives and tiring hours writing were suddenly brought to life. That design work is not Megan's full-time job but rather a hobby is remarkable. It's sheer dumb luck that I have a friend as talented as Megan who was willing to do this with me for so long. It's been one heck of a journey, but we finally got there. She should be very proud of what she has achieved – I know I am of her. Thank you for doing this with me, Megan.

I am also grateful to have had the remarkable abilities of my friend Alec Christie at my disposal, primarily helping in researching this book and proof-reading. A student at the University of St Andrews when I started this book, Alec is now a research fellow in biodiversity conservation at Downing College, Cambridge. That he was able to comprehend and provide excellent analysis of historical documents speaks volumes about his talents.

I am deeply indebted to Merle Read, from Glasgow, for her professional editorial assistance. Extremely professional, always meeting tight deadlines, and going beyond what could be reasonably expected, this book is infinitely better after having Merle's eagle eye cast over it. By the same token, I am very thankful to Maureen Smart, from Rugby, for her outstanding research abilities and astute suggestions which are present throughout this book. A special thanks to Dave Morgan from Stagecoach in Northampton for making the chance introduction to Maureen.

Annalise Thomlinson, from High Wycombe, was a somewhat late arrival to this book. Nevertheless, her dedication in testing 'lockdown' circumstances to performing a detailed proof of many chapters has resulted in a much-improved readability and removal of dozens of small errors.

This book would not have been possible without the professionalism of everyone at the Northamptonshire Record Office in Wootton, Northampton, probably the most under-appreciated asset in the county. If the Record Office is a historian's treasure chest, the staff are the key needed to open it. Over the years, through seemingly inconsequential small talk, new avenues of research have been opened. While, I'm sure, this has added to the time taken to write the book, I am confident it is all the better for it. In particular, thank you to Andy, Anjie, Daniel, Jenny, Lauren, Matthew and Victoria. Additionally, I appreciate the Northampton Museum and Northampton Central Library for access to their resources.

I've been privileged to have had very sympathetic employers who have supported my efforts in this book as well as my professional development. A big thank you to Steve Burd, my former managing director at Stagecoach Midlands, for always believing in me ever since he offered me a job in somewhat improbable circumstances. The job brought me to Northampton and helped enable further research for this book, but it is the kindness and generosity I was consistently shown that I'm most thankful for – also for letting me put my posters in every single Stagecoach bus in Northamptonshire at one point. I'd also like to thank my managers at Stagecoach, Chris Simes and Patrick Stringer, for their support and understanding over the years, and for never reprimanding me if I arrived in the office slightly late or slightly scruffy after staying up late working on this book (or playing tennis late at night – it was 50:50 with the book). Finally, I'm grateful to David Edwards, Matthew Coulson and Victoria Williams at the Department for Transport who have been a solid source of encouragement these last few years.

On that note, a special mention to Rushmere Tennis Club, Northampton, for distributing my request asking for relatives of former soldiers to get in touch. As a result the club coach, Maddee Blair, put me into touch with her brother, Stuart Blair, in New Zealand. Stuart kindly provided me with his own research about his ancestors Corporal Albert Charles Thompson and Lance-Corporal Henry Thompson, and constantly responded to my numerous follow-up queries. Both Thompsons are featured in the book.

I have been blessed with many volunteers who have dedicated hours of their time to improve this book, through proof-reading or research suggestions. My thanks to Marcheta Solomon, from Northampton; Ann-Marie Helsdown, from the Forest of Dean; Niall Cherry, from Lancashire for their proofing. My thanks to Damian Hobeanu, from Northampton, for his assistance with many of my IT-related requests and using his considerable talents to help streamline certain important tasks.

I am thankful to all those who have also provided me information on their ancestors, either in person, by telephone or via emails. While I have endeavoured to write in a reference regarding each of their ancestors, this has not always been possible, although their information has always been appreciated. Thank you to John Draper, Lynda Rich, Pat Twiselton, Stephen Cooper, Dianne Gadsden, Mary Driver, Jan White, Mark Frost and Jan Alibone. To the Pines Surgery, Kingsthorpe, Northampton, my thanks for putting up with the inconvenience of my bike during the very early months of this book's research process.

I also appreciate the encouragement provided by Kristy Ettles from Elgin, Scotland, for proof-reading the first chapter with an advanced design, offering much-needed assurance and for much-needed distraction during the writing of the book. My thanks also to my friend Kyle Gardener from Ullapool, Scotland, for his timely answers to my sporadic proofing questions. My thanks are also due to Deborah Starkey for her proofing help and very kind words.

Many others have helped bring the book to life, and my apologies if anyone feels forgotten.

Finally, I must thank my parents for their enduring support and the rest of my immediate family for their encouragement and belief over the years.

I hope this book does them proud.

Northamptonshire in the First World War

Figure 1.1: The 1st Battalion of the Northamptonshire Regiment march in formation as King George V looks on. Photograph taken on 22nd June, 1914. In a few months, this battalion was among the first in the country to leave for France.

Miss Talbot.   Parker   Mollie   Sybil   Daniels
    Miss Panther.   Miss Bland.   Ellie.

Figure 1.2: Nurses and soldiers help in the kitchen at Wellingborough VAD hospital; c1915.
Figure 1.3: A woman working on a six-inch howitzer exploding shell in a munitions plant in Abbey Works, Northampton; women accounted for 65% of the company's workforce at the height of the war as men were sent into the army, representing a sudden breakdown in traditional gender roles.

CHAPTER ONE

START OF WAR 1914

"This is not the occasion, nor have I the time, to make an impassioned address. You have been called out by your King to defend your King and your country. You have tremendous traditions of heroism left you by your predecessors; traditions of duty and discipline and endurance which have characterised the regiment in the past. You have to carry on those traditions. I ask you now to remember them. And to be true to your inheritance. I wish you God-speed and every possible luck in what lies before you."

Earl Spencer addressing the 4th Northamptonshire Battalion - Saturday 15th August 1914

"Armageddon has begun."

The Northampton Mercury, 7th August 1914

IT WAS THE SUMMER LIKE THE summer before it; children played happily in the streets, families flocked to beaches for a rest under the sun and quintessential village fêtes served up the usual combination of antiques, egg-and-spoon races and Victoria sponge. People headed to baby shows, enjoyed local cricket matches and summer weddings. To a tourist viewing these scenes all around Northamptonshire, this was a county at ease, at peace with itself.

This tranquil scene, however, hid dangers lurking below the surface. Dark clouds that normally interrupt an English summer this time engulfed the whole of Europe with the spectre of war — for this is Northamptonshire in July 1914. For many in society, the joys of summer were tempered by the escalating political events dominating the continent. Nor was it only the adults that had an anxious summer; the children of Wellingborough Winstanley Road Infant School were shocked to learn that their popular headmistress, Miss Lucy Webb, had been killed on 8th June after being struck by a car. For many of these children, this was their first experience of death, a situation their young minds would become very familiar with in just a few short months.

One hundred years ago, Northamptonshire was a much different place to now. A population of 350,000 lived in the area compared to over 730,000 in 2018. The people mainly worked in agricultural jobs or in the thriving boot and shoe industry. There were, however, some similarities with modern society; newspaper pages were filled with economic troubles as columns lamented price rises while people pushed themselves ever further into debt by profligate spending. The editor of *The Northampton Independent*, Mr W. H. Holloway, rebuked those in Northampton who did not know that "there is a time to save and a time to spend", and because "their money dribbles away and at holiday times the pawnbrokers and money-lenders have to come to their rescue". Another striking similarity with modern times is the headmaster of Delapre Infant School bemoaning the low attendance at the start of term as "several boys are abroad on holiday with their parents".

Since July, residents of Northamptonshire had been subject to a plethora of articles regarding Europe arming up for war. It is a common sentiment to hear that Britons in 1914 thought the war, if it arrived, 'would be over by Christmas'. In Northampton, there seems to be little evidence of this. When war was declared at 11pm on 4th August, after an ultimatum issued by Prime Minister Asquith's government to Germany expired, the following edition of *The Northampton Independent* reported that:

> "*The shadow of war which threatens to be the worst the world has seen hangs heavily upon us. The great gravity of the crisis facing us is reflected on every side. One can think of nothing but the War ... Even at the county cricket match, exciting as it was, holidaymakers sat as though they were participating in a drama, combined with a feeling that they ought to be doing something else in this hour of the nation's need.*"

Figure 1.4: Thousands of men across the county worked in shoe factories; photograph the Union Co-Operative Boot & Shoe Protective Society Ltd; Kettering c1910.

The British government, anticipating Germany's refusal to agree to their demands, had ordered the mobilisation of the British Expeditionary Force (BEF) earlier in the day. The 1st Northamptonshire Battalion received their orders to prepare for war in early evening. The battalion's history dates from 1741 when it was raised as the '48th Regiment of the Foot' during the War of the Austrian Succession. The battalion, known simply as the 48th, had won a famous victory against Napoleon's army during the Battle of Talavera in 1809; its sister battalion, the 58th Regiment, was raised in 1755 during the Seven Years' War.

In 1782, as part of an army scheme to aid recruitment, battalions without a royal title were given a county title. Both the 48th and 58th were awarded Northamptonshire and in 1881 were merged to form the Northamptonshire Regiment, affectionately known as The Steelbacks. In 1914, the BEF contained some 160,000 professional soldiers in six divisions, with the 48th belonging to the 1st Division as part of its 2nd Brigade. Consequently, the Northamptons would be among the first British soldiers to reach the shores of France with objectives to repel the German invasion. During the course of the war, many new battalions would be raised in the Northamptonshire Regiment as the demand for more soldiers seemed almost infinite.

The immediate consequence of the outbreak of war in Northampton, like much of the country, was a strange concoction of normality and panic. Sports events still continued even if spectators looked subdued and distracted, while the 32nd Annual Flower Show at Castle Ashby attracted huge crowds with over 1,200 entries. On the other hand, crowds rushed to panic-buy large quantities of food. In the week after the declaration of war, the corn market at Northampton was completely sold out, and prices of common food items such as sugar, butter and eggs all doubled.

The advent of the self-service shop had not yet arrived – it was not until 1950 when Baron Sainsbury imported the self-service model to the UK from America – and grocery shops were forced to shut early in order to cope with the overwhelming number of orders from customers. Crowds congregated outside closed shops anxiously, waiting for them to reopen. Those who went through unofficial channels did not fare much better, as it was reported that hoarders were refusing to sell their stocks despite price hikes. In an attempt to stem the tide, the Home Office immediately issued a statement to reassure people that the country had ample supplies of food.

Several editorials in *The Northampton Independent* also urged residents that there was no need to panic-buy. In a scathing piece, the editor severely criticised wealthy residents who had inundated stores with huge orders "relieving their own anxieties by adding to those of the poor". Very early on, it became clear that this war would affect all, rich and poor, and that all sections in society would have to play their part. It was said: "Liberals, Conservatives, capitalists, workmen, democrats, and aristocrats" would all be united in a "common peril that only hushes party feeling but makes us all akin." Clearly, it appeared in Northampton, or at least at *The Northampton Independent*, no one was under any illusions that the war would be 'over by Christmas'.

In a dark period which required the collective efforts of everyone, those who were not playing their part were angrily called out. In what would not be out of place in many of today's newspapers, the editor of *The Northampton Independent* said the level of drunkenness displayed in town was "disgraceful and depressing", before adding "had these beery brutes been forced to undergo National Service, they would have learnt something of what war means and the need of sober discipline in these dark days."

The country and government, aware of the high probability of war over the summer, moved quickly. *The Northampton Independent* revealed that many residents had been visited by a post office engineer who proceeded to dismantle their equipment to prevent the "leakage of secret service messages". On 8th August, just four days after declaring war on Germany, the House of Commons passed the Defence of the Realm Act (DORA), which gave the government sweeping new powers. Very quickly, press freedom was curtailed, the police were given extra authority, pubs saw their licensing hours reduced and were instructed to water down beer, and the government could take control of land and factories for war purposes. This act, passed without debate in Parliament, was revised over the war, each time giving the state more control and powers.

Perhaps most controversially, DORA allowed for the imprisonment of German nationals of military age. A site in Northamptonshire, in the sleepy village of Eastcote, was soon chosen for what would become a Prisoner of War Camp. The site in Eastcote was never actually intended to become a prisoner camp; one of the founders, former Liberal MP Joseph Havelock Wilson, was motivated to provide a safe, humane camp for German naval men. However, Eastcote (latterly known as Pattishall Prisoner of War Camp) would become one of the largest prisoner of war camps in the country, housing over 4,000 Germans at its peak.

Along with an upsurge of patriotism, there was an immediate rise in anti-German sentiment, as Germans in Britain began to be viewed with great suspicion. However, what was true in Britain was also true elsewhere on the continent. In the days after the British declared war, Mr and Mrs Wilkinson of Northampton were arrested while holidaying in Belgium. The Belgian authorities were on high alert after the German Army had invaded the country on 4th August in what became known as 'The Rape of Belgium'. At Namur, the pair were suddenly surrounded by soldiers and sent to a police station where they were subject to a lengthy interrogation on suspicion of being German spies. Eventually, the unfortunate couple were released and sent to a train station in the presence of soldiers tasked with protecting their carriage from the public. Once safely back in Northampton, *The Northampton Independent* ran a story on 15th August about the incident, going as far as printing a picture of Mrs Wilkinson – a well-known competitive swimmer in Northampton – claiming the woman's appearance "is not unlike a certain type of German" and thus explains "the cause of the trouble...".

Figure 1.5: *The Northampton Independent*'s article on a Northampton woman being mistaken for a German.

It was not just Namur that had a curious incident with suspected spies. Just one week later, the same paper reported that a possible German spy had been living in Northampton.

The individual in question is described as a young, unnaturalised man living on Kettering Road with a "particularly suspicious character". Eyebrows were raised when the man went to a local bank and asked for change in German gold. The bank was unable to meet his request, so he accepted the British currency offered and disappeared. The authorities, visiting his house, found wireless apparatus fixed on his roof for which he did not have the required licence. The paper suggested he might have received information from the equipment and urged readers to "be more cautious and on our guard against aliens within our gates". In over a month's time, Northampton would be asking itself just how literally this advice should be taken.

Meanwhile the 1st Northamptons, suited and booted, were at full strength with around 1,000 men. On 12th August, after joining their brigade, they left Blackdown, near Aldershot, and marched to Frimley station and entrained for Southampton. Here they embarked on *SS Galeka* and set sail for an unknown destination in France. The following day the battalion arrived in Le Havre and were greeted by rapturous crowds of the French singing 'It's a Long Way to Tipperary'. Such welcoming sights would become very familiar to the 1st Northamptons over the coming weeks as the battalion journeyed through French villages and towns, making its way to the battle line in eastern France. On 19th August, they billeted at Esquéhéries; such was the local gratitude that the town had an orchestra entertain the men throughout the night, finally ending by playing 'God Save the King' twenty times in succession.

Figure 1.6: The Northampton Independent published one of the last photos of the 1st Northamptons on 22nd August 1914, noting many of the men pictured wore "what appeared to be monocles in their eyes" but were actually their identity discs.

Despite the country being woefully unprepared for a major European war, when it arrived Northamptonshire quickly sprang into action, with several charities, hospitals and volunteers all gearing up for the war effort. By mid-August, the Northampton Red Cross branch was working in conjunction with St. John Ambulance Association. Work had already started to collect funds, enrol nurses, and prepare hospitals and convalescent homes.

Figure 1.7: For many residents, the reality of war quickly became apparent as 17,000 Welsh soldiers descended on Northampton. The pictures show the Royal Welsh Fusiliers in October 1914 marching down Wellingborough Road, Northampton, as they prepare to go to France and billeting in local houses when they first arrived. Notable in the bottom photograph is the square tower belonging to St Edmund's Church in the top right which was demolished in 1979, although the churchyard still exists. Many of the other buildings seen here have fared better over the years; the building in the middle of the picture with its distinctive curved turret is now home to a public house.

By the end of the month, no one could argue that Northampton wasn't doing its bit, the town having been transformed after the arrival of 16,000 men from a Welsh Brigade. Over fifty trains were used to bring the soldiers to Northampton, and they were greeted by flag-waving crowds who gave them an enthusiastic welcome. The men were accommodated in private houses, and with 20,900 homes in Northampton, almost everyone in the town had the war brought directly to their doorstep.

Some, however, didn't wait for the war to reach them. Speaking at Franklin Gardens, Northampton's very own England international rugby player, Edgar Mobbs, issued a rallying call to the crowd and his fellow sportsmen. Calling a meeting in the Plough Hotel on 3rd September, Mobbs received a great response from his fellow rugby professionals, with over 250 men soon enlisting and passed fit for service. Mobbs's efforts led to the creation of the 7th Northamptonshire Battalion. Mobbs wasn't the only Northampton sportsman to take a proactive approach: Walter Tull, Northampton Football Club's first black player, soon joined the Footballers' Battalion (Middlesex Regiment) along with his brother.

Vision of E. R. Mobbs at the Front.

Figure 1.8: The news that the popular Edgar Mobbs had enlisted was celebrated in humorous fashion in the local press; 19th September 1914, *The Northampton Independent.*

For many young boys seeing the army in full regalia enter their town, this was an exciting time. School attendance rates dropped as groups of boys took it upon themselves to marshal soldiers across the town. Several headmasters suspected in their logbooks that the military presence in town was contributing to low attendance, which was confirmed by the headmaster of Delapre Infant School, who noted two boys had been caught truanting "owing to so many military now being in the district". The same headmaster was more forgiving of low attendance for boys who had stayed home to help their "mothers who have territorials in the house".

Headmasters were understanding of these special circumstances, with school life immediately upturned with the arrival of war as attendance fell and lessons were focused on the events in Europe. In September at Guilsborough Primary School, Europe was made the main topic in geography classes: as the headmaster said, "the war is of much interest to all". By October, pupils at Blatherwycke Primary School were "very busy knitting mittens and scarves for the soldiers", wrote the headmaster, complaining the school "cannot work by the timetable". Later that month, the headmaster wrote that schoolwork "slightly suffered" as students had been "up all night" after a German Zeppelin was spotted over the village.

Very soon, however, the bleakness of war would be felt by schools. It appears that a former student of Guilsborough Church of England School by the name of Emerson was one of the first men from Northamptonshire to be killed in action. Serving in the Navy, it appears Emerson was killed in the first naval confrontation between Britain and Germany, the Battle of Heligoland Bight. A ceremony was held at his old school. Pupils, saddened by the death of one of their own, paraded in front of a Union Jack flying at half-mast and sang 'Eternal Father', a hymn for those at sea, before a performance of the Last Post filled the silent air. Unfortunately, little else is known about this fallen sailor.

While people were understandably worried about the war, it is important to remember the strong wave of patriotism that swept across the country – indicated by the large number of voluntary recruits. Indeed, by mid-August, the Northamptonshire Yeomanry told reporters that the regiment had too many men and was not taking further applicants. After all, in 1914 Britain still reigned over the largest empire the world had ever known, and the sight of the world's most successful army marching up and down the streets in full military dress would have been a remarkable sight. Young men, hoping to win the affection of their sweethearts, bring pride to their families and serve their King and country, were attracted by this irresistible prospect.

As the regiment departed Northampton to entrain to Derby, the images of young men leaning out of the train window, waving enthusiastically as their relatives said their final farewells, would be relayed widely across the town. Such images would serve just as well as any Kitchener poster in bringing recruits to the army; *The Northampton Independent* said Lord Kitchener's appeal in September for 100,000 men had "struck a responsive chord in the hearts of many Northamptonians" and that the recruiting officers at the Northampton Barracks "have been kept very busy by the number of men who have come forward at this crisis".

Back on the continent, the German Army had made rapid progress following an adaptation of the Schlieffen plan. The former Chief of the German General Staff, Alfred von Schlieffen, had devised a strategy to protect Germany in the event of a two-front war against France in the west and Russia in the east. Schlieffen's primary concern lay in defence but was altered by others, including the then Chief of Staff, Helmuth von Moltke, to provide for an offensive war. In essence, the

Schlieffen plan assumed that it would take Russia at least six weeks to mobilise its inferior army. A small Germany Army would secure the Russian front during this time, giving the remaining German Army just six weeks to conquer France by capturing Paris.

This was a hugely ambitious plan and its fate rested on the invasion of the neutral nations of Belgium and the Netherlands. Five German armies would invade Belgium, Holland and France in a 'grand wheel motion', turning through the Flanders plains. It was anticipated that the French would launch an attack on Germany via their shared border. Here, the French Army would be greeted by an under-strength German force which would deliberately encourage the French Army to invade Germany, just as its armies to the north progressed quickly through Belgium before heading towards Paris. Hence, the great bulk of the German Army would be free to attack the French from their rear (the grand wheel movement), encircling the French Army to bring about its destruction. This rested on the key assumption that the Belgians would allow Germany to march through their country or that their resistance would be pitifully weak. For the plan to work, Germany's army needed to move at lightning speed.

In reality, von Moltke did not invade Holland but focused his army on Belgium. Almost immediately the Schlieffen plan suffered a setback as the Russian mobilisation was quicker than anticipated; this was a remarkable feat for the one million strong army – the largest in Europe. The Russian colossus soon invaded the German territory of East Prussia scoring victories, forcing von Moltke to send large numbers of troops to that region. The Russians, hampered by the distance between their two attacking armies and stunned by German tactical superiority, saw their army annihilated at the Battle of Tannenberg. Victory brought great standing to the German Field Marshal, Paul von Hindenburg. The humiliated Russian general, Alexander Samsonov, committed suicide rather than face the Tsar. The remains of the Russian armies – they had lost around 150,000 men in less than a month – were on the retreat by the end of August and out of Prussia by mid-September.

The plucky Belgians, however, were proving to be tough fighters. While the German Army made swift progress through Belgium, they encountered just enough resistance to put the Schlieffen plan behind schedule and gave the BEF slightly more time to arrive. The atrocities committed by the German Army in Belgium were widely spread (and perhaps exaggerated) in Britain. This led to an outpouring of public opinion in favour of Belgium. Despite the best efforts of the small Belgian Army, the Germans, with numerical superiority, forced their way through the country, reaching the Belgian mining town of Mons. It was on 23rd August that the Germans were confronted by the British Army and fought one of the most decisive battles in the war: the Battle of Mons.

On the day of the vital battle, the 48th were billeted 9 miles from Mons in the small Belgian village of Roveroy. Three companies were sent nearer Mons but not one of them saw any action. The British had performed, given the odds, very well in their first major continental battle since the Crimean War, some sixty years earlier. The value of professional soldiers was evident as the Germans suffered a terrible death toll from the BEF's unparalleled musketry with their Lee-Enfield rifles. Nevertheless, in the face of German numerical superiority and relentless shelling, the BEF could only hold on for so long. At 0600 on 24th August, the order to retreat was given to the Northamptons, who had been in reserve. The Battle of Mons was over with the BEF suffering 1,600 casualties. The Great Retreat had begun.

The men fell back towards the Maubeuge–Jenlain line which was intended to be the major defensive line for the BEF to hold. It soon became apparent that the German advance was too strong and further retreat was needed to organise the British and French armies. France's army, under the command of General Joffre, had not planned that the British would aid their defence, and so both the British and French command were frantically trying to coordinate their respective army's movements.

The Northamptonshire Regiment had not yet participated in the fight and were now retreating under heavy shellfire from the advancing Germans. The men were not fully informed of what was happening and why they were falling back, but from their movements they deduced all was not well. Adding to these unsettling moments, the men came across roads crowded with refugees fleeing south. It was a tremendous sight of human misery made worse in the hot dusty weather, as German shells exploded near the displaced and desperate. The Regimental History Committee's book describes what greeted the men:

> "These unfortunate people had all sorts of household treasures with them, and the painful procession of old men, women and children, with carts piled with bedding and packages of every description, and perambulators with three infants abreast, brought home to all the reality of war."

For professional soldiers like the 48th, retreating without so much as firing a shot was not in their nature. One can imagine there was a lift in their spirits when they were ordered to march towards Favreuil on 27th August to reinforce the British troops fighting a fierce rearguard action there. However, the battalion once again saw no combat action and billeted at Oisy and marched to Wassigny the following day.

At midday on the 28th, news was received warning the men of a German contingent of motor lorries approaching the village. Soon enough, a small party of Uhlans, a light cavalry unit, were spotted. Not realising they were attacking a British stronghold, the Uhlans, to their great misfortune, opened fire. Immediately, the Northamptons took up positions and returned heavy fire, taking a young German soldier and his horse prisoner. The horse was subsequently named 'Uhlan' and served the battalion for almost the duration of the war.

The men would have had little time to celebrate their first taste of action. Around thirty minutes later, a German reconnaissance aeroplane flew over and within minutes the base was shelled – a novel experience at the time but one which the battalion would soon become very well acquainted with. Movement was detected in a plantation nearby from which the enemy soon emerged and charged at the Northamptons. As the Northamptons responded with brisk rifle fire, the Germans started their machine gun but the attack was repelled. The 48th continued their retreat, with D Company on the rearguard constantly on watch for the enemy who were hunting them down.

On the morning of 29th August, the 48th left Hauteville where they had stayed the night and marched on high ground near Thenelles on the River Oise. Here they took up defensive positions. At noon, they came under shellfire as masses of Germans were descending the slopes opposite. The Germans, however, did not continue with their attack and the Northamptons took their chance to withdraw safely across the Oise to Ribemont.

With very little sleep, late nights, early starts and continuous marches in the scorching heat, it was no surprise that the great physical toll exerted on the men was beginning to show. The Regimental History describes the men "staggering and hardly able to move from fatigue". Nonetheless, the march eastwards continued and on 31st August went into bivouac near Corcy.

The Regimental History describes around this time there were rumours circulating within the battalion that the Germans were closing in on Paris and were concealed by large woods. The battalion went as far as to make preparations for an imminent German attack which never appeared. The rumour mill continued apace the following day when the troops continued their march, allegedly towards Paris. It was not only those in England that agonised over a lack of information. Whether on the Western Front or in Northampton, the War Office needed to keep war morale up. Providing reports on the extent of the prolonged retreat would not serve to keep up the enthusiasm for war nor the record numbers of recruits joining Kitchener's New Army. On 22nd August, before the start of the retreat but after a series of German victories, the editor of *The Northampton Independent* penned a lead article complaining that "the only serious shortage is in the war news. As many a man would rather go without a meal than a paper just now, the crumbs and scraps vouched safe to use are about as satisfying as a bun to a bear." Tension was high both in France and back home, it soon became clear what was occurring on the battlefields was not positive.

The 48th were still marching eastwards through France and assisted in destroying bridges along the River Ourcq. On 2nd September, the men bivouacked just north of Meaux. The roads here, once again, were congested with French civilians. The Regimental History quotes an unnamed eyewitness:

> *"It was a sad sight. There were huge wagons of grain; there were herds of cattle, flocks of sheep; there were wagons full of household effects,*

with often as many as twenty people sitting aloft; there were carriages; there were automobiles with the occupants crowded in among bundles done up in sheets; there were women pushing baby carriages; there were dogs and cats and goats; there was every sort of vehicle you ever saw, drawn by every sort of beast that can draw, from dogs to oxen, from boys to donkeys."

Around this time, intelligence suggested the Germans were moving across the front rather than towards it. The truth was the German Army was severely stretched and fatigued from a month of continuous marching and fighting, while their supply lines were struggling to replenish their troops. The German high command knew that the Schlieffen plan had failed. After the BEF's stiff resistance at Mons and the rearguard action put up over the previous week, not even the most powerful army in the world could have traversed across the plains of Flanders and conquered Paris in six weeks. Regardless of the British and Belgian resistance, historians have cast doubt on the Schlieffen plan's potential to succeed due to scant attention being paid to the issue of supply routes and troop fatigue. Nonetheless, the Germans had made rapid progress into France and would not be forced out before offering a serious resistance – one that was to last four years.

On 3rd September, the 48th had a sudden change of direction as they marched near La Ferté-sous-Jouarre on the River Marne. They were now only forty miles from Paris, whose citizens were nervously preparing for invasion after witnessing their government leave for Bordeaux. Taking up defensive positions north of the town, the battalion readied themselves for the imminent fight. Soon they were given orders to prepare bridges across the Marne for demolition, cross the river and go into billets at Romeny, a small village four miles south of La Ferté-sous-Jouarre. On 5th September they entered Aulnoy, north of Coulommiers. The Battle of the Marne, one of the defining battles in history with the fate of Paris at stake, was about to begin.

Back home, the war effort was ramping up. To sustain the soldiers, a lead article in *The Northampton Independent* on 5th September urged readers to donate cigarettes for the front. A letter received from a soldier in the 1st Battalion asks readers to send them a packet of Woodbines as "the French cigarettes taste like poison to us". Several tobacconists had agreed to supply cigarettes at cost price; by the following week the paper reported 40,000 cigarettes had been sent to the 48th, which should have given each man around 40 cigarettes. Over the course of the war, the call to provide cigarettes for the front would become a staple feature in every edition of newspapers.

In another sign that the war would not be over by Christmas, by 12th September the town's famous boot and shoe industry quickly saw a colossal explosion in the number of boots ordered by both the British and French armies. The British had requested 400,000 pairs and a further 70,000 for the Navy. The French had ordered a staggering two million pairs of boots with a very precise

Figure 1.9: This cartoon with a pun in the caption, published in *The Northampton Independent* on 5th September, shows a light-hearted look at the war. In the early days of war, the public mood was upbeat, if wary of war. As the war progressed, and the number of casualties grew rapidly, cartoons became less jovial and more sombre.

THE SMOKE THEY LIKE.

specification of a "pronounced projection of nails on the sole to the extent of a sixteenth of an inch". The manufacturers, still adjusting production methods from commercial to military, were having trouble sourcing the correct type of nail and leather.

Meanwhile, the Battle of the Marne was raging in France along a hundred-mile front. If the Germans broke through, and they almost did near Paris, victory would be in their sights. Severely struggling against the force of Kluck's 1st Army, French commanders desperately ushered 600 Paris taxis to drive 6,000 French reserve troops to the battlefront. This famous incident became known as the 'Taxis of the Marne' and is credited with the French holding the line.

A large gap had opened up between the 1st and 2nd Germany Armies which the Allies were quick to exploit. By 9th September, with the gap growing larger in addition to a lack of communications between his forces, General Bulow ordered the 2nd German Army to retreat. The rest of the German Army soon followed. The Germans, having spent the previous month as the hunters, now became the hunted.

Closely pursued by the French and British troops, they managed to retreat 40 miles north to the Lower Aisne River and began to dig in. This marked a sudden end to the rapid movement seen in the very early stages of the war. For the next four years, the war would be characterised by brutal, prolonged trench warfare, with both sides constructing fortresses of complex trenches. Nevertheless, the French Army, assisted by the British, had succeeded in stemming the German tide, thereby ending any remaining German hopes of a swift victory. Over two million soldiers fought in the Battle of the Marne, with the French and Germans suffering around 250,000 casualties each. The British lost around 13,000 men.

During this battle, the 48th were bivouacked at Pézarches, waiting in reserve to reinforce the British-held line Crecy–Coulommiers–Choisy. On 9th September, the men crossed the Marne at Nogent-l'Artaud. Up until this point, and in stark contrast to the rest of the BEF, the Northamptons had suffered very few casualties and barely fired a shot. This bloodless trend would not continue for much longer. It is worth repeating the words of The Regimental History:

> "[The regiment] advanced over the decisive sector in one of the decisive battles of the world apparently without firing a shot. It was as if Fate were just 'nursing' the 1st Northamptonshire Regiment for a fuller vengeance. This, indeed, was so. And if a hundred years hence a bloodthirsty reader may become impatient at the narrative up to this point, he is asked to bide his time. Before he shall have read another hundred pages he will have blood – rivers of it, and will see the old 48th not merely decimated, but practically wiped out of existence."

As the battalion travelled north in pursuit of the German Army, they reached a small village called Priez. Reports of Germans holding positions north of the village were received and the battalion prepared to support an attack with the Royal Sussex and Loyal North Lancashires. The environment was bare: flat grassland with scarcely any cover, although there was a large copse on the left of the road. The Germans had positioned themselves in a low wooded ridge on the far side of the small River Ru d'Alland. As the men approached the copse, shells suddenly started to rain down upon them. The Germans had no intention of taking Priez. This was a rearguard action, much like the British fought during the Great Retreat, aimed at slowing down the British pursuit. Three men from the battalion were killed, with a further 25 wounded during this artillery assault.

On 11th September, the 48th continued their pursuit and were billeted in Paars the following day. The battalion received reports that the Germans had stopped their retreat north of the River Aisne. They were not going to fall back any more. The German command had earmarked this position as a line to withdraw to in the event of defeat on the Marne. Their position was formidable; the Aisne was 54 metres wide and 4.5 metres deep, with the river itself concealed by a steep

120-metre slope. It is no wonder The Regimental History said the area gave the "appearance of mountains". The German position was on a plateau some distance away from the stream. They wanted the Allies to cross the river, after which they would fire from their entrenched positions. The difficulties involved in crossing the river meant retreat was not a legitimate option.

On 13th September, Sir John French, commander in chief of the BEF, gave the order to attack along the German front. The Northamptons would have to confront this most hostile of territories.

The 2nd Brigade of the 1st Division, to which the Northamptons were attached, crossed the River Aisne and pushed to a point south-east of Moulins. A and D Company were sent forward north of the village and came under artillery and rifle fire from the waiting Germans. The Germans had taken a sugar factory on the famous Chemin des Dames D18 road, housing two batteries of artillery and some machine guns inside. Behind their lines, they also had four artillery guns supporting them.

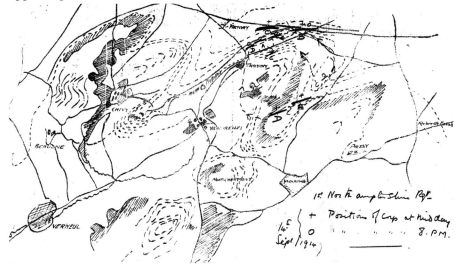

Figure 1.10: This map with handwritten tactical markings is part of the battalion's war diary and shows the troop's movements on 14th September in the Chemin des Dames area. The sugar factory described in the main text is marked near the top of the map.

The offensive began in terrible weather; stubborn rain and thick fog greeted the 48th, making accuracy difficult for the battalion. At 1130 came the order for the men to immediately advance and support the main thrust of the British offence. The sugar factory was left to the Loyal North Lancashires to take and, despite putting up a valiant effort, they suffered severe casualties and abandoned their position, leaving the German artillery guns free to wreak havoc elsewhere. Meanwhile, B and C Company had forced their way through to the Chemin des Dames. The 1st Northamptons had amassed 102 casualties and dug themselves in for the night on the slope of the ridge. The next days were spent improving their hastily contrived trenches. During these days of fighting, some of the first Northamptonshire Regimental officers were killed. Captain White and Lieutenant Paget were killed north of the small village of Troyon. Paget, from Great Houghton, was only 23 years old. His death, only reported in late October, would serve as a dark realisation to those at home that the war would devour their youth and that a higher rank would provide no protection.

On 17th September, an infamous incident in the history of the Northamptonshire Regiment occurred. After Captain Gordon was killed alongside seven men from his company, on 15th September, the command of A Company transferred to Second Lieutenant Burlton. At around 3pm, the German guns came to an abrupt halt and the Northamptons saw a flurry of hands raised along the German lines. Burlton ordered his company to stop firing and nervously stood upon the parapet sensing victory.

A German soldier was walking along No Man's Land and Burlton cautiously went out to meet him. Upon inspection, the lieutenant realised that the German was only a private. Standing exposed in the middle, Burlton ordered the private back to his line and told him to send a senior officer to discuss the terms of surrender. After some confusion, an officer did make his way to the middle but did not understand English. Burlton told him he accepted their surrender and that the Germans must lay down their weapons.

While Burlton was making arrangements, a large body of Germans climbed their parapet and began to make their way towards him. In the confusion, it appeared some of the soldiers were carrying their rifles while others had their hands up. By this stage, Burlton was growing anxious and demanded that the German officer order his men to drop their guns. The officer, seemingly unable to understand Burlton, did his best to reassure the worried British officer of his surrender.

Already isolated from his men, the lieutenant was now surrounded by hundreds of German soldiers. Recounting the incident, Burlton said:

> *"Firstly, I thought it was a 'bona fide' surrender, as many of the enemy came without arms and with hands up; and, to make the illusion complete, some of those who were armed delivered their rifles over to some of our Tommies, who had come out on their own to meet them. It would have been a dirty business to have opened fire on men who were advancing with their arms because they did not understand English."*

Burlton, therefore, took the German officer and his command of around 400 soldiers back to the Northamptons' trench. Things appeared to be going smoothly and some of the German ranks even shook hands with the Northamptons. Suddenly, however, a German soldier shot dead one of the Northampton soldiers. Burlton, probably horrified at the situation he and his men found themselves in, demanded that the German officer command his men to stand down. However, the officer had other plans:

> "… and the officer, on my saying that if he did not order an immediate cessation of his fire I would order mine to open, informed me that I was his prisoner. We then all set to in earnest, so to speak, and at point-blank range, of course; no accuracy of shooting was necessary – the men used their butts and bayonets lustily. We were, however, far outnumbered, being but some seventy odd, I believe against 400."

Luckily for A Company, the Queen's Regiment had observed the peril and went to the 48th's rescue:

> "The Queen's (I think) on our right, seeing we were in trouble, and seeing that the Boches were, for the most part, standing on our parapet and firing down into us in the road, turned on their machine gun and the spectacle was one never to be forgotten. They fairly enfiladed the Huns on our parapet, and the execution can only be compared to that of a harvesting machine as it mows down wheat."

One can imagine the bloody scene as A Company fired indiscriminately in an attempt to save their lives from the German deceit. The Germans were taking heavy casualties from two sides and chaotically began to abandon their positions, frantically sprinting back to their trenches. Not all Germans managed to escape. Those that were left behind put their hands up in surrender. They were not shown any mercy by Burlton:

> "… but we declined their offer, and, in fact, I think we only kept one prisoner – a souvenir, no doubt."

Meanwhile, an officer from D Company, Captain Savage, had been sent to take over the command of A Company. Before he met up with his battalion, he went out with an officer of the 60th King's Royal Rifles to discuss terms of surrender with the Germans opposite them who had also muted their guns. After a short talk, it became apparent the Germans were not interested in surrender. As the two British officers turned around and were walking back to their trench, the Germans started firing. Savage was shot in the back and died from his wound. The other officer fared better and was unhurt.

The Northamptons had suffered gravely on this day with 161 casualties – the majority from D Company. On 19th September, the tired battalion were relieved by the 18th Brigade and went to billets in Pargnan. Here, they received their first parcels of cigarettes, chocolates and other comforts.

Unsurprisingly, this appalling incident was heavily featured in the local press albeit with differing accounts. It was another month before the town learnt of this occurrence of German treachery, when *The Northampton Independent* contained a report with the headline "How Captain Parker Died – Victim of White Flag Treachery." The article contained an account from Private H. Corcoran of C Company who said the men were charging at Noyons "in the face of a flaming hell of bullets and shrapnel" with Captain Parker leading. As the men approached the enemy trenches, Corcoran says the Germans displayed a white flag. Captain Parker stopped his men from charging but then "the cowards picked up their rifles and fired". Parker was killed after receiving a wound to his chest, while Corcoran was struck by a shrapnel bullet in his right leg but managed to crawl to safety.

This account does not corroborate with the version found in The Regimental History, written in 1932. For instance, Noyons is around 40 miles north-west from Pargnan, where the battalion was billeted on 19th September. However, some points appear to correlate with the battalion's official war diary. The entry on 17th September does mention, although briefly and with no detail, a charge – although it says "Captain Parker killed leading the charge" before the Germans had shown the white flag. The discrepancy may originate from the battalion's war diary. The white flag incident is explicitly recorded on 17th September and the entry does say Captain Parker was killed leading a charge, but these were likely two separate events.

On 24th October, *The Northampton Independent* contains a report about another white flag incident. On this occasion, it resembles more closely the account found in The Regimental History. The paper reports the Germans suddenly raised

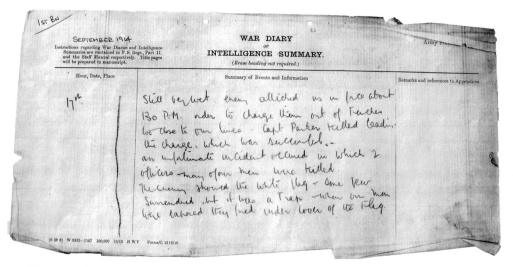

Figure 1.11: The battalion's war diary wrote: "An unfortunate incident occurred in which 2 officers + many of our men were killed. The enemy showed the white flag – some few surrendered but it was a trap – when our men were exposed they fired under cover of the flag."

their rifles as if to surrender. It appears that a German soldier met a Northampton officer in the middle. On seeing how few soldiers were in the British trench, the German told the Northampton officer, "You are my prisoner," and gave a signal to his men to rush forward. The Northampton officer, whose name is not provided in the account, is then said to have shot dead the German officer with his revolver. The Germans immediately responded, and the Northampton officer was only saved after a bullet hit the regimental badge on his cap.

The Germans then pushed forward to the Northamptons' parapet and opened fire at point-blank range. Like The Regimental History account, the paper reports most of the Germans (300–400) were killed with assistance from the Queen's Regiment. The enemy were so close that bayonets, rather than bullets, were the primary method of killing the enemy.

Figure 1.12: The Northampton Independent portrayed the white flag incident in dramatic fashion.

These divergent accounts provide excellent examples of the misinformation provided to the public during the war. Even information sourced from official battalion war diaries might not be strictly accurate. The battalion diarist was a soldier too and subject to stresses of war: incessant shelling, tiredness and a shortage of food. It is not uncommon to find diaries containing wrong locations or inaccurate timekeeping.

Nonetheless, it is highly likely the Germans did misuse the white flag in an attempt to rout the Northamptons. Other British units reported similar German activities in 1914. Regardless of what exactly happened to the Northamptons on that day, when reported in the press it would have served to increase the growing animosity towards the Germans and reinforce the principled case of war to protect western civilisation from German savagery. Throughout the months of September and October, *The Northampton Mercury* and *The Northampton Independent* contained numerous first-hand accounts from soldiers in the regiment which described their movements across France. Many accounts told of German atrocities committed in Belgium and France. For example, on 24th October, *The Northampton Independent* quoted a soldier who "found two peasants who had been shot; one had his wrists nearly severed, and the other had had his arms bound and then shot".

One unavoidable evil of war was now beginning to appear. Casualties from earlier stages of the war were now being reported in a regular feature titled "The Roll of Honour." Almost teasingly, a prominent advert from Barrett & Son Goldsmiths appeared right next to this section on 26th September in *The Northampton Independent*, tempting men with engagement rings. For the thousands of men reading this section and preparing themselves to join the army, the insinuation would not have been lost.

The Battle of the Aisne raged on without any decisive breakthrough. After a great period of movement, supply lines were still catching up and both sides faced a shortage of shells. Instead, the focus switched to defence, with armies developing and fortifying their respective trenches. Attention swiftly turned to trying to outflank each other from the north. A complex series of trench lines were constructed along northern France and Belgium in the 'race to the sea'. Sir John French was concerned about the prospect of Germany controlling the Belgian channel ports and received the support of General Joffre to divert resources up north.

During this period, the Northamptons often stayed in the caves near Paissy when not in the trenches. On 18th October, the battalion entrained at Fismes to make their way to Cassel, where they went into billets.

Back home in Northampton, after months of first-hand accounts of German butchery of the Belgian people and white flag treachery, the town was growing increasingly divided over a rather peculiar situation. In late August, the editor of *The Northampton Independent* asked his readers whether Germans living in Northampton should be treated with tolerance or "wholesale expulsion".

The Engagement Ring

HOW valuable a possession is the Engagement Ring, and its value is not judged by the price paid.

While it is in a man's heart to give the best that money can buy, circumstances limit him to the best he can afford. It is, therefore, up to him to go to the Jeweller who has a reputation for quality, and has a wide and varied stock from which a satisfactory ring may be chosen. We have the selection, and every ring in stock has been chosen with great care and . . . deliberation. Our values, too, cannot be bettered. If you are contemplating making such a purchase you ought to call round here before going elsewhere. You will save money and make certain of getting just what you want.

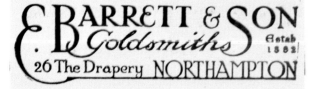

E. BARRETT & SON
Goldsmiths Estab 1882
26 The Drapery NORTHAMPTON

Figure 1.13: An advert for engagement rings in *The Northampton Independent* on 26th September 1914. Such adverts became extremely frequent after the declaration of war and were a lasting feature throughout the war.

Figure 1.14: This image shows British troops marching through Cassel, a town where the Northamptons stayed.

In October, the realities of this question would become all too true for editors, councillors and the general public, for there was an issue that, in the words of the editor, Mr Holloway:

> "...caused splits in political parties, sundered private friendships, created no end of factory feuds, embittered the sweets of many a five o'clock tea party, caused sleepless nights and anxious days for super-sensitive Town Councillors, provoked committee meetings and petitions galore, a town's meeting of protest culminating in a special meeting of the Town Council, which from seven until eleven discussed him until everyone was utterly weary of the whole subject."

The person that was the cause of all this tension was Mr Julius Gottschalk, the manager of the Northampton Corporation Tramways. Gottschalk had lived in England for 27 years since arriving when only 18. Indeed, his late wife was English, while his son even served in the British Army. Of steady character and fine ability, he had been promoted at the Tramways. By all accounts, Gottschalk was a model citizen. However, Mr Gottschalk also happened to be German.

On 3rd October, *The Northampton Independent* contained a lead article titled "Should Gottschalk Go?" The paper notes he had not applied for his naturalisation papers since arriving in England, leading many to question his allegiance. Although

Gottschalk had now applied for the papers, and despite the application being approved, a resolution at the Town Hall was "almost unanimously" passed protesting against Gottschalk's continued employment as the Tramways manager. Holloway gives his personal opinion, stating: "I always feel that when the man for the job is not to be found in the town we ought at least to employ an Englishman." However, he also takes a more conciliatory approach than some in the town by suggesting Gottschalk be suspended without salary for the duration of the war.

On Monday 12th October, the issue that had been slowly simmering was set alight. In an extraordinary four-hour session finishing at 11pm, Northampton Town Council decided to allow Gottschalk to continue his employment at the Tramways, with a vote of 28–18 in his favour. This was a decision that was not received kindly by some councillors nor the public. No concessions were given to the 'anti-Gottschalk' camp, which fuelled widespread anger. As Holloway wrote, the decision "does more credit to their hearts than their heads, for it threatens to place the peace of the town in serious peril".

Figure 1.15: Mr Julius Gottschalk, in *The Northampton Independent.*

In a special feature, titled "The Most Talked of Man in Northampton", *The Northampton Independent* listed the arguments for both sides. Essentially there were two camps. One argued Gottschalk was a loyal subject who had been made "the innocent martyr of persecution worthy of the worst Prussians themselves". The other saw "certain sinister possibilities" that included rumours about concealed mines in the River Nene or guns hidden in Abington Park. The report actually censored this as "A------- P---", although everyone in the town would have been aware of the area being referred to.

Supporters of Gottschalk argued he had not naturalised himself sooner because he "never conceived the possibility with our present civilisation that war could possibly occur" and that he applied for his papers as soon as war broke out.

The 'anti' side countered "Once a German always a German" and that Gottschalk was "nominally as loyal to his Fatherland as to England" at the start of the war. Additionally, they felt that he only applied for naturalisation in order to save his salary. The debate, far from over, led to the local elections that month being coined 'The Gottschalk Election'.

Amid rising tensions and heated political discourse, Gottschalk acted decisively to defuse the situation. On Wednesday 21st October, Gottschalk met the Tramways committee and presented a written statement which requested: "with a view of bringing the strife to an end, that I be relieved from duty for such period and on such conditions as the Committee may determine".

The Committee passed a resolution relieving Gottschalk of his duties for the war while paying him one-third of his salary. The deal, however, did not satisfy the 'anti' camp which, by now, were beyond reconciliation after several earlier snubs by the Town Council. They wanted unconditional expulsion with no salary, although were generally supportive of some compensation being paid for his discharge.

This incident dominated the town, filling up newspaper columns for over a month. While this episode was, on consideration, relatively mild with no violence, it serves as an example of the murky potential war can have on society. It is important to remember that Northampton, in a few short weeks, had been completely changed. A peaceful quiet summer had been disrupted by the engine of war. Hundreds of families had witnessed their sons go to fight an enemy which had committed terrible atrocities in Belgium and France, thousands suddenly found staple foods and items were in short supply, and social events were cancelled and pub opening hours curtailed. While certain sentiments expressed by segments of the population might seem unduly reactionary, in October 1914 it was very much Germany's war. News of the German retreat to the Aisne had not yet fully been issued to the public, yet the British retreat from Mons had. People were understandably angry and turned towards the easiest target to display their rage.

If any judgement should be made, it is somewhat heartening to see that even in one of the darkest moments in the nation's history, Northampton did not resort to more perverse methods of discourse. As Mr Holloway said, seeking to arrive at a compromise solution for all, the town strove to display the "spirit of Christian toleration", despite "the stern, if sad, reality that in war time human nature is not normal. Men's passions and prejudices are easily stirred and we must make allowances accordingly."

Passions that have been stirred can also lead to remarkable good deeds. The Marquis of Northampton, in France with the regiment, sent instructions in October to his agent to accommodate Belgian refugees at Castle Ashby. It is reported the refugees' "gratitude is beyond expression". Fundraising efforts for the Belgians were stepped up in October with first a Belgian Relief Fund organised by a Northampton councillor, G. W. Beattie, which raised £500 within days. On 24th October, Belgian Rose Day was organised by town ladies with the Belgian flag proudly flying over the council offices and items dressed in Belgian colours sold to raise funds. That month, *The Northampton Independent* reported that, such was the generosity of Northampton, there was actually a shortage of Belgian refugees, with demand outstripping supply. To help accommodate refugees, the council had set aside funds to help with maintenance for those who took in refugees. Further help was routinely provided by Charles Spencer, 6th Earl Spencer of Althorp Estate. One of Northamptonshire's more prominent peers, Earl Spencer quickly set up a fund and donated large amounts for soldiers at the front. His fundraising efforts carried on throughout the war, with his fund a regular feature in newspapers.

Figure 1.16: Parades and charity events in aid of Belgian refugees were held across Northamptonshire. Photographed is a parade in Thrapston sometime in 1914.

The first Belgian refugees had started to arrive in Northamptonshire throughout September and October. With Northampton homes housing the Welsh Brigade, the first arrivals were sent to Kring, Wellingborough and surrounding villages. One such refugee was Maurice Thomas, who settled in Abthorpe. There he found a tranquil scene, a world apart from the chaos and devastation of his native land. He describes Abthorpe in the early war as one would find it during peace:

"... a few peaceful walkers attracted by the rusticity of the area; a herd of cows returning to the farm and then going back to the field after being milked and, at harvest time, the huge farm wagons heavily laden with hay and stray; and finally children walking along in groups, singing

and dancing ... The Church ... the deep voice of the hour sounded by its clock is the only sound which awakes echoes in this lost corner."

Rather amusingly, Thomas goes on to describe the old-fashioned, reactionary attitudes held by some of the village's elderly residents when young women arrived in the village to work in the fields. For example, women in trousers cutting trees was "anything but feminine" which "gave rise to a veritable burst of indignation". As the war progressed and women entered more areas of work previously the sole domain of men out of necessity, these attitudes would be continuously tested with debates on what women could or should do.

Figure 1.17: This photograph shows the Women's Land Army hard at work on a farm near Brackley in 1917, a scene that would have been unthinkable just a few years prior.

Similarly, like Northampton suspecting German spies in the town, so too did Germany have its own 'Gottschalk incident' involving a Northampton man.

In the pages of *The Northampton Independent* on 7th November, an episode that had occurred in late August surfaced about the treatment of Mr Henry Dexter. Dexter, whose brother lived at 105 Birchfield Road, had lived in Bavaria in his role with the British Council for some twenty-five years, also holding a high position at a local brush factory. On 21st August, Dexter found his telephone line had been cut and he was later arrested. Two police officers escorted the British official to prison without showing their warrant for arrest. Marching through town, by sheer coincidence, they encountered Dexter's wife and the couple said their brief goodbyes. Dexter was put in a prison room with two Russian journalists.

The conditions in the prison were appalling. His cell was cramped, subdued with darkness, and only a small beam of light and air was allowed in via a small slit in the wall. Later on, a prison warden appeared and shouted "Hop!" after which the prisoners were taken to the bathroom, stripped and administered a bath. So terrible were the sanitary arrangements and treatment that Dexter actually suffered a heart attack but was refused medical treatment.

Later, he and the Russians were taken into the courtyard for some brief exercise. Still feeling unwell, he was finally allowed to see a doctor. After complaining to the doctor at the standard of his treatment, the doctor remarked, "You do not say anything about how the Germans are being treated in England." Dexter replied he was confident they would not put a German who had been there for 25 years in solitary confinement and treat him like a criminal. Indeed, Gottschalk was never put in prison in Northampton; he remained living in his house at 214 Wellingborough Road until his death at the age of 93 in 1954 and is buried in Northampton Cemetery. Dexter was finally released on 24th August after his wife waited three hours to see the Generalissimo, refusing to leave until she had secured her husband's release. The couple took the first train out of Germany to Geneva and then Paris. Arriving on friendly soil, the two were said to be in a state of "nervous exhaustion".

While long-term German residents in Northampton, such as Gottschalk, were not put in prison, and as the county read the Gottschalk and Dexter cases in October and November, the prisoner camp in Eastcote had already changed significantly since its inception in September. In early October, it was announced in the local press that a huge influx of Germans would arrive, increasing the camp's population from just 50 to 2,000 men. At this time, the camp's original purpose was to provide a safe location for German seamen. One of the camp's founders, former sailor and Liberal MP George Wilson, sympathised with German sailors whom he had known in his past career and ensured camp conditions were favourable. Recounting these early days of the camp in 1917, Wilson said:

> "They had wooden huts to sleep in and four good meals a day. The only guards were fourteen policemen, who were never allowed actually to enter the camp. They had concert halls, cinema shows, and all kinds of musical entertainments. They had bottled beer three times a week … imprisonment [was] far more comfortable than any freedom they had ever known."

Indeed, thousands of pounds had been spent making the camp suitable, with the purchase of toilets, showers, beds, kitchens and also the land. While the camp was segregated from the local villages, some neighbourly tensions emerged. The vicar of Pattishall, Rev George Gibson, complained to the Towcester Rural District Council that sewage from the camp was being directed into a local brook. The Council investigated Gibson's concerns but could not substantiate any of the claims.

On the whole, the Eastcote prisoner camp had very little discernible effect on day-to-day life in the village, although the presence of extra police and arrivals of heavy cargo and camp equipment were noticeable. Even Alfred Stockhurst, the first prisoner who escaped from Eastcote, on 29th October, did not cause too much of a stir in the village. Stockhurst was found less than a mile away and sent back to the camp. He would not be the last to escape – and to get recaptured.

In early October, the Germans had begun a bombing campaign on Antwerp and by the ninth day of that month it was under their control. The Belgian Army retreated to the Yser. On 12th October, Lille also fell to the Germans. It was clear that the enemy were targeting Ypres, this ancient city being the last major obstacle between the Germans and the Channel Ports. Sir John French, determined to prevent the enemy gaining control of these ports, sent the British Army to assist the French and Belgians and arrived near Ypres on 14th October.

Figure 1.18: This image shows prisoners in front of the Dining Hall at the Eastcote POW camp. Date unknown. Images of the camp are rare, with not more than a dozen photographs known despite the camp's lengthy operation in the war.

The Northamptons, with the rest of the 2nd Brigade, had arrived at the Ypres front on 20th October, by which time the battle for the city had commenced. After spending the following day in a small nearby village called Pilckem cleaning their rifles, clothes and equipment, the battalion was sent into the trenches on 22nd October. The men were in the northern extremity of the Ypres salient, now forming to assist the 1st Camerons of the 1st Brigade, who were struggling desperately against a numerically superior German force.

At a crossroads from a lane south-east of Pilckem, there were a small group of buildings with an inn standing near the village centre. These were now occupied by German forces. The battalion waited silently through the night as A Company readied themselves for their mission to infiltrate the inn. Private Sam Weston of the 1st Northamptons participated on the raid and later wrote:

> *"We waited till night, and crept to within a hundred yards of them. Then we heard the charge, and were at them like the wind. Before they could realise what was the matter we were in their trenches playing at pig-sticking."*

However, the German position was too heavily fortified for the Northamptons to make any solid gains. After their commanding officer, Captain Russell, was killed the men had to retreat. This was far from straightforward, with the battle continuing throughout the night; the flashing lights, the roaring sounds, the cries of men never subsiding. Not all men successfully retreated. Weston had been separated from his section. Attempting to find somewhere safe, Weston saw a farm with some buildings and cautiously entered it and lay down for some rest:

> *"Happening to see a farm, I made for it, and was soon inside. Imagine how I felt when I was woken up by the Germans. One of these patrols had got lost and had come for the same thing as I had. They took my rifle and kit, and then had a look in my pockets. I had some cigarettes which they were soon smoking. They put a guard over me, and the rest of them were soon asleep. But not for long. In company with the Queen's our regiment made a big advance that night, and I must say I was very pleased when a dozen of our chaps took the farmhouse and the Germans, who did not show any fight at all. I relieved one of them of his cigarettes for mine. As he had three times as many as I lost, I was better off after all..."*

After being rescued from the German-controlled farmhouse, Weston was put in hospital with frostbite where he wrote to his mother. The above accounts appeared in the local press in late December depicted a thrilling account of battle to readers, crucially portraying that British troops were making decisive progress. Sadly, this could not be further from the truth.

By afternoon on 23rd October, things took a turn for the worse as the Germans launched a fierce counterattack, retaking the inn. All throughout this period the powerful German artillery was pounding the 48th's trenches, inflicting on them a steady stream of casualties. Finally, at 1930, the Germans retreated. The Regimental History records that: "House and Haystacks were on fire in all directions, and when dusk fell the whole countryside was lit up by bright jets of flame."

This was the battalion's first real experience of trench warfare. Unlike anything they had experienced before, the pressure was unrelenting; constant fire, continuous shelling and the never-ending wails of beaten men put the greatest of strains on even the most seasoned soldiers. During the night it was announced the 48th would be relieved by French troops. As the French arrived, a nearby mill suddenly flared up, illuminating the night and prompting the German rifles to spring to life. At 0300, the Northamptons finally arrived at Pilckem, where they were served tea and allowed a period of rest. The battalion had suffered 150 casualties over the last three days of nonstop fighting. The men were billeted in a school on the outskirts of Ypres to recover.

Meanwhile, the Battle of Ypres was growing in intensity. From La Bassée to the sea, the thinly spread British line was in serious danger of breaking. The situation was so desperate that all soldiers, regardless of their condition, were sent back to the front. Over the next few days, the 1st Northamptons were in a state of flux, constantly being ordered to where the immediate danger was.

On the morning of 30th October, the 48th with the Royal Sussex were ordered to hold a defensive position in a small wood now known as Bodmin Copse, around 1.5 miles west of Geluveld. As the troops arrived in the wood, they immediately began digging trenches. C Company remained in the battalion headquarters on the western side of the copse, the rest of the battalion took the southern and eastern edges, and the Royal Sussex held the northern side.

The Germans launched a forceful attack on 31st October, starting with a heavy bombardment in the early hours of the morning. By noon, they had captured Geluveld and were now only 200 metres from the copse and unleashed heavy machine-gun and rifle fire. The commanding officer of the Northamptons soon received an order to withdraw towards a nearby forest.

Their withdrawal from the copse should have been relatively straightforward, with a small sunken lane offering protection to the forest. However, the men were spotted by the enemy, who issued a blaze of gunfire on their exposed positions. The Northamptons scrambled to their checkpoint and were lined along the forest, for a German charge was imminent. The enemy had already torn through the copse and were now moving briskly through the opposite side of the forest.

The brave 1st Northamptons, side by side with troops from the Royal Sussex and Gordon Highlanders, were all that remained between the Germans and their relentless charge. With bayonets fixed, rifles gripped tight, backs straight and their minds focused, a loud cheer erupted from their ranks. The British soldiers charged at the oncoming Germans; bloody chaos ensued as the British put up a gallant fight. After the melee, dozens of German soldiers lay motionless on the blood-soaked soil around the forest, and those that were still standing fled for safety. One Northampton soldier later said:

> "I have never seen so many German dead at any other time of the war. They were lying in heaps in a shallow ditch which ran on both sides of a ride in the wood."

After one of the rare incidents of the war involving hand-to-hand combat, the Regimental History records that at least 200 German corpses lay scattered around the forest. The battalion's war diary was lost during this time. As a result, between 26th October and 15th November the diary simply reads "The Regiment was heavily engaged during this period."

The 48th, buoyed with this victory, decided to attempt to recapture Bodmin Copse. However, after their ill-fated charge, the Germans were not going to concede any of their captured territory. They defended the copse with heavy machine-gun fire and the Northamptons could not make any progress; instead the Northamptons improved their defences on the edge of the forest over the next couple of days. Finally, on 4th November, the exhausted battalion were removed from the front line.

A week later, the elite Prussian Guards made a final attempt to break the British line. At 9am, the battalion received a message informing them that the enemy had broken the British line at Polygon Wood (a few miles north of Geluveld). The battalion were immediately rushed to a position nearby and at 11am the order to invade was given. As they entered, a torrent of fire was unleashed, forcing the battalion to alter their direction and find cover along a hedge. They had more luck at this position providing supporting fire.

No further attack was made. Indeed, 11th November marked the end of what would become the First Battle of Ypres. This Belgian city, once full of magnificent medieval architecture, was now unrecognisable after shells had reduced much of it to rubble; the worst was still to come for this city, with fierce battles in spring 1915 and much of the second half of 1917. The First Battle of Ypres had seen the BEF obliterated: 7,900 killed, 30,000 wounded and 18,000 missing. In total, there were around 56,000 casualties from the 160,000 soldiers the BEF had deployed. It had taken the destruction of the world's best army, but Ypres was still in Allied hands and with it the Channel Ports. The 48th were now only a fragment of the battalion that had left England in high spirits three months ago. Only 350 men remained fighting fit.

Figure 1.19: A man cycles in peaceful Ypres in 1911 before the war destroyed the town's beautiful architecture.

The Germans too had lost dearly: 20,000 killed, 83,000 wounded and 31,000 missing. It was estimated the Northamptonshire Regiment alone had killed over 1,500 of their soldiers, taking a further 600 prisoners. The Belgians too fought fiercely for their ancient city, amassing 21,000 casualties. France also bled deeply: between 50,000 and 85,000 casualties were incurred. The First Battle of Ypres was the first major trench battle which would come to epitomise the war: suffering of unimaginable scale on both sides, with no clear victory. Hostilities would resume in Ypres in April 1915.

The First Battle of Ypres also ushered in a marked change in the freedom of the press. In the early months of the war, regular accounts of the battalion were published, with some going as far as to include locations. Despite the valour shown by the troops at Ypres, scant information was to be found in the local papers. Ypres is only a passing reference in December when *The Northampton Independent* reports the death of Major Norman, who was killed in the battle.

As a curious side note of history, around seven miles from where the 48th were fighting in Wijtschate, a young German corporal was participating in his first major battle. Such was the bravery he showed when rescuing a wounded comrade, the soldier was awarded a second-class Iron Cross. His name was Adolf Hitler.

Figure 1.20: This patriotic cartoon, published in the early months of the war in The News of the World, depicts a nation enthusiastic in its quest for victory as evidenced by a stirring portrayal of Britannia, the female personification of Britain.

Figure 1.21: Taken in November 1914, the photograph shows St Martin's Cathedral in Ypres severely damaged.

Figure 1.22: A dead horse lies abandoned on the Menin Road near Ypres in October 1914.

Figure 1.23: The famous Ypres Cloth Hall – once the largest commercial building in medieval Europe – barely stands after being hit by shells during the First Battle of Ypres.

Figure 2.1: The ruinous aftermath of battle. A street in neighbouring Laventie after the Battle of Neuve Chapelle, April 1915.

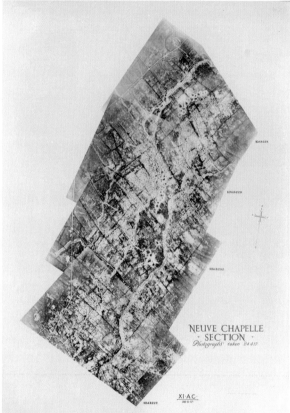

NEUVE CHAPELLE
· SECTION ·
Photographs taken 24.4.17.

XI·A·C·

Figure 2.2: Scorched earth. An aerial image of the Neuve Chapelle section taken in April 1917, showing the destructive effects of years of shelling.

Figure 2.3: A church in Laventie barely stands after the bombing, April 1915.

CHAPTER TWO

THE BATTLE OF NEUVE CHAPELLE

"Our battalion suffered very heavily, but the General said to what few remained,
"I am proud of you, you fought like lions. I knew you would"

Anonymous Northampton officer writing in
The Northampton Independent – 3rd April 1915

"The battle began with the desultory boom of long artillery, which developed into a positive inferno. The din was terrific. We had over 300 guns pouring a continuous hail upon the German positions, which were blown clean into the air one after the other, men, earth, shelters and trench debris all being scattered and shattered to bits. It was a fearful sight, but it had a sort of hypnotic influence over most of us, and made us gaze with a kind of awe indifferent to the German shells streaming and showering all round us.
Then came the charge."

Anonymous Northampton officer writing in
The Northampton Independent – 27th March 1915

THE EARLY MONTHS OF THE WAR had seen the British Expeditionary Force retreat at Mons, the French Army suffer heavy losses and the Germans' rapid march falter to a mere amble. By the winter of 1914, the murky realities of prolonged trench warfare were beginning to sink in for the soldiers.

Back home, the war had quickly changed the makeup of society and the full effects were just beginning to be understood. Northampton had seen the arrival of thousands of Welsh soldiers in September, and also their departure to war before Christmas; towns like Kettering and Wellingborough had received hundreds of Belgian refugees; thousands of German sailors had arrived at the Eastcote Camp. Schools had also been strongly affected, with efforts made to incorporate the war into school life – for example, in January 1915, Delapre School in Northampton issued 43 medals to boys whose fathers or brothers were serving in the British Army.

To compound matters, as the county entered 1915, the weather took a turn for the worse. Arthur Dryden, owner of Canons Ashby, wrote in his diary that heavy rain "changed to snow which lay 4 or 5 inches deep". This further worsened existing agricultural pressures caused by a shortage of manpower as farm labourers left for France. At the start of 1915 old attitudes that farm work would be too difficult for women prevailed, and so the industry lobbied to have boys leave school to work on farms instead – a request that was supported by Northampton County Council. A glimpse of similar old-fashioned attitudes is found in the memoirs of Belgian refugee Maurice Thomas. Then living in Abthorpe, Thomas notes the reaction of some of the village's residents to the arrival of a group of twenty girls from the Land Army:

> *"as soon as the group of young women appeared, the whole village rushed to their doors and windows and the military step of the 'Landgirls' was still ringing on the pebbled surface of the road when already comments were flying around. However, in order to fully comprehend the intensity of the consternation produced by the appearance of the female workers … women in trousers … in this small English village, where concepts of decency and modesty were pushed to their extreme limit, it gave rise to a veritable burst of indignation."*

Older residents complained that jobs such as cutting trees "is anything but feminine" and such jobs should be done by men. In a sign of societal change brought about by the war, such opinions were not universal among the villagers. Thomas notes there was discussion on the role of women when all the men were at war and jobs like cutting trees could not be done in skirts. As the war progressed and as women went first into the fields, then into the shoe and munition factories, such debates were always a feature. Ultimately old attitudes were supplanted with new ways of thinking and by the realities of warfare.

Along with his French counterparts, General Haig, then commander of the First Army, spent the early months of 1915 attempting to devise a plan to break through the German lines and end the current stalemate. The stage was to be a little village called Neuve Chapelle, which was occupied by the Germans from 27th October 1914. Lying between Bethune and German-controlled Lille, it would not only act as a base to stop the Germans – who were only around 50 miles from Paris – but would also provide the gateway for an assault to take the high ground at Aubers Ridge. As things stood, the British faced being surrounded by the Germans on three sides in waterlogged land while the Germans held a strong advantage to defend the Lille–La Bassée line. With the 'race to the sea' spreading through north-eastern France and spilling over into Belgium, culminating in both forces trying to take Ypres – the last major barrier the Germans faced before they could take the Channel Ports – the only option left was to break through the German trenches.

As a result, in early March 1915, four British divisions comprising 40,000 men gathered on a front less than 2 miles wide and began preparations. Amidst this crowded scene, the 2nd Northamptonshire Battalion were to be found as part of the 24th Brigade of the 8th Division.

The Northamptons had arrived in the Neuve Chapelle sector in November 1914, and spent the first few months of 1915 in billets at La Gorgue. Here they were intermittently sent to the trenches while their casualty list steadily grew. Indeed, by the end of January, at least twenty men had been killed in action. One of these fatalities was Lance Corporal Henry Thompson. From Kingsthorpe, Northampton, Thompson had joined the Northamptonshire Regiment in 1909 aged 17. Six years later, aged 23, he was shot in the head as he wrote a postcard intended for his family in Northampton. His obituary appeared in *The Northampton Independent* in February. He is buried in Estaires Cemetery, France, alongside 874 fellow Commonwealth soldiers.

These first few months, however, were relatively quiet compared to what was to follow. General Haig has received heavy criticism from historians for his reliance on old war strategies during the conflict. It is a curious incident, then, that he was in charge during a battle which displayed several tactical innovations for the first time in the war. Despite the fact it served as a laboratory for forms of warfare which were to become a mainstay for the duration of the war, the Battle of Neuve Chapelle is largely forgotten. The battle was the first British offensive starting from static trench lines. While not necessarily a new phenomenon of war, it was the first time soldiers and officers alike would have experienced anything like this compared to the old forms of warfare. The effectiveness of the 'lifting barrage' strategy was to be tested here. It involved a large concentrated fire by the artillery on one enemy target for a short period of time, before locking on to a new target. In the meantime, soldiers at the front would rush into the bombed area, in the hope that the enemy would be disorganised, in chaos, and unable to mount an effective resistance. The most critical component of this tactic, as Neuve Chapelle would tragically show, was the accuracy of the artillery.

Figure 2.4: (Above) The view from La Gorgue, looking towards Neuve Chapelle and Aubers.

Figure 2.5: (Left) The gravestone of Henry Thompson at Estaires Cemetery, France, adorned with his regimental crest.

On 7th March 1915, the 2nd Northamptons went into the trenches with Neuve Chapelle in their sights. They were given orders to simply hold this position for two days before the main assault. Normally the troops would be tasked with cutting and removing wire in anticipation of the troops going 'over the top'. On this occasion they were under strict instructions not to remove any wire – lest the Germans get wind of the impending assault. For the artillery assault and subsequent trench invasion to be effective, it was vital to ensure that they kept the element of surprise for as long as possible prior to the attack. Two days later, on 9th March, operational orders were issued. A three-pronged attack would commence on the 10th. On the left flank would be the 7th Division, with the Meerut Division of the Indian Corps operating on the right. The 8th Division, and therefore the Northamptons, would be positioned in the centre, with the Indian troops, sharing Neuve Chapelle as the main target. The plan did not mark out the Northamptons to play a major role in the assault. Indeed, as part of the 24th Brigade, they were to be used as a reserve in the attack, with the 25th Brigade in the front line initially supporting a battalion of the Royal Berkshires in building roads for their artillery. In the stillness of night, the troops moved to their stations with no enemy engagement. The silence would not last long.

At 0730 on 10th March, the morning stillness was interrupted by the British bombardment. In the Regimental History Committee's book, the authors describe how the ferocity of the British shells was unlike anything ever seen "in the history of war", as the German line was instantly covered in thick smoke. The heavy fire continued for thirty-five minutes. One officer later recalled the bombardment:

> *"We had over 300 guns pouring a continuous hail upon the German positions, which were blown clean into the air one after the other, men, earth, shelters, and trench debris all being scattered and shattered to bits."*

At 0850, the Northampton men watched as the attacking troops quickly climbed their ladders and rushed over the field to invade the German trench. Meanwhile, the German fightback had begun. Their guns, free from British bombing, rapidly began firing shells on the reserve troops in the trenches. It became disastrously clear that something had gone wrong. The thirty-five minutes of heavy bombardment was meant to render the German guns useless or at least severely limit their capabilities. In fact, the Germans replied with such force that casualties were even recorded across the reserve troops, including the Northamptons.

The invading troops were having a more successful time taking control of Neuve Chapelle, although they too came under fire. Reinforcements were needed to shore up these newly won positions and, as planned, the Northamptons started to play an active role. C and D Companies were chosen to assist the 25th Brigade in digging trenches beyond Neuve Chapelle facing Bois de Biez. Ordered to go 'over the top', they charged head on into the German onslaught and were slaughtered before they could reach the village.

A first-hand account of the carnage is presented by the same wounded officer quoted above:

> *"My senses swim as I think of the slaughter in our ranks. Officers and men dropped until we felt that the regiment would be almost annihilated, but on we rushed. There were moments in those rushes when we felt a dread despair seize us."*

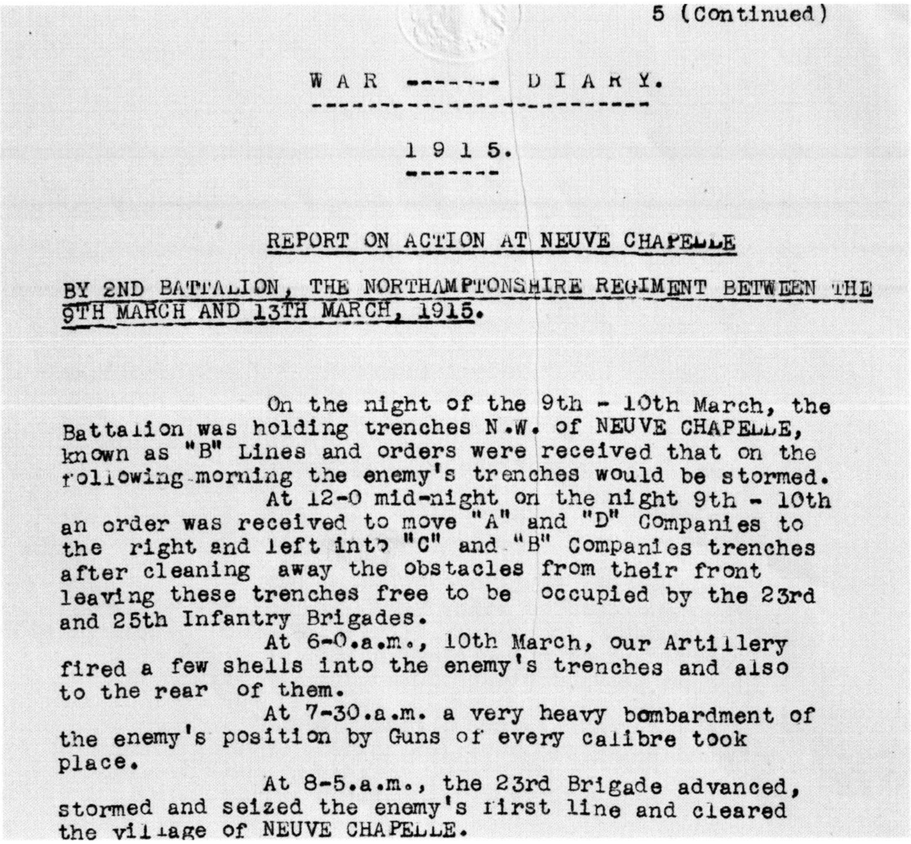

W A R ------- D I A R Y.
----

1 9 1 5.

REPORT ON ACTION AT NEUVE CHAPELLE

BY 2ND BATTALION, THE NORTHAMPTONSHIRE REGIMENT BETWEEN THE 9TH MARCH AND 13TH MARCH, 1915.

On the night of the 9th - 10th March, the Battalion was holding trenches N.W. of NEUVE CHAPELLE, known as "B" Lines and orders were received that on the following morning the enemy's trenches would be stormed.

At 12-0 mid-night on the night 9th - 10th an order was received to move "A" and "D" Companies to the right and left into "C" and "B" Companies trenches after cleaning away the obstacles from their front leaving these trenches free to be occupied by the 23rd and 25th Infantry Brigades.

At 6-0.a.m., 10th March, our Artillery fired a few shells into the enemy's trenches and also to the rear of them.

At 7-30.a.m. a very heavy bombardment of the enemy's position by Guns of every calibre took place.

At 8-5.a.m., the 23rd Brigade advanced, stormed and seized the enemy's first line and cleared the village of NEUVE CHAPELLE.

Figure 2.6: A section of the battalion's report of the action at Neuve Chapelle

At 0830, A Company were ordered to clear a barricade in the road to the now ruinous village. The area had been littered with the dead from both sides; British soldiers dangled on German wire beside dead German bodies whose skins were yellowing from lyddite shells. One private describes the moaning from the wounded as "something dreadful". B Company arrived at this location around 1100. In the midst of heavy fire, their task was to help consolidate the position by digging a communication trench up to the captured enemy line and to bring up supplies.

The regiment was split, incessant German shelling was causing heavy casualties and communication lines had been destroyed. It was clear to soldiers at the front that reinforcements were needed urgently. That's not, however, what was being planned. The divisional headquarters, not completely aware of the situation on the ground, prepared for a renewed offensive. The regiment was collected and at 1620 advanced along with the rest of the 24th Brigade. At 1700, they reached their target with little engagement but were unable to rendezvous with the 7th Division. Under the darkening sky, the commanding officer of the Northamptons sent a message to brigade headquarters asking for instructions. A reply soon came back, informing them to advance immediately.

The men rushed forward as ordered, covering a short stretch of ground before lying flat on the ground to avoid the bullets darting over their heads. The Regimental History quotes a platoon commander of B Company who recounted that "the terrific din of musketry seemed to increase in intensity" every time the men made one of their dashes forward. During this chaotic advance, now in full darkness, it appears the Northampton Regiment once again became split up and was mixed amongst other regiments as casualties were mounting up. The Northamptons persevered and managed to reach the front line, only 300 yards from the enemy lines, where they began digging holes to protect themselves from German bombs. Unfortunately, these holes did not provide adequate protection later on in battle: dug quickly in frantic circumstances, they were not deep enough because of the waterlogged ground. In fact, the men were so close to the German trenches that W. H. Holloway, in his book, *Northamptonshire and the Great War*, said that fragments of German corpses were blown on to the British side along with earth, dust and fumes.

As a result of continuous heavy fire from the Germans, ammunition running low and a dispersed regiment, Lieutenant Colonel Charles Prichard rushed back to the brigade headquarters and informed them that the regiment had lost contact with the Sherwood Foresters, who were supporting the Northamptons on the right, and that any attempt to carry out a further advance would be futile. Prichard said the assault should now wait for dawn; the planned British bombardment would clear the way for invasion while the postponement would give Prichard time to reorganise his battalion. The Lieutenant Colonel's advice appears to have been heeded, as the division headquarters issued orders at 2320 that the 24th Brigade must advance at 0700.

Figure 2.7: Lieutenant-Colonel Prichard. This photograph, taken in 1913, shows a 52-year-old Prichard with the 2nd Northamptons in Malta.

The resumption of the advance on the 11th was mired in confusion from the off as a thick fog replaced the dark sky, reducing the visibility. As a result, artillery observation was unable to produce an accurate overview of German fortifications and the bombardment was completely ineffective. When the order was given for the Northamptons to go 'over the top', they were almost immediately gunned down by heavily armed and well-prepared German soldiers. An idea of the severity of the German guns is to be found in the normally impassive battalion diaries which recorded that the battalion was "suffering very heavy casualties". It was here that the popular Lieutenant Gordon got fatally hit. Lieutenant Coldwell of D Company recalled that:

> "About 7am, Gordon and I were looking over the top of the trench with a view to our line of advance, when a bullet took him straight through the throat. I gave him a morphia pill – poor devil, it was quite hopeless, but I think it kept him out of pain."

A mere forty minutes after the start of the attack, the Worcesters, second in the line, sent a desperate message back to brigade headquarters informing them that the Northamptons were held up at the front and more artillery support was urgently needed. This was not possible due to the adverse weather conditions. Despite the day's action only being two hours in, it was clear that the chances of meaningful progress were painfully slim. The attack, as per orders, carried on, although D Company's advance was cut short after they were "repulsed by heavy fire". Lieutenant Coldwell gives a graphic account of D Company's offence, providing a rare insight into some of the brutal aspects of the war:

> "Off we went; dead silence for three or four seconds, and then came the German bullets, and that, as far as I am concerned, was the end of the attack of D Company – practically everyone who left my bit of trench was blotted out … the Germans then started to shell our line and things were decidedly unpleasant, so those of us that could made a painful crawl back to our line … I remember talking to a wounded man close to me as he lay out there. He was badly hit and he wanted me to finish him off, but I was too much of a coward to do so, with so many of our own people about … This man must have been killed soon after I saw him, as I remember a shell which appeared to burst slap on top of him."

As morning came, so too did the realisation that it was now the Germans' turn to counter-attack. A large number of German soldiers were spotted some 400 yards in the distance. Frantically, the Northamptons began to fire at once. As light broke out, the Northamptons were greeted with the sight of masses of wounded German soldiers barely moving on the ground. The battalion diary records that the Germans were "nearly all shot down" – one soldier wrote that "we simply mowed them down like ninepins". Feeling buoyed after stopping the German advance and perhaps remembering the Army Order circulated on the eve of battle that reminded soldiers "the army and the nation are watching the result", the British thought they could still salvage some form of victory. Lieutenant Colonel Prichard ordered an attack and the Northamptons, once again, went into No Man's Land with Prichard leading the charge, trench map in hand.

On this occasion the men reached the German lines, and some even occupied a few enemy trenches which they found to be empty. The battalion were under heavy fire from the well-armed German forces; unable to secure any gains, they were soon in retreat after an order for withdrawal was issued by Prichard. During the withdrawal, Prichard's adjutant, 28-year-old Captain H. Power – son of Lieutenant C. E. Power of the 1st Northamptonshire Battalion – was killed. The rest of the day was spent in their dugouts seeking shelter from German bullets and shells. In the evening, the Northamptons were relieved of their positions, with the battalion diarist after the battle, Captain L. A. Haldane, simply stating that they had "suffered severe losses".

It is illustrative that Haldane gave no precise details on the casualties, preferring a simple unemotional note. Indeed, when the retreat orders were issued he blandly records, "This order was carried out, some few men reaching the enemy's trench and found it vacated," underplaying the struggle to reach the enemy line. Perhaps this was because of the personal circumstances Haldane found himself in. He was now acting adjutant to Prichard due to the death of Captain Power. Weary from fighting a fierce battle, now fulfilling the adjutant role after his predecessor's death in that battle, Haldane was also tasked with writing the diary report – a task he clearly took no joy in. Haldane would soon assume greater responsibility after Prichard was shot in the lungs shortly after this battle.

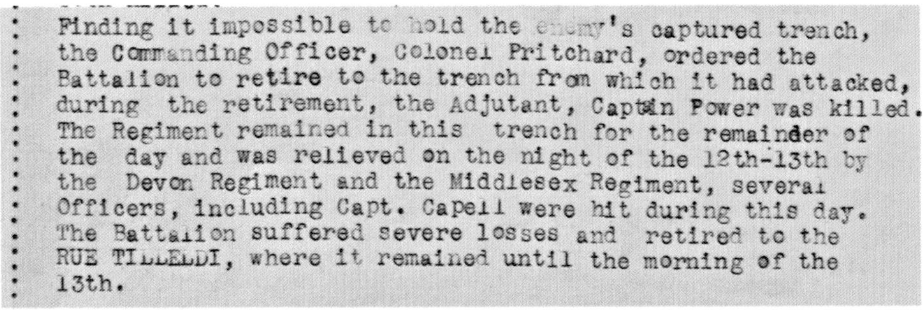

```
Finding it impossible to hold the enemy's captured trench,
the Commanding Officer, Colonel Pritchard, ordered the
Battalion to retire to the trench from which it had attacked,
during the retirement, the Adjutant, Captain Power was killed.
The Regiment remained in this trench for the remainder of
the day and was relieved on the night of the 12th-13th by
the Devon Regiment and the Middlesex Regiment, several
Officers, including Capt. Capell were hit during this day.
The Battalion suffered severe losses and retired to the
RUE TILLELOI, where it remained until the morning of the
13th.
```

Figure 2.8: The battalion's war diary contained a summary of the battle, candidly writing of "severe losses".

The battle continued until the following day, although by this time the intensity of the fighting had diminished and both sides spent the day consolidating positions and digging trenches. The Germans had repelled the British offensive and thus deprived the British of the strategically advantageous high ground at Aubers Ridge. However, this outcome had not come cheaply for the Germans, with their casualties amounting to over 12,000. The British casualties numbered 11,200 (7,000 British, 4,200 Indian). The 2nd Northamptons had suffered tremendously. Every single officer in B Company was either killed or wounded; the battalion's total losses numbered 107 killed and 207 wounded, with a further 83 missing, which meant that a shocking 64% of the battalion was destroyed in three days. The shattered remnants of the 58th were sent to billets for some much-needed rest.

The British commanders, Sir John French and General Haig, did learn some valuable lessons from this battle. It must be remembered that Neuve Chapelle was the first planned British offensive of the war, and hitherto it had been thought impossible to break into enemy trenches. The battle showed this was indeed possible. The hard part, however, was to defend newly won positions in the absence of good communication lines. Neuve Chapelle also revealed the vital importance of artillery observation posts with good visibility. One of the main failures of the attack was the lack of effectiveness of the British bombardment despite the sheer number of shells fired. Indeed, the thirty-five-minute bombardment at the start of the battle was found to be too long, as it gave the Germans precious time to rush in reinforcements to fend off the impending invasion.

Neuve Chapelle was first reported in the papers as a heroic sacrifice in late March. The editor of *The Northampton Independent* in a lead article wrote that "our gallant sons fought like lions and fell like heroes with their faces to the foe", and despite the battalion suffering more than any other unit, the Northamptonshire Regiment had "gained a fresh lustre" by the 2nd Battalion's bravery. With the grieving and worried relatives at the forefront of the author's mind, the column pleads that their sons "died the noblest of deaths in giving their lives for their country" and that they "have died so that we may live".

The paper also reports a special order issued to the 2nd Battalion and other units in the 24th Brigade which actually portrays Neuve Chapelle as a "brilliant success" and says that the men should "fully realise that what they have accomplished in breaking through the German lines is an achievement of which they should all feel proud". This, of course, was nonsense. The artillery effect had done little noteworthy damage, while the breakthrough in the German line had not been held. Lack of reliable information from the front was a feature ever since the start of war and would only get worse.

Media silence and limited official information meant families were left in the dark about the situation for their sons. The Marchioness of Exeter, wife of the Lord Lieutenant of Northamptonshire who resided at Burghley House, received a letter in September 1914 from her friend Ada Foundes, complaining that:

> *"It is a ghastly war, and I do feel sorry for the wives and mothers of the Expeditionary Force, as it seems so very difficult to get any information, and the numbers missing is ghastly. Probably a large number will never be accounted for. Uncertainty is the hardest thing to bear."*

One year later, Burghley House, like many noble estates, was used for Northamptonshire's convalescence requirements, housing dozens of beds for wounded soldiers.

Six months on from Ada Foundes' letter, Northamptonshire mothers would strongly feel this uncertainty as the truth about Neuve Chapelle was slowly revealed. Edward Charles Mapley, from Far Cotton, Northampton, was only 16 when he joined the army in 1910. Stationed in Bombay, India, when the war broke out, he returned to England in October and was in France with the 24th Brigade of the 8th Division under General F. Carter by 4th November 1914. Preparing for the offensive at Neuve Chapelle, he died in Flanders on 14th February 1915, aged 21. How Mapley died is unknown, and his remains were never recovered. After his death, his family back in Northampton received his few belongings from the front: two Christmas cards he had kept, a photo of his family and a Princess Mary gift box. His is just one of thousands of examples of Northamptonshire soldiers being killed and their bodies never being recovered. Mapley is commemorated at the Le Touret Memorial, for those whose bodies were never found or identified.

Figure 2.9: Private Mapley, standing proudly in his uniform before war broke out in 1914.

To its credit, as the true realities of what happened on that fateful day in March became clear, *The Northampton Independent* didn't shy away from exposing the truth. On 10th April 1915, the paper issued a desperate plea for the authorities to "Tell us the Truth." In a dramatic lead article, the editor asks "when are we going to be told the truth about what was officially represented as a brilliant victory at Neuve Chapelle", before adding, "What about the shattered bodies of our brave boys?" The article touches upon the issue that the truth will eventually be known as letters of the wounded arrive home. On 17th April, five long weeks after the battle, the paper is able to dramatically report that the battalion had been "practically wiped out", although exact details of the battle are missing. Once again, the editor fiercely criticises the war authorities, claiming that the British press have been restricted in their coverage more than that of any other country. While accepting the need for censorship to prevent important details being known to the enemy, it is suggested that unless the public know the "enormity of the suffering and sacrifice" the soldiers face, they won't make the necessary sacrifices for the war effort.

Inside the paper, the reader would find the usual spread of soldiers who were from Northamptonshire or part of the county regiment who had recently been killed in action. Unusually, in this edition all the photographs were of men belonging to the 2nd Battalion and who had perished at Neuve Chapelle. This symbolic mark was no accident: the editor would have been aware of the impact of filling the pages with casualties from Neuve Chapelle instead of soldiers from various battalions in several battles as usual. Finally, on 17th April, the newspaper could report the 'official' story and the editor again criticises the censorship authorities for "needless concealment and reticence".

Despite the stark realisation of war now being fully understood, support for the war was still strong in Northampton. In April, the Oxford University MP, Lord Hugh Cecil, addressing the Northampton Recruitment Committee, delivered a strong justification for war:

> *"The claim upon the nation is one of honour, of interest, and national security ... we are also fighting against the new German theory that Germans are so much superior to the rest of the world that they may properly force upon us German ideas and the German standard of thought and cultivation in all relations of life."*

It is noteworthy that this quote refers to Germany in the First World War. It could understandably be interpreted for events in Europe a quarter of a century later. It was also an opinion shared by many, including some of the Belgian refugees displaced by the war. One can sense the anger felt by the previously mentioned Maurice Thomas, in Abthorpe, who wrote in his diary of "barbaric Germany" as the "bringer of brutal violence". Many refugees of fighting age took up arms after securing their family's safety. Arthur Dryden, of Canons Ashby, employed a

Belgian refugee on his estate in January 1915 and provided shelter to his family. This refugee's stay was short, however, as he left to fight in France by June that year.

The Battle of Neuve Chapelle would in time become a prime example of the formulaic, vicious series of events that came to characterise the Great War. Thousands of men lay dead on both sides, but neither the Germans nor the Allies had much to show for their efforts. For all the bullets, bombs and bodies spent, the British had only advanced a mere two kilometres.

Stagnant trench warfare had begun.

Figure 2.10: With the first mass casualties experienced by the Northamptonshire Regiment in the First World War, those who fought and fell at the Battle of Neuve Chapelle were lauded as heroes by the local press and were afforded extensive coverage.

Figure 3.1: This aerial photograph of Aubers village and the surrounding area taken in July 1916 shows the extent of the trench work and the fields darkened from shelling.

Figure 3.2: A scene from Aubers after the battle, showing the village in ruins.

CHAPTER THREE

The Battle of Aubers Ridge

The Journey of Life

He knoweth the way that I take.
The way he has ordered for me,
And though to my gaze it is hid,
Right on to the end He can see,
And this do I know, come weal or come woe,
His way is the best that can be.

He knoweth the way that I take,
And lest I should falter or stray,
He walks by my side as my friend,
Nor leaves me by night or by day.
Along the rough road He carries my load,
And gladdens the whole of the way.

He knoweth the way that I take,
Then why should I e'er be distressed,
Though trials my pathway beset,
Though Satan my spirit molest,
I shall pass one day, at the end of the way,
To heaven and rapturous rest

Private W.H. Pacey, 2nd Northamptons.
This poem was contained in Private Pacey's last letter home.

He went missing during the battle of Aubers Ridge.

DURING THE BATTLE OF NEUVE CHAPELLE, the 1st Northamptons were manning trenches at Festubert. They left for Oblinghem for what was to be a short period of rest. However, they were soon given orders to prepare for action. Along with the 2nd Northampton Battalion, they were to play a leading role in the British offensive at Aubers Ridge. The army was gearing up for a second attempt to take the area, which offered several strategic advantages, only months after the failure at Neuve Chapelle.

In early 1915, the German Supreme Command moved forces from west to east, determined to defeat Russia while holding strong on the Western Front. The French High Command, observing German movements, began to draw up extensive plans to exploit what they saw as an opportunity to break through the enemy lines. Soon after the losses at Neuve Chapelle, the French Commander-in-Chief, Marshal Joffre, asked Sir John French if the BEF could assist the French Army. Sir John, seeing the opportunity presented, gave his support to Joffre. The French generals had planned three strikes along the front: the primary aim was destroying German communication lines and thereby preventing the Germans from defending the large salient that had grown into parts of France during 1914. A lack of men and resources meant that these plans were abandoned in favour of focusing the first wave of attacks on the Artois region with the aim of gaining control of the high ground at Vimy Ridge.

The attack was planned for 7th May 1915, with the main thrust of the attack falling to the 10th French Army, who would be supported the next day through two flanking attacks by the British. However, heavy rain on the 6th and thick mist on the 7th led to the offensive being postponed until the 9th, on which both the French and British attacks would take place.

The mood among the 1st Northamptons was upbeat. Private C. G. Freir of A Company wrote that "everybody was cheerful and pleased that we had been chosen for the post of honour, the first line of attack," and after learning of the attack being delayed, there was some "slight disappointment which soon cleared off when the men realised that it was only one more day to wait". Their excitement was unsurprising given the magnificent build-up the attack had received; the attack was to give the Allies a decisive advantage in the war, providing a breakthrough that would bring an end to trench warfare. Indeed, the Regimental History states one officer thought the attack "was going to work wonders". On the evening of the 8th, the men left the billets in good spirits reciting popular songs. The singing soon stopped as they reached their positions, being replaced by the occasional bullet whizzing overhead. With the enemy front just 300 yards away, the 1st Northamptons relieved the Black Watch and started preparations for the morning's attack. The men were allowed a short rest at 0200, but were back up at 0400, when each man was given a biscuit for breakfast; for many, this would be their last meal.

Figure 3.3: This photograph, taken at La Gorgue during the early days of the war, shows the French countryside as a tranquil scene, with rolling hills and thick forestry. The villages of Auber and Neuve Chapelle, where the Northamptonshire Regiment would see fierce fighting, are seen in in the distance.

The scene at Aubers on the morning of the 9th was a calm one as the men were greeted by a colourful sunrise. This tranquil scene – "as if there was no such thing as war in the world," as one soldier wrote – would dramatically change.

At 5am, as morning began to break, the Allied bombardment commenced, directing its fire at the German barbed wire. Half an hour later, 9-inch and 15-inch howitzers showered the German trenches with high-calibre shells. A machine-gunner in *The Northampton Independent* provided a dramatic quote: "The racket was appalling, and the earth under our feet trembled and rocked as though Mother Earth had got violent pains under her 'pinny'."

However, the Regimental History claims those who had fought at Neuve Chapelle knew this fire was less intense from the sound of the guns. Additionally, to the bewilderment of the men, the German line was constantly firing back during the British bombardment. At 0540, the British guns shuddered into silence. At once, B and D Companies of the 1st Northampton Battalion climbed their ladders and entered No Man's Land with A and C Companies behind them in support. It was quickly apparent that the British artillery had failed at causing any meaningful damage to the German defences. The Regimental History commented, "what followed was less a battle than a massacre". Indeed, it was. The next moments would go down in history as one of the most depressing situations in the Great War for the British Army, even surpassing the failures at Neuve Chappelle.

The Germans, well prepared and organised, rushed their guns to the front and fired a deadly hail of bullets upon the hapless troops stranded in the middle of No Man's Land – the flat ground providing very little natural cover. The Northamptons and other British troops were gunned down in their scores. Some of the few soldiers who did manage to make progress were impaled by hidden German barbed wire; left dangling on their torn, bloodied limbs, they made easy targets for the German rifles. One Northampton soldier at the scene of battle said that once the men "got their clothes caught they were as helpless as flies on flypaper, and it was good-bye to this world". Another eyewitness account was printed in *The Northampton Independent* on 29th May 1915:

> *"In war theory and practice don't always harmonise, and so the poor Cobblers, as we call the Northants, found themselves hanging on like grim death to that little wire-covered slope. From the top of the trench the Germans were pouring down lead by the ton from their rifles and carefully-posted machine guns. It was more than flesh and blood could stand, and if the Northamptons had turned and run for their lives there isn't a man in the Army that saw the whole thing who wouldn't have acclaimed them as heroes."*

But the Northamptons did not turn around. They soldiered on despite the mass slaughter around them. A small contingent of B and D Companies had managed to reach the German barbed wire which they found to be perfectly intact. The prior British bombardment had barely scratched the surface of the German defences. Unable to get through, the men desperately sought cover in the open, flat ground. Retreat was futile in the daylight as survivors would be instantly shot down. Firing back to the German line was also useless. For one, the British forces on the ground were severely outnumbered. Secondly, German defences had been constructed in a manner which concealed their machine-gunners. Lastly, rising to fire their weapons from whatever limited cover they had found was akin to a death sentence, such was the ferocity of the German guns.

As a result, the men found themselves desperately stuck in No Man's Land with a flood of bullets raining over them. A soldier manning the British artillery wrote in *The Northampton Independent* that, "The bullets were spluttering about like hailstones in a heavy shower, and God alone knows how any of the poor chaps missed being hit." At 6am, orders were given to stop the attack and return to the trenches. It was decided to lie still until nightfall before attempting to retreat back to base. In these extremely horrific times, with hundreds of bloodied corpses scattered on the cold ground, the regiment's officers provided outstanding leadership. The composure, bravery and selflessness displayed by Second Lieutenant Pitcher and Lieutenant Bourdillon earned them both the Military Cross. Pitcher was instrumental in making contact with the battalion headquarters and informing them of the disastrous situation. He also managed to maintain his composure in the heat of the battle, calming his men down and detailing plans for a night retreat. Bourdillon was a medical officer who worked tirelessly throughout the battle, risking his own life to tend to wounded soldiers in the field. Even when he arrived back at his trench, he worked through the night – an indication of both the compassionate nature of the officer and the magnitude of the morning's calamitous events.

Around 1700, the sun began to set, to the relief of those stranded in the middle of No Man's Land. The soldiers had been awake with no rest for 36 hours, having worked vigorously through the previous night making preparations for the morning's attack, and had now spent the last 12 hours in the muddied field. Indeed, the non-combatant, physical role of the soldier is often forgotten about; with irregular, short sleeping hours, often working through several days without any sleep before a major offensive, it is no wonder that the machine-gunner quoted in *The Northampton Independent* also said, "Some of them didn't look quite awake, and went past our position rubbing their eyes." Slowly, the weary survivors began to crawl back to base. One unnamed sergeant quoted in the Regimental History reported that "It took us about two hours to get back, crawling along ditches, stopping to bandage up wounded, rushing over short open spaces, and slithering carefully through the long grass."

For those who were left in the middle for several long hours, many were shot en route back to their base. Private F. S. Whiting of the 1st Battalion later wrote of the incident: "The shell fire was terrific, and after that we had to run through a hail of hundreds of bullets." It appears that the Germans had increased the vigour of their bombardments to maximise casualties on the men's retreat from No Man's Land. Writing in *The Northampton Independent* after the battle, perhaps with grieving relatives in mind, Private C. F. Wheeler described how "the German snipers picked off our officers, and those who fell were mostly shot through the head and therefore died instantly". The knowledge of a quick and painless death was perhaps the only flicker of comfort available to loved ones. The men eventually trickled back to their trenches, where they were greeted with a "rousing cheer" from other troops who realised their losses had been terrible. Soon the shattered survivors of the 1st Northamptons were transported to Le Touret for rest.

The 2nd Battalion of the Northamptonshire Regiment also played a major role in this battle; built up with recruits from 'Kitchener's Army' after the calamitous losses at Neuve Chapelle, these new arrivals would also suffer terrible casualties in their first 'baptism of fire'. As part of the 7th Division, they were assigned the front-line position in an attack aimed at making a breakthrough in Rouges Bancs, just to the left of the 1st Northamptons. The battalion officers had spent the preceding week preparing for the attack by training enthusiastic recruits to go 'over the top'. Late in the evening on 8th May, the men left their base to go into the trenches between Petillon and Rouges Bancs. A and D Companies were in the front line, while B and C Companies occupied the trenches behind them near a beautiful orchard – a grim contrast to what they would face in the looming battle. As the British bombardment finished at 0540, numerous whistles began to blow along the battalion front line. The men climbed their ladders and marched straight into the Germans, who were ready and waiting. For many of the new recruits, this would be their first and last experience of war.

Figure 3.4: This photograph taken at Neuve Chapelle shows Aubers and Bois du Biez. The terrain the men had to cross is visible: rough, loose ground with deeply dug trenches all protected by barbed wire.

In a matter of minutes, the whole of A Company was almost annihilated. B and C Companies bravely tried to press on but were incurring heavy casualties. Around 30 men of D Company led by Lieutenant Parker actually managed to reach the German breastwork but were not able to secure any gains as they found it impenetrable. Two hours later, at 8am, an order was received from battalion headquarters telling C Company to withdraw from the battle. Orders were also given for the rest of the battalion to retreat, but these instructions were not received, as the communication equipment was blocked by trees. Therefore, Private Lapham bravely volunteered to go into No Man's Land to inform battalion officers. Miraculously, he succeeded in contacting the men at the front and brought back news to the trenches of the dire situation in the middle of No Man's Land. With this, the battalion sent a report to brigade headquarters informing them that no further progress was possible.

Like their sister battalion, the 1st Northamptons, the men of the 2nd were left in the middle of No Man's Land praying for nightfall to come early so that they could begin their long, arduous retreat. Private Fred Larkman, of 51 Dunster Street, Northampton, was one of those who was stuck in the middle along with his comrades in C Company. After being shot in the elbow, he wrote to his mother while in hospital at Halifax:

> "I had a bit of luck to get back to our trenches, for I don't quite know how I managed it, as I was about 100 yards away from them, and was under heavy fire. I had a river to cross and about four rows of trenches, which were about two feet deep in water. I had to crawl on my side to get back to safety, but I got there with a struggle."

Typical of letters sent back home during the war, the message has a notable lack of emotion and absence of information about casualties. Partly because soldiers knew their letters would have to pass the censors, the lack of detail was also because they did not want their loved ones to know the terrifying realities they faced.

The few remaining soldiers who had gone into battle first, along with A and D Companies, did not make it back to their trenches until 2000. The battlefield was now completely shrouded in darkness and the stretcher-bearers began the unenviable task of collecting the wounded, always mindful of German snipers on the prowl. The battalion was formally relieved in the early hours of the morning and went to Laventie to recuperate.

In what was the single worst day in the Northamptonshire Regiment's history thus far, the 1st Battalion suffered greater casualties than any other battalion – 560 men in total. The 2nd Battalion was scarcely better off, amassing 426 casualties, of whom 67 were killed. A further 157 men from the 2nd Battalion were recorded as missing. As a result of these losses, the 2nd Battalion was amalgamated with the 5th Battalion of the Black Watch. In total, the British Army had 4,500 casualties from this single day of action.

The Northamptonshire Regiment had suffered gravely, and the town would soon start to grieve for their fallen. The first mention of the battle in *The Northampton Independent* was on 15th May. The paper printed a short letter it had received, which ominously states:

> "We went into action about five o'clock on Sunday, May 9th, and lost between 600 and 700 of our Regiment alone, as far as I can say. It is a wonder I am alive to tell the tale."

As worried families read the rest of the newspaper, they would find no further details about the battle. One can imagine the psychological strain that such a short, hopeless article would have on relatives wondering if their loved ones were among the casualties. With the first year of the war just coming to a close, reports of large casualties would still have the capacity to shock, frighten and panic people back home. Day by day, month by month, the war was growing older and its reality far bleaker. Industries began to have severe labour shortages, young men had suddenly disappeared from the high streets, and theatre productions, musicals and summer fairs were cancelled. These occurrences, combined with the news that around "600 or 700" men had either been severely injured or killed on a single day of battle, would make it crystal clear that this was a horrific war – like no other before it.

A horror that, if it ever needed to, became extremely vivid for those back home with one of the pivotal events of the Great War. A few days before the Battle of Aubers Ridge, on 7th May 1915, a German U-boat torpedoed the British luxury passenger ship RMS *Lusitania*. The Germans justified their actions because their intelligence suggested the *Lusitania* was carrying munitions from America for the British. The Germans were correct in this respect, and while the exact location of the ship's cargo is not known – probably having sunk to the bottom of the North Atlantic Ocean, near Old Head of Kinsale, Ireland – the ship was carrying millions of rounds for small-scale weapons and thousands of shrapnel shell casings. The British Navy had also provided funding for the ship's construction with the agreement that the ship could be used for military purposes if war ever broke out. Within twenty minutes of being hit, the ship had sunk, taking the lives of 1,128 people. Among the deaths were 128 Americans, a fact that generated huge anger in Washington, DC, and across America, setting off a long chain of maritime events that eventually led to the Americans declaring war on Germany.

Shortly after the sinking, inmates at the Eastcote Prisoner of War Camp had organised a concert, one of several activities that was allowed in the prison to occupy the men. The founder of the camp, Joseph Wilson, learnt about the concert on a visit and, in front of 1,000 prisoners who had gathered in the main hall, announced that it would be postponed "out of respect" for those who had died. Wilson recounted what happened next:

> "There was dead silence. I was scarcely outside the door before the men began to sing 'The Watch on the Rhine' and other German patriotic songs."

Edward Tupper, a trade union activist and close friend of Wilson, was present and later described Wilson's reaction:

> "[Wilson] turned to stone ... I have never in my life seen any man's face change in a moment as his changed then. He gripped my arm, and I saw moonlight glittering on the tears streaming down his face."

Hitherto, the camp was run by Wilson's affiliated union, the National Sailors' and Firemen's Union (NSFU) and provided a degree of comfort to prisoners that would come to a swift end. Incensed by the prisoners' reaction, Wilson made arrangements to hand over management of the camp from the NSFU to the War Office. This eventually happened over the following year, but more immediate changes such as the erection of barbed wire and armed guards patrolling the site signalled to the prisoners that their fortunes were taking a turn for the worse. It is perhaps these developments that prompted three prisoners to escape in August. Not much is known about this incident, though a short report in The Northampton Herald on 13th August does state the escapees were soon recaptured.

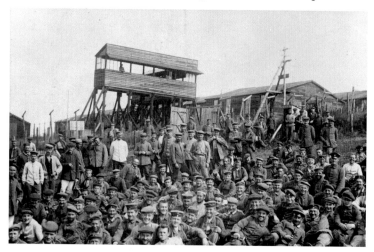

Figures 3.5 and 3.6: German prisoners outside the POW Camp at Eastcote, Northamptonshire. Date of photographs circa 1915-1916.

On 18th August, a full three months after the Battle of Aubers Ridge, a prominent editorial in *The Northampton Independent* finally informed readers that their "worst fears" had been confirmed regarding those who were recorded as "missing", since no prisoners were reported as having been found. The editorial also added that "this sad news will tend to remove the last shred of hope from those still suffering an agony of suspense concerning their dear ones". Remarkably, a month after this article, the paper on 18th September reported that a Private George Barber of the 2nd Northamptons had been taken prisoner after fighting at Aubers Ridge. The editor, aware of the paper's reports a month earlier, told readers not to "buoy themselves up with the belief that there can be many, if any, more".

Indeed, others were not so lucky. It was not until 29th August that the father of Second Lieutenant G. F. Blacker of the 58th received news that his son had been buried near an orchard in Fromelles after fighting at Aubers Ridge. The reason for the long delay was that Blacker, like many around him, had been killed near the German line. It was too dangerous to attempt to retrieve their bodies until many months after the battle, if at all. Private John Joseph Tarry, from Duston, Northampton, had joined the army in 1913 and was part of the BEF in B Company of the 1st Northamptonshire Battalion. A lively character in the battalion, Tarry was known to his superiors before the war as a bit of a rebel after a series of run-ins involving gambling and not complying with orders. Tarry was killed at Aubers Ridge on the day of the battle. His father, living at 27 St Spencers, St James, Northampton, was only informed on 29th September, over four months later. By this time, relatives would have read several press reports speculating on casualties and possible survivors, before receiving the sad truth. As was often the case, John Joseph was one of several brothers from the same family that served: Herbert Frederick Tarry was wounded in France in October 1916 and returned home, while Francis Stephen Tarry enlisted in October 1917 and was discharged in March 1918.

Figure 3.7: Private Joseph Tarry, second row, fourth from left; No 8 Platoon, B Company, 1st Northamptonshire Battalion, 1914.

In the immediate aftermath of the battle, however, relatives had to settle for a report in *The Northampton Independent* on 22nd May, where the editor announced that the battalion was almost annihilated after being "ruthlessly mown down" by German machine guns at close range. The editor, taking a brave stance by departing from the official government line, prints a revelation from The Times of London in bold text which read:

> *"Men died in heaps upon the Aubers Ridge on May 9th because the field guns were short, and gravely short, of high explosive shells."*

When reading newspaper reports during the war, one must always have the intended audience in mind. This was a local paper covering an event where local soldiers had died in their hundreds. There exist common perceptions of the war – not entirely unfounded – of a patriotic public who were wholly supportive of the war effort, of millions of young men eagerly enlisting in Kitchener's 'New Army' and a press muted by the war censors. The Battle of Aubers Ridge serves as quite an interesting example to test such impressions. While it is always difficult to measure public opinion, it appears the initial fervour for war was clearly declining; already new recruits to the army were falling month by month in their tens of thousands and the press, not yet completely straight-jacketed, could fiercely criticise the government. In the article of 22nd May, the editor demands to know "who is responsible" for the munitions shortages.

The scandal was far from over with the following week's *The Northampton Independent* carrying the headline: "Why the Northamptons suffered." Alluding to the previous week's report of munitions shortages, the German defences were said to be "practically intact" after the British bombardment, with the enemy "safely entrenched behind them". In a courageous move, the editor, Mr Holloway, disclosed highly controversial information he had received from private sources. Shockingly, shortages were revealed not to have been limited to munitions but also of basic tools such as wire cutters. He cited one of the Northampton battalions – a thousand men strong – having a measly 24 wire cutters between them. Even if the men overcame the odds greatly stacked against them by reaching the German wire, they had no means to force their way through it. With no safe passage back, the men had little alternative but to attempt climbing over the barbed wire where their limbs would be penetrated by the cold steel and while dangling would attract the attention of the German gunners. In an act of desperation, an unnamed Commanding Officer of the regiment appealed to the editor of the newspaper for help. The paper, through the generosity of its readers, was able to send the battalion hundreds more wire cutters. It is not hard to imagine the anger the wire-cutter shortages would have provoked.

The editor of *The Northampton Independent* was perhaps encouraged by another military scandal playing out in the national papers. After the disaster at Neuve Chapelle in March, Sir John French had spoken to his personal friend, The Times war correspondent Colonel Charles Repington, on the reasons for the failure. Sir John had pointed to the severe lack of munitions available, the quality of munitions produced and also Lord Kitchener – the man responsible for munitions. The Chancellor, David Lloyd George, encouraged Lord Northcliffe, proprietor of The Times and The Daily Mail, to publish Repington's article about the shortage of shells on the Western Front. On 14th May, just five days after another colossal failure at Aubers Ridge, the article was duly printed to huge public outrage, and the phrase 'Shells Scandal' was born.

So devastating was the scandal that the Liberal government collapsed on 25th May. A new coalition government was formed, with Herbert Asquith continuing as prime minister, but with several new departments created, including the Ministry of Munitions headed by Lloyd George. The new ministry was extremely successful: 16.5 million shells were produced by the end of 1915, compared to the 500,000 shells produced in the first five months of war. Part of the dramatic production increase was the result of scientific innovation of converting grain, via a process of anaerobic fermentation, into acetone – a key material needed for cordite. There also began the unprecedented employment of women in factories helping to cover the growing labour shortage.

Partly for his role in leaking the Shells Scandal, Sir John French was recalled as Commander-in-Chief at the end of 1915, to be replaced by Sir Douglas Haig. Lloyd George, on the other hand, continued to grow in stature and replaced Asquith as prime minister in December 1916 with the support of Lord Northcliffe. Repington, who had personally witnessed the failure at Aubers Ridge, was banned from visiting the Western Front until 1916. After Aubers Ridge and the Shells Scandal, war news and battle reports had to go through a longer censorship process before being published, lest they dampen public approval of the war.

Soldiers' letters home were also subject to strict censorship, with no mention of location or casualties allowed. There were, of course, cracks in the system and on some occasions prohibited content leaked through. Arthur James Ette, a soldier from Northampton serving in the 2nd Northamptonshire Battalion, sent a letter to his parents on 4th October 1915 after the battalion had seen action at Aubers Ridge. The letter's lucid content is remarkable. Ette writes about coming under "heavy fire" from the Germans, and that while he is safe, "hundreds have not" survived. He writes to his worried parents that his experience has "been simply hell!"

Battalion war diaries by custom are dry, monotonous logs that simply list key facts in an unemotional manner. While a useful tool to monitor the progress and whereabouts of a battalion, they give little insight into the experiences of soldiers.

The contrast between Ette's letter and the official battalion war diary is striking. The soldier describes to his parents in vivid detail the battalion's activities on 21st September 1915. He writes:

> "On the 21st our artillery started, knocking the enemies' works down, I might add that we had 23 batteries on the go. R. H A [Royal Horse Artillery] quite up to the trenches near the Canadian guns 8 miles away. They done considerable damage the first day, and our machine guns kept up a steady fire all night to keep the enemy from rebuilding there [sic] lines again. The Germans brought their big guns up and retaliated. We had to shout to each other to speak so awful was the noise. You might guess angry chaps go mad in the midst of such an awful time. You should see the way old Lloyd Georges [sic] ammunitions bursted up everything. The Germans artillery was the same. He put them over 3 at a time. It was enough to scare you to death, let alone the shells flying in all directions. The force of the explosions will knock you down. As I was saying we had 4 days of this and at night the 25th Brigade came into the trenches ready to face the foe."

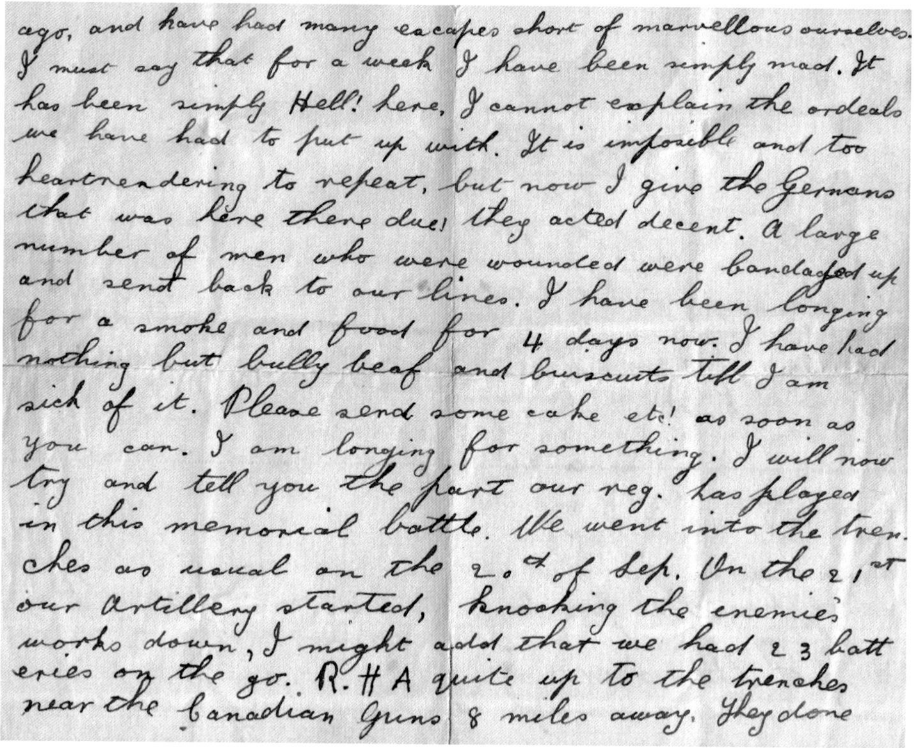

Figure 3.8: An extract from Arthur James Ette's revealing letter which reached his family unscathed by the censors.

The battalion diary on 21st September simply states:

> *"Our artillery bombarded the enemy's position at BRIDOUX FORS. The enemy did not reply very much."*

For the next three days, the diarist just records "artillery bombardment continues" without further embellishment, although Captain Latham being wounded is noted.

On the 24th, the battalion were relieved of their positions by the 2nd Lincolnshires and were given a period of rest before the impending attack. Ette's account paints a harrowing scene:

> *"Well the morning came, a big gun sounded about 4 and then the whole lot spoke out together. We were watching the affect [sic] and all along the German lines it was nothing but red fire. This kept on for an hour and then the boys advanced and took the German positions capturing 102 prisoners. About 9 oclock, a mist came over and with it came thousands of Germans. The Germans came up in motors and anything to get them up quickly. Our chaps fought like lions but were compelled to retire a bit. The Northamptons then went up in the firing line, and dug a new trench between ours and the enemy, and we have been in it since. They have been trying to force us out of it with shells and mortars and grenades but they cannot. The right reg were holding it I haven't had a wash since I have been in. Dare not move sometimes. On the night of the 5th we saw some awful sights when we were coming through the old trenches. Men lay dead and wounded all over the place, but the stretcher bearers worked like heroes and cleared them away. Well this gives you some idea what Tommy is doing today in France, and I hope that people who have the means will try and help us out here who have not got the means to help ourselves."*

Meanwhile, the battalion diary records:

> *"The German position was assaulted by the 25th INF BDE. The 24th INF BDE were in support [...] The Battalion was ordered to send up its Grenadier platoon to assist in bombing the enemy's second line [...] At 1pm 2 Cy [Company] were sent up under CAPT LATHAM to support the counter-attack [...] At 8PM the Battalion moved up the trenches and relieved the LINCOLNSHIRE REGT. Two Cy dug themselves in between DEAD TREE and the CINDER TRACK."*

From the battalion diary, one would not grasp the intensity of the fighting in normal trench positions despite no major battle being fought. The severity of the fighting was even worse after a vital battle like Aubers Ridge, and it is unsurprising the 2nd Battalion, utterly bruised and battered, were given a period of much-needed rest. What remained of the battalion enjoyed games of inter-company cricket on a makeshift pitch. Sadly for C Company, they capitulated to a massive defeat at the hands of D Company. Despite D Company scoring a modest 112 runs, C Company made a pitiful 27 runs in their first innings. D Company duly enforced the follow-on, putting C Company in the wicket once again. A slight improvement was displayed by C Company as they scored 69 runs, although this did not save them from suffering the embarrassment of an innings defeat.

After the terrors witnessed just over a month ago at Aubers Ridge, the game would have provided some well-earned relaxation, relief and fun for the men. Public perceptions of the war are almost solely of soldiers lying in rat-infested muddied trenches, suffering from frostbite and being ordered to march to their deaths in No Man's Land. The image of 22 soldiers playing a gentlemen's game, situated on a pleasant, albeit uneven, field under July's warm sun is not something that would immediately spring to mind in common imaginings of the First World War.

The battle had been a hopeless failure for the British Army, and the British effort had no positive effect on assisting the main French attack 15 miles south. Some of the failures from only two months previously at Neuve Chapelle had come back to haunt the army. Firstly, the effectiveness of the field artillery had been grossly exaggerated; the shock and awe bombardment did not come close to having the desired effect on the enemy defences, with the barbed wire appearing untouched. Secondly, other German defence structures such as their breastworks had withstood the barrage, leaving the machine-gun loopholes at their bases intact and free to fire without reply on the invading troops. Subsequent histories of the battle have even recorded that the British received information from several sources about the bolstered German defences – information that was clearly not acted upon or paid sufficient attention. Finally, any advantage to be gained by the element of surprise was somehow lost. If any positives can be found at Aubers Ridge, the battle may have persuaded Colonel Repington to author his article on the dire shortage of shells, thus setting in motion dramatic and long-lasting changes to both industry and government.

The Battle of Aubers Ridge fits the mould of typical impressions of the First World War: horrifying trench-based warfare with men mown down in their thousands and no gains in territory. Indeed, the battalions who fought this battle would bear little resemblance to those that had landed at the start of the war and also to those that would finish the war – such was the scale of losses for many units, including the Northamptons.

(From top to bottom)
Figure 4.1: The 6th Battalion walking through rubble in France.
Figure 4.2: The battalion being inspected in France, photographed in 1915
Figure 4.3: Officers of the 6th Northamptonshire Battalion in 1915

CHAPTER FOUR

The Somme

Trones Wood
July 14, 1916

Three times the khaki line had leapt and surged
Among the up-torn trees, and won the wood;
Three times the furrowed earth of foes was purged,
But still the blue-grey flood

Wave after wave, returned all ridged with flame,
Flashing with steel, and surfed with bursting shell;
Triumphant - till the Sixth Northamptons came
Undaunted to that hell.

Then dying eyes, despairing of the day
Lit with new hope; and tortured forms
Upstood,
Staggering to help, or cheering where they
Lay,
As swiftly to the wood

The Sixth Northamptons charged. Nor bomb nor blade
Could stop that splendid thrust of Neneside men:
The wild, impetuous tide was met and stayed
And tumbled back again.

Slowly it ebbed; but every yielded yard
The Sixth Northamptons held - till all the wood
Was one impervious rampart, grim and hard,
Cemented with their blood.

This is the story that in farm and fen
Factory and field for countless years to be,
Will still be told where runs the silver Nene
From Naseby to the sea.
A.

Poem printed in '*The Northampton Independent*, 2nd September 1916.

"With true British tenacity they broke all efforts to drive them out, and earned a noble share of that brilliant success on July 1st which spread fresh heart and hope through every corner of the Empire"

The Northampton Independent, 15th July 1916

THE ABOVE REPORT REFERS TO THE OPENING DAY of the Battle of the Somme. In fact, it was not a "brilliant success". Instead, 1st July 1916 would go down as the darkest day in British military history; over 19,000 men were killed, with another 35,000 wounded – this was the greatest number of losses ever suffered by the British Army on a single day. Unsurprisingly, almost all subsequent accounts of the Somme offensive have condemned it as an unequivocal failure. For three months the battle raged, and by the end of November the Allies had only advanced a paltry nine kilometres. The human cost was tragic: the British suffered 420,000 casualties; the French, 195,000; and the Germans, 650,000.

By spring 1916, the country was truly feeling the full force of the war. In a sign of the perilous situation, on 21st May the British government introduced the Summer Time Act, which advanced the clocks one hour. Arthur Dryden, managing his estate at Canons Ashby, wrote in his diary that the change was done "to obtain a saving during war in the consumption & consequent expense of artificial light and cause the people to live more by natural day-light."

Substantial efforts were also being made to increase medical facilities. Just 192 beds in five key locations across Northamptonshire existed for wounded soldiers at the start of the war, which proved woefully inadequate. By spring 1916, total beds had increased to over 1,000 and were spread across seventeen locations. Northampton General Hospital had taken control of nearby buildings to cope with the growing demand; 260 beds were put in Barry Road School, while Abington Avenue School also took 64 beds. In a few months, as casualties from the Somme returned home, even more beds would be required.

The weather took a turn for the worse in late March as heavy snow and violent winds played havoc with infrastructure. Telephone poles were ripped out of the ground, cars were stuck in the snow and train services were cancelled. For two days, Northampton was effectively cut off from the outside world – a feeling that the prisoners at Eastcote would have been all too familiar with.

By April 1916, there were 1,660 inmates at the camp, the majority of them German nationals, and there were also five Turkish men. Most of these were still civilian prisoners, despite the War Office working to transfer control of the camp's running from the National Sailors' and Firemen's Union after the response from German prisoners to the sinking of the *Lusitania* in May 1915 [1]. An American Embassy report from February 1916 gives some indication of the living standards

---

1 Covered in Chapter 3, Battle of Aubers Ridge.

at the camp: each shower was shared by 65 men while there were 30 men to each toilet, an infirmary was on site staffed by two doctors while a fully equipped hospital was under construction, and only one of the four compounds was in use. As the process of transferring control to the War Office continued, efforts were geared up to increase capacity.

It appears that prisoners self-policed themselves at this time, with officers loosely involved in the camp's internal function. It was this structure that led to the organic formation of societies for sports, bands, theatre and even a school with a library containing over 2,500 books. This insight into day-to-day life is illuminating, as scarcely a thought is given to how such camps functioned. Not only was it a huge task to procure all the resources needed for thousands of men, the prisoners needed to be occupied in some capacity. Indeed, Chapman and Moss state in their book, *Detained in England 1914-1920: Eastcote POW Camp Pattishall*, that one of the reasons breakouts occurred, despite humane living standards, was out of pure boredom.

Early in 1916 on the Western Front, the French had been suffering severe losses at Verdun, 130 miles east of Paris. General Joffre, wary of this precarious position, requested that General Haig help relieve his army and called upon Lord Kitchener to dispatch more army divisions to France. As a result, the Allied High Command decided to launch a major attack to the north of Verdun to help take pressure off the French. The British planned to attack a fifteen-mile front between Serre and Curlu, with the French attacking an eight-mile front south of the Somme. The date for the attack was set as 1st July.

The Somme was hoped to be a decisive moment in the war, the moment when the Allied forces would unleash such a ferocious offensive that the Germans would be forced to retreat, thus heralding the end of war. The scale of the offensive can be gleaned from how many Northamptonshire battalions were called upon for action; the 1st, 2nd, 6th and 7th Battalions were all involved. Soldiers were aware that there was a big push being planned but could not inform their families. One soldier, Arthur Bonham, not serving with the Northamptonshire Regiment but with the 27th Brigade in France, wrote to his mother at 33 St Giles Street, Northampton, on 29th June – just two days before the battle. Rather ominously, he said, "Don't be surprised if you don't hear from me for some little time now as something is on the board … all leave is stopped."

The 2nd Northamptons, part of the 24th Brigade, were temporarily assigned to the 23rd Division. At 2130 on 6th July, the battalion arrived in Fricourt and they were given a briefing for a major assault the following day on the town of Contalmaison. However, the attack did not go as planned, as supporting attacks by other divisions failed, thus delaying the 24th Brigade. The battalion were promptly given revised orders, with C Company and D Company moved to the trenches in Lozenge Wood, while A Company and B Company were sent to Crucifix Trench. B Company advanced right up to Contalmaison and were ordered to occupy the

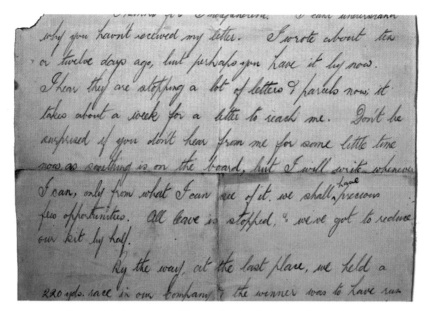

Figure 4.4: An extract of Private Bonham's letter to his mother.

town. In the Regimental History, the authors state the following events are mired in confusion with conflicting accounts. It is clear that the trenches were in an already terrible state – crowded with the dead bodies from previous attempts to take the town – which meant navigating the trenches was a slow process, made slower by heavy rainfall.

The Regimental History suggests it is likely that C Company moved up to Birch and Shelter Alleys to support the 1st Worcesters, who were also on the front line with the Northamptons. Meanwhile, A Company marched up a sunken road towards the town, with D Company following closely behind. However, the enemy artillery was proving too powerful, launching a steady volley of shells halting the advance of the invading troops. This left the Northamptons with little choice but to retreat as casualties mounted. What was left of the battalion regrouped at Birch Alley, where they dug themselves in for the night and cleaned their mud-ridden rifles.

The following day news came in that Contalmaison had been evacuated by the Germans. Cautiously, the Northamptons and the Worcesters advanced. Soon the Germans revealed themselves and were launching heavy machine-gun and rifle fire, ambushing the advancing British troops. The Northamptons suffered heavy casualties but managed to reach a relatively safe spot near Peake Wood, where they rested. On 10th July, the 2nd Northamptons were relieved by none other than their sister battalion, the 1st Northamptons, a historic occurrence that "evoked great enthusiasm in both battalions". Earlier news that Contalmaison had finally been taken also added to the jovial mood. It was a rare opportunity for some cheer after a bloody month. By 31st July, the battalion was 808 strong after suffering 300 casualties over the course of the month. Soon after, the 2nd Northamptons rejoined the 8th Division and were sent to the Cuinchy sector, fifty miles north of Contalmaison.

The battalion's efforts at Contalmaison were never formally revealed in Northampton. On 29th July, *The Northampton Independent* made a reference to the 1st and 2nd Battalions but with infuriatingly little detail. However, a dramatic quote from an unnamed soldier was printed which said, "We are at present back in billets trying to make something of what remains of the battalion." One last cryptic mention was finally printed on 7th October – three months after the incident had occurred – under the simple heading "Northamptons Capture Another Stronghold." With no information regarding which battalion fought and where the victory had occurred, the editor sadly told his readers to prepare for another long casualty list, claiming that:

> *"this time the sacrifice has not been in vain. The awful experience of Aubers Ridge has not been repeated ... our men have tasted the sweets of triumph in defeating some of the proudest infantry regiments in the world."*

This passage perfectly illustrates the difficulties editors faced during the war. In possession of knowledge that was of critical importance to their readers, but unable to breach censorship laws, they resorted to vague mentions to provide encouragement and reassurance. In this instance we find an editor trying to brace his readers for big losses while at the same time providing reassurance that their sons' sacrifices were worthwhile. It had now been two years since Britain went to war: the "heroes who have fallen" section in the paper got ever longer, rations got ever smaller, tribunals were introduced with the power to send the few remaining young men to war and there seemed to be no end in sight.

Back in France, on 8th August, the troops were moved to the Quarries Sector. Here the trenches were among the worst in France, prompting the normally bland war battalion diarist to record that "trenches were appallingly filthy and that no work had been done for ages". As troops dug new lines they would often discover dozens of rotting corpses, while the parapets were littered with mangled bodies chewed up by rats. The men were soon moved to the Hohenzollern Redoubt, where on the 24th two Northampton parties launched a night raid. However, the Germans were well prepared and immediately began shelling No Man's Land, forcing one of the raiding parties to return to their line. Nevertheless, one group made it to the German lines, killing five enemy soldiers before returning to their trenches. These small raids could not impose any significant damage on the enemy and nor were they designed to. Instead, the aim of such missions was to capture a German soldier for interrogation purposes. On this occasion, the Northamptons were not successful.

Figure 4.5: "Died for their Country" – *The Northampton Independent*, 29th July 1916. Newspapers across the country had similar features detailing men who were injured or killed, often providing a small biography of the soldier.

However, their luck soon changed. On the 25th, the battalion war diary records that "during the early morning a Bosche was seen lying in No Man's Land". Realising he had been spotted, the German soldier began to run back to his trench, but was shot by a Northampton man on sentry duty. Around 1400, Lance Corporals Lovell and Vickery went out of their trenches and brought the German soldier back for interrogation. Lovell and Vickery were awarded the Military Cross for their actions. There was little major action over the next few weeks and the battalion's time was brought to an abrupt end as the 8th Division were sent back into the Somme area.

The 1st Northamptonshire Battalion arrived in the Somme region on 10th July where it met its sister battalion, the 2nd Northamptons. The battle had been fiercely raging for over a week and the British had made little progress, reaching a position two miles beyond the original German front line. While the 2nd Battalion was occupied attacking Contalmaison, 400 men from the 1st Battalion were sent to the front line carrying wire, stakes and ammo. They were, however, not left untouched by the battle raging nearby. They came under fire from German shelling from Contalmaison and 11 casualties were incurred. On 17th July, the battalion were sent right into the forefront of action near the north-west corner of Mametz Wood. Situated in front of them lay the second German line. A few days previously the 3rd Brigade had launched a successful night attack on the enemy trenches. However, there was a limit to the progress that could be made, and the Northamptons were charged with continuing the attack. Unfortunately, the Germans quickly launched a counter-bombardment. For the seasoned soldiers of the 48th, experiencing shelling was nothing new. On this occasion, however, it was unlike anything the men had witnessed before: it was their first taste of gas shells.

The Northamptons occupied a most perilous position. To their right flank, they had support from other British units. On their left, however, the trenches were occupied by the enemy. All that separated the 1st Battalion from the Germans were two barricades built across the trenches. Adding further danger to their position, the village of Martinpuich was located north of their trench. In between their trench and Martinpuich, the Germans had constructed a strong defensive position to stop further British advancement. The Somme's whole overriding aim was that it was not meant to be yet another stalemate, with troops in trenches merely holding ground – the onus was to move and move fast. The Northamptons would have been all too aware of this and knew that they would soon be invading heavily armed German trenches.

The wait was a short one, for on 20th July, the 1st Battalion received instruction to capture a trench junction immediately behind the German barricades. Four storming parties of ten men plus one subaltern officer were chosen to launch a surprise attack during the early hours. Following closely behind them would be several consolidating parties. At 0230, the parties left their positions and slowly moved forward. The Germans, as on so many occasions, were on high alert and had their machine guns at the ready. The assaulting troops were forced back by German bombing and the order to retreat was soon issued. The attack was a dismal failure, incurring dozens of casualties. After some progress in the early weeks of July, the Somme battle had become yet another bloody stalemate.

After a short period of rest in Albert and with new recruits, the battalion were sent into the front line in the Bazentin area on 15th August. Soon after its arrival, the battalion sent two reconnaissance patrols to scout the enemy trench. Lieutenant C. Nye and Second Lieutenant N. L. Giddy reported that the German trench was lightly defended. Encouraged by what they saw, they persuaded the battalion headquarters that a surprise attack without any prior artillery involvement would be enough to capture the trench. Keen to make progress, the battalion sent a small detachment from C Company to attack that night.

The decision turned out to be a fatal mistake after an instance of ill-fated luck. Just as the invading Northamptons rushed into the trench, a large German working party had arrived in the trench. The patrol was hopelessly outnumbered and now exposed. Second Lieutenant Giddy was shot dead, while Lieutenant Nye was reported missing. Nye, however, returned back to his trench on 16th August after hiding in a shell hole. The Regimental History says that Nye brought back information of "great value" for a new operation being planned – now that the element of surprise had gone. The war diary records Nye as being "absolutely confident of success should the Regiment attack again". Nye, possibly to make amends for his previous ill judgement, volunteered to lead the attacking force. This decision would cost him his life.

On 16th August, at 2200, the orders for attack were issued. C Company and D Company were sent to invade the German trenches with the 2nd Royal Sussex on their right flank. Although artillery support succeeded in quietening enemy fire from the trenches, it quickly became apparent that things were not going as planned. In a saddening episode, the pace of D Company's advance was too fast, and they surged straight into the bombardment issued by their own artillery and incurred severe casualties. Elsewhere, a German counter-attack had forced the Sussex men out of a portion of trench they had previously taken. C Company, led by Captain Clark, bravely resisted further German assaults on their positions, including attempts to bomb them out of the trenches. It was during this defensive stand that Lieutenant Nye was killed along with three others, and there were dozens of further casualties. Despite the losses, C Company successfully held their trench and spent the rest of the day consolidating their position. They didn't have much time as the Germans made yet another counter-attack the following day, where they managed to drive out the Royal Sussex men from their trench. However, they were unsuccessful in scattering the Northamptons from their positions. For their leadership over the last few days, Captain Clark and a junior officer under his command, Second Lieutenant J. Lingham, were both awarded the Military Cross. Since the attack beginning on 16th August, casualties had been extremely high, with around 150 men either killed or wounded.

With the Germans now tired from their failed exertions, the Northamptons went on the offensive. The following afternoon on the 17th, working with the 1st Loyal North Lancashire Regiment, the men invaded enemy positions, aiming to recover the trenches lost by the Royal Sussex men. The attack plan was executed impeccably, with strategically placed machine guns and artillery fire. In a war where winning new territory was a rare feat, any advantage gained was to be built upon immediately lest a period of rest allowed the enemy to draft in reinforcements.

As a result, A Company was sent out on 19th August at 1400 and succeeded in establishing a line of posts on the top of a ridge. With units from other regiments, the men started to construct a communication trench connected to Clark's Trench. While the men worked through the night, a party of around 50 Germans launched a surprise attack from a wood to the rear of the ridge. In a space of a few moments, sudden confusion engulfed the area as the Northamptons tried to organise a defence. In the obscure darkness, Captain Clayton appeared to have mistaken a group of English soldiers for Germans and began firing at them. The soldiers returned fire and shot dead Clayton and two of his men; a further twelve were wounded. The 1st Northamptons war diary describes the incident:

> "In the dark about 50 Germans got round on right ... amongst this party and caused considerable confusion as a result of which Capt Clayton was killed and 2 Lt."

However, the Northamptons managed to fend off the Germans, and by morning had built a reasonable standard of defences.

The men were now exhausted after near constant physical exertion. The Germans, perhaps conscious of this, organised an attack on the Northamptons' exposed flanks. The officer commanding A Company considered their position too exposed and ordered a retreat. When the men got back to Clarke's Trench, the Regimental History claims that Lieutenant Colonel Bethell was furious. The battalion war diary does not directly record this incident, simply stating the ridge was "counter attacked immediately". The fight lasted all day with several waves of attacks, but with the Germans on higher ground, the Northamptons could not force a breakthrough. The war diary took an optimistic view of the situation, recording that their new position 300 yards from the ridge provided an "excellent view" for the artillery and for observing enemy movements. The 1st Battalion were finally relieved on 21st August after a week of intense fighting: 61 men had been killed, 252 had been wounded and a further 60 were missing.

At the same time that the 1st Northamptons were engaged in relentless warfare, Northampton itself had just held a military funeral for a German soldier. On 15th August, the funeral of Johann Riesberg, 26, was held at Billing Road Cemetery. Riesberg was a POW being treated at Duston War Hospital (later renamed St Crispin's Mental Hospital), where he died. Riesberg was one of 25,000 convalescing soldiers that passed through Duston during the war. A newspaper report of his funeral states that he was treated with the same level of care as English soldiers – "an impressive lesson to the Germans in chivalry", as *The Northampton Independent* put it. A large crowd turned out for Riesberg's funeral and the German was given military honours; his coffin was covered by a German flag and three volleys were fired over his grave. Despite two years of brutal war with the "evil Kaiser", the people of Northampton still respectfully recognised this young

German's sacrifice for his country. This small story of gentle humanity contrasting with the ritual massacres of both armies on the Somme is an incident worthy of the same level of appreciation as the Christmas Day truce in 1914.

Figure 4.6: The kitchen of Duston War Hospital, which fed over 25,000 soldiers over the course of the war. Duston later became St Crispin's Mental Hospital.

Elsewhere in August, the 7th Northamptons found themselves heavily engaged in the Somme area. After the start of the Battle of the Somme, they spent weeks in the trenches in and around Bray-sur-Somme, Carnoy and Montauban-de-Picardie. After sunset on 17th August, as the men prepared for an attack on Guillemont, the battalion suffered a huge blow. The popular former England rugby captain Colonel Edgar Mobbs and several officers were hit by a shell - a stark reminder of the threat from bombs even in reserve positions. Mobbs suffered a bad wound to his shoulder blade, while his deputy, Major Grierson, was also seriously hurt. Both men had to leave the trenches for treatment just as the attack was launched, with Captain H. B. King now in command.

Figure 4.7: German trenches near Guillemont after the British shelling in September 1916. Craters from the British shells can be seen alongside several German corpses.

The left flank of the Northamptons had reached their checkpoint but the right could make no progress and became isolated. The Germans had slaughtered the 13th Middlesex, who were in front, and were now firing on the Northamptons. Luckily for these men, the battalion's Lewis gunners managed to hold off their German counterparts until relief arrived. Nevertheless, the casualties borne by the battalion were steep: 50 men had been killed and 273 wounded, with a further 50 missing. The men would get little rest as they were quickly built up with "raw recruits" who had not seen active service before and put into the line by Delville Wood.

Figure 4.8: The Northamptons would likely have encountered this ominous sign declaring a part of Deville Wood to be the "Devil's Trench". Photograph taken on 3rd July 1917.

The men also had another enemy during this period – thirst. The Regimental History states that it was common to see the "poor fellows quenching their parched thirst with water scooped from muddy pools". The men would have to endure many more months in similarly foul conditions as they were sent intermittently into the trenches until Christmas. Like the 6th Battalion, it is important to remember the men of the 7th were not professional soldiers; men from the 6th were largely recruited from farms and factories, while the 7th contained a large number of sportsmen who fought valiantly in the face of indescribable conditions for which they had little training. For many of these men, the Somme would be their first and last experience of active combat.

The men themselves were also aware of what awaited them on the Somme. Private Alexander Morley of the 7th Battalion kept a secret diary during the course of the war. In an emotional entry on 2nd July, Morley is undoubtedly scared but nevertheless determined to meet his fate:

> *"For weal or woe; for victory or defeat; for life or death; for lifelong sorrow or eternal rest. And from afar off I can hear the guns mutter; onerous & moody they are, boding death & the conflict of peoples.*
> *And so tomorrow I go a way that may lead me to my death & I end my life. Anyway, I shall see something of active war."*

In the event, Morley was taken ill with typhoid having a temperature of 40.5°C just before he was to depart to the Somme. After suffering through training drills, he was ordered bed rest by the doctor. Ignoring the doctor's advice, he took the opportunity to relax in the surrounding French countryside. While buying fruit and newspapers in the local village he met the same doctor. Embarrassed, Morley remarked, "I don't know what he thought of me breaking his prescription." After a long journey with stays in military hospitals across France, he was eventually sent back to England to recover. Morley would rejoin his battalion in early 1915.

The 7th Battalion were then sent to the woods near Bécordel-Bécourt, a small village two miles east from Albert, for a short period of rest. On 9th September, the battalion were ordered to move up to High Wood and prepare for a large coordinated sweep on the German trenches. Organising thousands of men in narrow trenches was problematic; so heavily congested were the trenches that it took B Company and D Company around two and a half hours to reach their spot in the front line. A Company and C Company fared even worse; given support and reserve roles, they were completely blocked off from the dense crowds in the trench and could not reach their position until the attack was over. When the attack eventually did launch, the Northamptons had a torrid time.

The prior mortar bombardment had been completely ineffectual, and the Germans launched a precise counter-attack on D Company's exposed flank. Another regiment was supposed to be covering D Company, but owing to the cramped trenches they did not reach their positions in time. As a result, many Northamptons were shot dead before they had even left their parapet. The Germans, sensing the British attack had collapsed, began to move their troops to D Company's exposed flank. Alert to the impending danger, Second Lieutenant F. G. S. Martin moved a small group of men to cover the exposed area where they were able to prevent the Germans advancing any further. This was a physically demanding battle, with men having to manoeuvre around the thick forest and avoid tripping over fallen trees. After sunset, the sounds of the German guns finally began to fade, and the men made their way back to the British lines. The total casualties numbered 140. The 1st Battalion were finally moved out of the

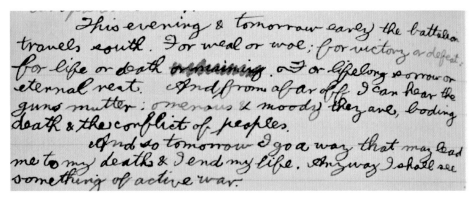

Figure 4.9: An extract from Alexander Morley's secret diary.

Somme in late September and billeted in a small village called Acheux-en-Vimeu in northern France.

In Northampton, the papers were not allowed to report on the number of casualties or what had happened. The only recognition the 48th received was from a small article printed on 2nd September in *The Northampton Independent* which ran through vague notions of warfare – "heavy shell fire", "a fearful hail of rifle fire", "mine explosions" – before adding that the "losses were inevitably heavy". No other details could be given, for the "fog of war" had silenced the press.

The 2nd Northamptons, meanwhile, had a quiet September. They spent time either training or in billets in northern France, but were back in the Somme region in October, where they were involved in a series of minor assaults. Not much had changed in their absence. The British had made pitiful progress despite becoming the first nation in the history of warfare to use tanks, during the Somme Battle of Flers–Courcelette. A significant battle for the 2nd Northamptons occurred on 23rd October near Gueudecourt, where they were to help take the neighbouring village of Le Transloy which ended in yet another deadlock. This was the 2nd Battalion's last major call to action at the Somme and they finally left the region on 17th November.

The Regimental History notes that morale amongst the troops was at a "low ebb". It is easy to see why. The battalion had been in almost continuous action since the start of July. They had experienced defeat after defeat, setback after setback, and had suffered tremendous losses. The Somme was promised in both the army and at home to be the decisive breakthrough in the war. While people back home might be none the wiser due to heavy censorship, the soldiers knew how little actual progress had been made. The men had spent months in horrific conditions; the Somme offensive that had begun under a hot July's sun would end under the frosty skies of November. An extended quote from the Regimental History portrays the dismal situation that the men had to live in:

"The effect of the weather had made this Somme country the most God-forsaken and miserable area in France, bar possibly the salient at Ypres ... Constant rain was varied by spells of intensely cold weather and some very heavy snowfalls. Everything was mud, mud – and again mud. There was thin, liquid, watery mud – mud like inferior gruel. There was a slightly thicker mud – a porridgey kind of mud. But the bulk of the mud was mud like simmering glue – in everything but the temperature, for it clung with icy chill. Billets in the back area were camps of dirty, wet and decrepit huts – gloomy archipelagos rising from mud seas. The front 'line' beggars description. It consisted of a mass of shell holes; of an ocean of mud; of gulfs, inlets, lagoons and lakes of icy water ... Villages there were in profusion – on the map; but in reality they were flattened brickwork. Looking back on those days, it is hard to realize how human beings could have existed in such conditions. Mud, mud, nothing but mud. Mud that squelched; mud that gurgled; mud that gripped the ankles like a vice; mud that often wrenched the boots off a man's feet; mud that made movement a painful, dragging labour. Thin mud, thick mud, never-ending, incredible mud. Mud that made reliefs a nightmare and ration-carrying like a scene from Dante's Inferno. A watcher from Mars might well have conceived that the earth was covered with a festering sore, and might have mistaken the million or so combatants for loathsome bacteria swarming in the oozy putrescence of the Somme."

Figure 4.10: A Somme battlefield with mud stretching as far as the eye can see, near Le Transloy; c1916.

Equipment issued by the army was inadequate for such conditions, leading soldiers to suffer terribly from trench foot. It is no surprise that Arthur Bonham wrote to his mother requesting a "pair of gum boots, you know made of India rubber", before adding "several of our fellows had some last winter & they are jolly fine things for keeping the wet & mud off your legs ... I never had a dry foot the whole of last winter." Given his plea to his mother to "put plenty of labels on the parcel so that it don't get lost", one can imagine how desperate men were for simple comforts.

The 6th Northamptons, a service battalion raised in August 1914 as part of Kitchener's second army, were attached to the 54th Brigade in the 18th Division. They too were involved in heavy fighting during the Somme battle and suffered terrible casualties. However, the casualties inflicted did not come without a moment of triumph: one of the most famous victories of the Northamptonshire Regiment belongs to the 6th Battalion for their role alongside the 12th Middlesex in the capture of Trones Wood located around four miles east of Albert. Situated next to the German-held village of Guillemont, the wood served as an important strategic defensive point along the Western Front. An attack had been launched by the 30th Division on 8th July 1916. On several occasions after fierce fighting it was thought that the British forces had won the woods, but each time new reports arrived that the Germans still controlled large parts of the area. On 14th July, as troops were receiving their orders for the day, it emerged Trones Woods was still under German control. In light of this startling information, orders were quickly issued to recapture the woods – whatever the cost.

Before the men could actually enter the woods, they first had to charge across a thousand yards of open ground in the face of a strong German barrage being directed against them. Once they had reached the woods, the battleground was one of the most challenging the men would encounter, with tall, thick trees engulfing the sky and hidden German traps everywhere. The Regimental History describes the battle environment:

> "The wood proved to be a positive wilderness of fallen trees, thick undergrowth, a maze of trenches and barbed wire, with snipers and machine guns everywhere. Enormous shells were bursting all the time, and trees flying bodily in every direction."

Inside the woods, the situation was a blaze of turmoil, with bullets fizzing through gaps between trees. Major Charrington, commanding the 6th Battalion on this occasion while Colonel Ripley was working at the brigade headquarters, said "the inside of the wood was an absolute inferno, all the officers and men fought like heroes". One such man was machine-gunner Sanders. Sergeant Cas. R. Kightley of C Company later recounted that Sanders "did glorious work with his machine gun". Spotting a large group of Germans numbering around 200

Figure 4.11: (Top) The once thick forest of Trones Wood casts a dilapidated view after the fierce fighting; photo taken in September 1916. (Bottom left) The remnants of a railroad that ran through Trones Wood to Guillemont paint a bleak scene; c1916-17. (Bottom right) The Germans had heavily defended Trones Wood; pictured is an observation post in the woods on 10th August 1916.

assembling on their flank, Sanders unleashed a deadly wave of fire which crushed any hopes of a German counter-attack. Kightley had himself a fortunate escape during the battle, narrowly avoiding two bullets – one of which went through the head of the Sergeant's understudy. Throughout the battle, they were repeatedly commanded to carry on pushing forward – a task he later wrote was "of course suicide for them [soldiers]".

One soldier who heeded the call to push forward was Sergeant W. E. Boulter, who won the Victoria Cross during the battle. Boulter had already been shot in the shoulder by a sniper and now found his company being attacked by a machine gun. Without a thought for his personal safety, Boulter grabbed a bag of bombs and charged alone across the woods, avoiding bullets from both sides. As he neared the German machine gun, he threw his bombs, successfully hitting his target, thus rendering the machine gun out of action. This incredibly brave act cleared the way for his company to advance.

Sergeant Boulter's courageous actions were some of the many that contributed to the hard-fought victory at Trones Wood. The price of this rare victory was dear: 32 men were killed, with a further 204 wounded and 35 missing. The battalion were shattered and had to be given time to rest and to be built up again with new recruits.

Figure 4.12: The 6th Battalion's victorious actions at Trones Wood were celebrated enthusiastically in the local press as good news stories became rarer; 12th August 1916, *The Northampton Independent.*

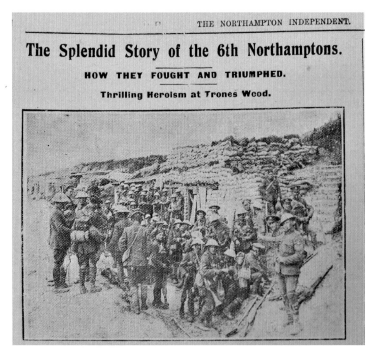

The news of the victory at Trones Wood was proudly celebrated in the Northampton press. The first mention of the battle was surprisingly only a day after the victory, when on 15th July the lead article in *The Northampton Independent* lavished great praise on the 6th Northamptons. The short leader gives no specifics on the battle or location, but says the 6th Battalion had "earned a noble share of that brilliant success on July 1st which spread fresh heart and hope through every corner of the Empire". This is notable for two related reasons. The first is the absence of references to the 1st, 2nd or 7th Northamptons, who were also engaged in heavy fighting at this time but did not participate in a clear British victory. The second is that the start of the Somme battle is referred to as a "brilliant success" that "spread fresh heart and hope" throughout the country. While the lead article does make a passing reference that the 6th Northamptons' success had to be paid with "precious lives", the reality was that the first few weeks of the Somme offensive were the bloodiest and most brutal the British Army had ever seen, with their gains meagre.

On 26th September, the 6th Northamptons were sent into battle again in the attempt to capture Thiepval Ridge. Once more, they were to play a major role, yet again incurring severe casualties. This area was the Germans' last observation point over the Albert area, and they were determined to hold it. As a result, the enemy bombardment was all the more intense. One shell hit the battalion headquarters directly, shattering it to smithereens. In the attempt to move headquarters to another trench, Colonel Ripley and his Adjutant, Lieutenant Barkham, were hit by the same shell. The Colonel's right arm was severely wounded. After the battle, Ripley had his arm amputated and returned home to England, where he was nursed by his wife. However, he had caught tetanus from the shrapnel in his arm, which was followed by heart failure as a result of blood poisoning from the wound. He died on 16th October. He was one of the highest ranked officers of the regiment to die during the war.

Figure 4.13: The men of the 6th Battalion pose for a group photo in France; c1915-18. Among the faces seen in this photograph would be men who had worked on farms and in factories before they enlisted for military service. The battalion would suffer severe casualties over the course of the war, but would also win great distinction for their actions.

Colonel Ripley was one of many casualties from the attack on Thiepval Ridge. As the men marched out of their trenches, they were decimated by a flood of deadly fire. By the time they reached their first objective, only three officers remained, which caused great organisational problems. Nevertheless, the men pushed on and by the afternoon most of Thiepval Ridge was captured. The men were wounded, broken and shattered. Their losses were tremendous: 105 dead, 235 wounded and 23 missing. For all their heroics, the battalion's ultimate sacrifice was never reported in the papers due to censorship; there were no detailed reports or articles about Thiepval Ridge, unlike that of Trones Wood. Just as the tribunals were starting to send men over to the Western Front, stories about horrendous casualties would not serve to encourage recruits.

The only news report Northampton received of the 6th Battalion's involvement at Thiepval Ridge was through the reporting of Colonel Ripley's death. In a long obituary printed on 21st October, the newspaper lavishes great praise on Ripley for being "courageous, considerate, and scrupulously fair". A veteran of the South African War, Ripley had spent the early years of his retirement as a member of the Northants Territorial Force Association and as a Justice of the Peace. When war was declared in 1914, despite being 50 years old, Ripley didn't want to sit on the sidelines and immediately applied to command his old battalion. However, the authorities decided it would be better for a man of Ripley's talents to serve in one of Kitchener's battalions, and he was given the newly formed 6th Battalion. There he made a great impression on the young men, so much so that they "would follow him anywhere". In what turned out to be one of his last acts, Colonel Ripley recommended Boulter for the Victoria Cross for his actions at Trones Wood. Boulter later said, "No officer at the front was more beloved. He was just like a father to us all."

The people of Northamptonshire were soon able to celebrate their Victoria Cross winner, as Boulter was sent home in late October to Northampton to recover from his wounds. Unfortunately, the Sergeant would get no immediate rest. First, Kettering, where he worked as a drapery assistant at the Co-Operative Society, organised a fete in his honour. Thousands of people cheered him as he was driven through town, before making a humble speech on Market Hill. There he said, "I feel I do not deserve all this. I have only done my bit, the same as others are doing, especially so in the Somme district at present. Everyone out there is a hero."

Later in the week, Boulter visited his old primary school in his home town of Wigston, Leicestershire. Addressing the schoolboys, Boulter gave a heart-warming speech: "I only went out to do my duty, and if I succeeded it was not my fault," which elicited laughter from the boys. In what turned out to be a sad prophecy, Boulter added: "I hope when you all grow up you will try and do your duty noble and well. You never know what you may be called upon to do … I hope you will all have good luck and that there may be no more wars for you to participate in." Some of the boys addressed that day were likely to have followed in Boulter's footsteps and served their country in the Second World War.

Northampton too buzzed with excitement for a glimpse of a Victoria Cross recipient in their county regiment. In a lavish ceremony that had been arranged on 4th November, a full procession took Boulter, his family, fiancée, and military and political dignitaries through The Drapery, St Giles Square and Palmerston Road, culminating in Abington Park. The procession was lined by hundreds of spectators, soldiers and boy scouts; the war offered few opportunities for celebration and Northampton was determined to make the most of their own Victoria Cross recipient. On a specially erected stage, the Mayor, J. E. Pearse, gave a short address

Figure 4.14: Sergeant Boulter, newly recipient of a Victoria Cross, is pictured during a visit to a Rushden shoe factory aimed at boosting morale. Boulter was lauded across the county and in the press, with several parades held in his honour during his visit to Northamptonshire.

in which the Sergeant's actions at Trones Wood were recounted, and presented him with an "18 carat gold Waltham lever wristlet watch, of the very best type". As a volunteer band played "See, the Conquering Hero Comes", a shy-looking Boulter rose to make a curious speech in which he appeared to criticise the political order:

> *"I feel that you are honouring not only me but the whole of the 6th Battalion. I went out to do my duty the same as others are doing. They are doing quite as good work as I have done. My only hope is that they will soon be back among you, and that we shall have no more war; and that it will no longer be in the power of one or two men to make wars. I only hope you will not forget the boys at the front."*

It is a telling sign of public opinion that the editor chose to include this last passage in the report. With the introduction of tribunals earlier in the year, perhaps this is a small glimpse into the real public opinion of the war.

Boulter was far from alone in receiving an enthusiastic welcome home. As large numbers of those wounded at the Somme began to trickle into hospitals around the country, soldiers were treated to a wide range of entertainment provided by local groups and schools. For example, the Rushden Rifle Band and the Rushden Town Male Choir were regular performers in hospitals around the county, where they would delight soldiers and nurses alike with popular contemporary pieces.

The treatment of men in hospitals was, by most accounts, good, despite the arduous demands placed upon staff. An insight into the quality of the care received by soldiers can be gained by the letters and pictures the men at the Weston Favell hospital in Northampton sent to Nurse Alice Robbins in the form of a memory book. The soldiers, wounded physically and mentally, clearly appreciated the care and attention provided by this popular nurse. Some of the men wrote affecting poetry, each stanza containing a tenderness which spoke to the horrors they had borne witness to. A soldier, F. Plumpton, of the Lancashire Fusiliers wrote:

> *"You cared for us in sickness*
> *You cared for us in health*
> *And we can't repay your kindness*
> *Even if we had the wealth*
> *What you've done you call it 'duty'*
> *And did it without fuss.*
> *So we ask for one more kindness*
> *By above Remember us."*

Not all letters or poems to Nurse Robbins were so emotional. One soldier, F. A. Laws of the Warwickshire Regiment, drew a cartoon for the nurse in January 1917, depicting two German soldiers having a conversation.

While generalisations should not be made based on a few sources, this cartoon was one of many in the book that displayed great wit amongst the soldiers. Like Laws, many soldiers do not paint the Germans in a dark light, preferring a slightly mischievous tone. These letters and drawings also speak of the morale in hospitals amongst the soldiers – at least in Weston Favell – which appeared to be high across the war. In typically British fashion, these soldiers were making the best of things with an easy-going humorous attitude.

Some hospital staff, however, were perhaps too enthusiastic in their desire to help. James Campbell, a wounded Canadian soldier, had been resident in Duston War Hospital since August 1916. During his stay in Duston, he befriended local resident Emily Smith, a widow with two young children after her husband had been killed at war. On 21st November, feeling bored and unwell, Campbell went to visit Smith from whom he received some whisky in return for a one-pound note. Campbell stayed the night and returned to the hospital the next evening smelling of liquor, which set off one hospital sister's senses. Both Campbell and Smith were arrested, with the latter given a six-week prison sentence. A senior military officer in the area said it was "a great danger to men in the hospital to have a place so near where they could have a drink"; presumably alcohol was not part of a soldier's convalescent care plan.

Figure 4.15: This cartoon by F. Lawson was less than complimentary towards the officer class. The caption reads:
Officer (to new recruit on "sentry go" for first time): "Now mind you let no one go by without challenging them."
Recruit: "That's all right guv'nor. Don't you worry. The slightest of noise wakes me up!"

After the flurry of news reports about Trones Wood and Boulter's VC in November 1916, there is a notable lack of information about the regiment's activities on the Somme. Very little was officially reported throughout the battle and the exploits of the 1st, 2nd, 6th and 7th Battalions scarcely received a mention. This is unusual because there were regular reports about the 4th Northamptons in Palestine at this time. Perhaps the censors and press wanted to switch focus from a battle that was framed to be the "great offensive" but ended in bloody stalemate.

After an extraordinary loss of life on both sides and pleas from officers, General Sir Douglas Haig, who wanted to end the campaign on a winning note, finally called off the battle in November as the troops gained the remaining territory of Thiepval Ridge and Beaumont Hamel, while the weather made further troop movements impossible. As the Australian historian Robin Prior has noted, both Beaumont Hamel and Thiepval were targets marked for capture in the first hours of the first day of the battle.

While initially he was seen as a hero after the end of the war, historians have severely criticised the commander of the British Army and architect of the Somme battle, Haig, for the enormous casualties that occurred under his watch – earning him the nickname 'Butcher Haig'. Historians have accused Haig of incompetence, indifference to the many casualties and a stubbornness against changing tactics when evidence showed his plan was failing. First and foremost, Haig has been criticised for his unwavering belief in old forms of warfare: tactics involving slowly marching towards the enemy line (the slower the better to maintain control) followed by a cavalry charge. In the face of machine guns, it is no surprise that thousands were slaughtered on the Somme.

While British intelligence may have underestimated the strength of German defences, the responsibility of the bloody failure on 1st July can be attributed to Haig's flawed strategy. Haig had great faith in his huge artillery to break the German line, clearing the way for the cavalry. However, the artillery was too spread out to break through the enemy defences along the Somme front. Dispersed and not focused on a precise location, the British did not have enough fire power to destroy several lines of German defences. As a result, most German machine guns and artillery survived the initial British bombardment, and the Germans stealthily waited for the first line of British men to walk into No Man's Land to their deaths. One of the earliest criticisms of Haig comes from Winston Churchill in July 1916. In a letter circulated to his ministerial colleagues, he directly reprimanded Haig, saying that "the results of the operation have been disastrous; in terrain they have been absolutely barren … from every point of view the British offensive has been a great failure".

Nor was Lloyd George any more forgiving. Always suspicious of Haig, the Prime Minister began an intrigue, working with his French counterpart, Marshal Foch, who sought to subordinate Haig to his command. Only when Haig threatened to resign in 1917 did Lloyd George back down. Nevertheless, Lloyd

George's memoirs, published after the Field Marshal's death in 1928, successfully diminished Haig's reputation.

While Haig has his large share of detractors, he hasn't been without his supporters. More recently, military historian Gary Sheffield argued that Haig did learn from his mistakes, culminating in the successful defence of the German offensive in 1918 and the 100 days counter-offensive which forced Germany to sign the armistice of 11th November 1918. Additionally, the war was a period of rapid technological change with the introduction of tanks and aeroplanes. No one knew at first how to effectively utilise these untried and untested machines. Countering charges of emotional apathy in the years after the war, Haig was heavily engaged in charity work for ex-servicemen wounded in the conflict. He was an influential founder of the Royal British Legion in 1921, and the words 'Haig Fund' were initially inscribed on the black button in the centre of the poppy. Although the debate on Haig's reputation is far from settled, two things are clear: firstly, he presided over the bloodiest period in British military history; secondly, he did eventually lead his country to victory – victory that, without the benefit of hindsight, was far from certain.

Perhaps the lasting effect on British consciousness resulting from the huge loss of life on the Somme was because of the recruitment innovations resulting from Kitchener's Army. While the 1st and 2nd Battalions had historically contained a reasonable proportion of men from Northampton or Northamptonshire, there were actually a significant proportion of men from other parts of the country. With an urgent need for new recruits, army commanders decided to allow groups of friends to enlist and serve together; the Somme was one of the first instances where the new 'Pals' battalions would fight. However, it would take just one shell to kill a large group of men from one area. For some small villages, this meant that most of their young males would never return. For towns like Northampton, whole streets would have their curtains drawn as news arrived that a platoon had been lost. Like towns and cities across the country, the Battle of the Somme had left its bleak mark of death on Northamptonshire.

Figure 5.1: A 'Notice of Appeal' document filed by Charles Henry Percy White, who argued significant hardship would fall on his family if he was sent to the army as his grocer business would fail.

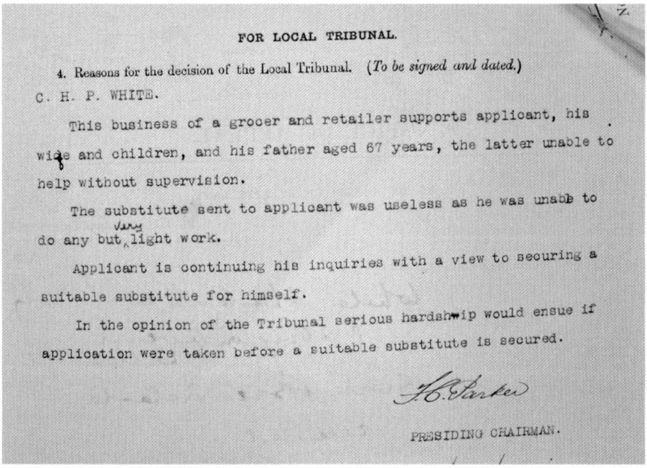

FOR LOCAL TRIBUNAL.

4. Reasons for the decision of the Local Tribunal. (*To be signed and dated.*)

C. H. P. WHITE.

This business of a grocer and retailer supports applicant, his wife and children, and his father aged 67 years, the latter unable to help without supervision.

The substitute sent to applicant was useless as he was unable to do any but light work.

Applicant is continuing his inquiries with a view to securing a suitable substitute for himself.

In the opinion of the Tribunal serious hardship would ensue if application were taken before a suitable substitute is secured.

PRESIDING CHAIRMAN.

Figure 5.2: An applicant to the Tribunal for military exemption states he has seven children to care for; a butcher on his Tribunal Appeal form states he provides meat for nearly 2,000 customers through his family business of 35 years; a mother pleads for exemption for her son. She writes she has already given three sons to the army, two of whom were killed. Her son was granted a temporary exemption by the Tribunals.

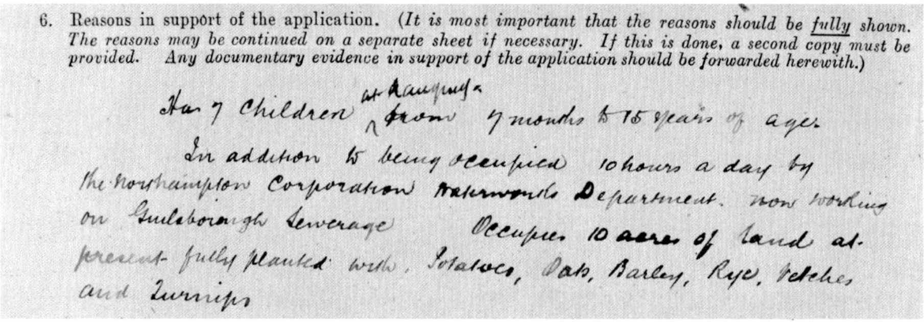

6. Reasons in support of the application. (*It is most important that the reasons should be fully shown. The reasons may be continued on a separate sheet if necessary. If this is done, a second copy must be provided. Any documentary evidence in support of the application should be forwarded herewith.*)

Has 7 Children at Hanpny from 7 months to 15 years of age.

In addition to being occupied 10 hours a day by the Northampton Corporation Waterworks Department. now working on Guilsborough Sewerage. Occupies 10 acres of land at present fully planted with Potatoes, Oats, Barley, Rye, Vetches and Turnips

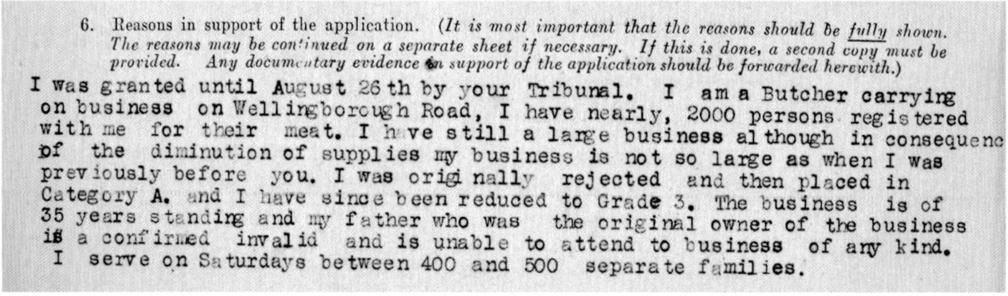

6. Reasons in support of the application. (*It is most important that the reasons should be fully shown. The reasons may be continued on a separate sheet if necessary. If this is done, a second copy must be provided. Any documentary evidence in support of the application should be forwarded herewith.*)

I was granted until August 26th by your Tribunal. I am a Butcher carrying on business on Wellingborough Road, I have nearly, 2000 persons registered with me for their meat. I have still a large business although in consequence of the diminution of supplies my business is not so large as when I was previously before you. I was originally rejected and then placed in Category A. and I have since been reduced to Grade 3. The business is of 35 years standing and my father who was the original owner of the business is a confirmed invalid and is unable to attend to business of any kind. I serve on Saturdays between 400 and 500 separate families.

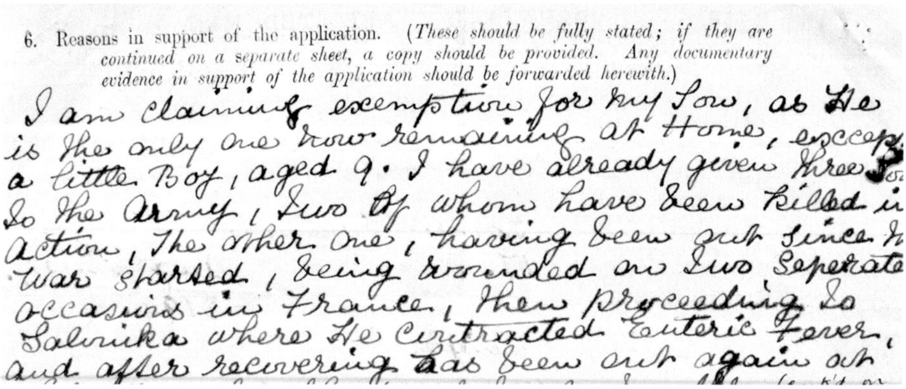

6. Reasons in support of the application. (*These should be fully stated; if they are continued on a separate sheet, a copy should be provided. Any documentary evidence in support of the application should be forwarded herewith.*)

I am claiming exemption for my Son, as He is the only one now remaining at Home, except a little Boy, aged 9. I have already given three Sons to the army, two of whom have been Killed in action, The other one, having been out since the War started, being wounded on two seperate occasions in France, then proceeding to Salonika where He contracted Enteric Fever, and after recovering has been out again at

CHAPTER FIVE

THE TRIBUNALS

Father: This one (points at son, George). The other would not be much use.

George: If one goes, I must go. I don't think my brother would shoot a German if he went.

Father: You can't keep him in the fields if it thunders and lightens; I don't know what he would do with the guns firing round him.

Stopford-Sackville (Chairman): So's Tipperary. We cannot stand between George and the Germans. I wish you good luck, George, and I hope your 'bag' of Germans will be a big one.

Tribunal Judge: What would you do in case a German threatened the life of your father or mother?

Applicant: I should not kill the German.

Judge: Supposing you had a revolver?

Applicant: I do not intend to carry a revolver.

Judge: But supposing you had one?

Applicant: I cannot suppose anything as to what I should do with a revolver, because as I say, I should not carry one.

Judge: You recognise the fact that if all people held the same views as you, England would be conquered tomorrow?

Applicant: Not if everybody held my opinion. If all the people held my opinion they would not have quarrelled and made war.

Tribunal cases reported in *The Northampton Mercury*, 17th March 1916

In August 1914, the vast majority of the British public were fully supportive of declaring war on Germany. Iconic posters such as Lord Kitchener, conqueror of Sudan, with his large accusing finger and stern eyes staring into yours, were part of the undoubtable wave of euphoria that swept Britain in September 1914. Streams of girls cheered as they watched their men, buoyed by pride and duty, march straight to the local recruitment office, while brass brands performed a catalogue of patriotic anthems for the adoring public.

As the war continued and casualties mounted, this eruption of patriotism soon subsided – a faster decline than is often recognised. Only in the very early months of the war did the commonly held notions of young men, in their scores, marching enthusiastically to war bear resemblance to reality. In August 1914, 298,923 men enlisted in the British Army or the Territorial Force. This figure, in the first month of war, would only be surpassed the following month, which saw a record 462,901 men join the colours. Never again would the army see more than 200,000 men enlist in one month despite all the publicity campaigns, numerous recruitment schemes and even the introduction of conscription.

One year into the war, after disastrous losses at Gallipoli, fierce fighting in the Middle East and, most significantly, the ruin of the BEF on the Western Front, enlistment had faltered to 71,000. Despite war propaganda and media censorship, the authorities could no longer turn a blind eye to the suffering of the British people, as wounded men returned home in their tens of thousands – each one of them a piece of evidence that the Great War was going badly wrong.

Britain was unique amongst European Powers for being the only country not to have a policy of conscription enshrined in law. By the summer of 1915, the government was beginning to realise that this could not be maintained, with the demand for more men becoming ever more critical. To this end, the National Registration Act was passed in July 1915, aimed at recording all men aged 15 to 65 and their occupations. By the middle of September, the results of this census found that there were at least 5 million men of military age who were not in the army, of whom 1.6 million were in 'starred' jobs deemed to be essential to the war effort.

To solve the growing crisis in recruitment, Lord Edward Derby, the Director-General of Recruitment, designed what became known as the Derby Scheme. Men aged 18 to 40 were given the option to attest with an obligation to join the military if they were called up later. Married men were given the added reassurance and incentive that they would only be called upon when all single men had been drafted. The men were placed into forty-three groups according to age and marital status. For example, Group 1 was single men, aged 18, while Group 40 was married men, aged 40. These groups were called to enlist throughout 1916. For example in June, Arthur Dryden of Canons Ashby writes of one of his staff leaving:

"W Cross, the under carpenter left to join the army to fight against Germany in the great war. He formerly attested under the Derby scheme."

This short passage is noteworthy for several reasons. Writing before the Somme – where, on the opening day of the battle, the British Army suffered their largest number of casualties on a single day – Dryden is referring to the war as the 'great war'. That this phrase had already entered the common lexicon is illustrative of the impact this war was having. Furthermore, Dryden goes on to describe details of Cross's life, writing that he is married with children. There is no reason for Dryden to write this, indeed most of his diary refers to the running of the estate, with occasional mentions of the war given in a typically detached factual manner. The fact that Dryden has written this perhaps reveals some hidden emotion. Cross was not the first, nor the last, staff member to leave Canons Ashby due to the war, and Dryden, who housed refugees on his estate, was personally touched by the pains of war.

The Derby Scheme was a complicated system that caused much confusion for employers unsure about their future manpower. The County War Agricultural Committee was worried the Derby Scheme would deprive them of much-needed manpower. Indeed, so great were agricultural demands already that the Northamptonshire Regiment had released men from military duty to work on farms. The local boot and shoe industry was also extremely concerned; they had supplied much of British and French requirements since the start of war, but pressures to deliver increased after the Italian government ordered up to 200,000 pairs of boots.

The scheme was intended only to run until the end of November but was extended into December, with a widely publicised campaign informing men that this was their last chance to voluntarily enlist. Despite a last-minute burst of enlistment, when Lord Derby rose in the House of Commons on 20th December 1915 to announce the results of the scheme, it was widely deemed a failure. Out of 2.1 million single men in the country, only 53% enlisted or attested – interestingly, more married men attested. In total, 59% of British men attempted to register for military service. Once the number of men in 'starred' occupations was taken into consideration, it was estimated only 830,000 could be sent into military service. A huge disparity clearly existed between the number of men who wanted to enlist and the number the army needed to fight.

In Northampton, however, the editor of *The Northampton Independent*, Mr Holloway, highly praised the town for their enlistment numbers, under a lead article titled "Bravo! Northampton." In Northampton, 11,050 out of 12,850 men aged 18 to 40 attested (86%). The editor said these figures were even more impressive when one considered men in "starred" occupations and those physically unable to join the army, which left only "450 slackers". Holloway wrote that Northampton had responded "magnificently" to the Derby Scheme and that "if other towns had followed Northampton's lead there would be no question of compulsion".

The failure of the Derby Scheme led to the government passing the Military Service Act in January 1916. Effective on 2nd March, this act ushered in conscription for the first time in the nation's history. Every man between 18 and 41 would have to enlist with the military. Anticipating this would be unpopular, the government also created a system of tribunals where a man could seek an exemption certificate or postponement in front of an independent panel of tribunal judges. Grounds for exemption included that a man's occupation was vital for the nation; that serious hardship would occur to his business or family if he was sent to war; as a result of ill health on medical grounds; and – most controversially – the issue of conscientious objection.

A man would obtain a hearing at a local tribunal if he applied within four days of receiving the call to join the army. The man could represent himself, nominate his employer or hire a legal counsel. If his case was rejected, he would have the opportunity to have his case reviewed at an appeal tribunal. In exceptional circumstances, a case might be heard at the Central tribunal based in Westminster. The military too would have a representative sitting in proceedings and had the right to appeal an exemption given by the local tribunal. Both the individual and military representatives were given three days to appeal.

The tribunals were a complex system devised in little time, aimed at reassuring applicants of a fair hearing while achieving the government's aim of more men. Almost immediately, however, it became clear that its creation had been poorly designed. Firstly, they were to be staffed by men and women, known as tribunalists, with no legal training or relevant experience. The tribunalists, on one hand, were under huge pressure from the government to make sure the army received greater numbers of men. On the other, they were the sole arbiters, with no training, pressured by local industry and newspapers, ultimately deciding who would go and who would stay. James McDermott, in a pioneering book titled "British Military Service tribunals" dryly observes:

> *"Ironically, responsibility for implementing legislation that effectively buried a venerable British tradition of voluntarism was to be devolved entirely upon a group of volunteers."*

Overwhelmingly consisting of men, tribunalists held some form of local distinction, be they leaders of business, MPs, councillors, lawyers, union bosses or retired soldiers. For example, Northampton's appeal tribunal included the retired colonel and former Conservative North Northamptonshire MP George Stopford-Sackville. Only one female member, Beatrice Cartwright, sat on the tribunals in Northampton.

Within weeks of the tribunals' first sittings, two key implications became apparent. Firstly, conscription was not having the desired effect. As McDermott details, the first month of the appeal tribunals saw 25,931 extra men secured for the army but over 58,000 exemption certificates granted. Secondly, fierce public opposition to conscription was laid bare. In April 1916, just one month after conscription took effect, a demonstration by up to 200,000 men in Trafalgar Square, London, ended in violence, with uniformed soldiers and sailors storming through the crowd. Despite this, or perhaps as a result, the government was soon compelled to extend the Military Service Act so that married men were included, thus widening the eligibility. The tribunals were also given the power to include a 'finality' clause on temporary certificates (of which the vast majority were) which meant no further exemptions would be issued.

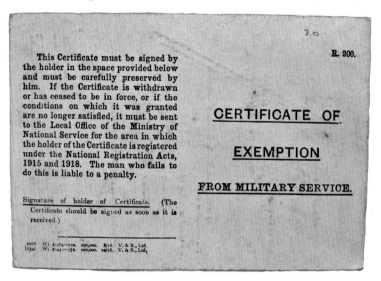

Figure 5.3: An example of a certificate of certificate from military service.

Despite conscription, recruitment targets were still not being met. Throughout the war, conscription's net was cast ever wider. In January 1917, instructions were issued to tribunals to consider men aged under 31 to be more important to the army, regardless of their occupation. In April 1917 further legislation was introduced, this time aimed at men who had been previously exempted, which allowed their medical certificates to be re-examined. By September, the government culled the number of occupations deemed to be essential for the national good.

In May 1918, conscription was expanded to include men aged up to 51. With hindsight, this may seem strange considering the war would come to an end in November. However, the fact serves to highlight the stark reality the country faced at the time: despite the growing presence of American power finally being felt at the Western Front, there still seemed no end in sight. The extension also exposed the calamitous consequences of war in Britain, that so many young men had perished, the government, in desperation, had to call on men the same age as the life expectancy at birth of a boy born in 1911.

The end of warfare did not bring the end of conscription – it was extended until 1920 so the army could maintain trouble spots in the Empire – but it did bring the end of the tribunals. Often accused of being a law unto themselves, ruling with prejudice and condemning unsuitable men to the army, it was unsurprising that few mourned their demise. For reasons not fully known, the government instructed local government boards to destroy all tribunal record papers. Only the Middlesex Appeal Records were intentionally preserved in England. It has been suggested that records were destroyed to preserve the reputations of those who served on the tribunals and to limit post-war criticism of the state. Regardless of the reasons for their destruction, historians are left with few resources from which to conduct an objective analysis of conscription; newspaper tribunal reports cover only the most newsworthy incidents, which generally are the rarest and controversial, such as conscientious objection cases.

Curiously, again for reasons unknown, the Northamptonshire tribunal records were never destroyed. Due to the excellent work of volunteers at the Northamptonshire Record Office in 2014/15, every known tribunal document has been examined, with key information recorded.

While the records only provide evidence relating to Northamptonshire, uncharacteristic of the rest of the country due to its vital boot and shoe industry, they do help provide a deeper insight into a part of British history which very little is known about. It is not possible for a statistical analysis to show whether the Northamptonshire tribunals were 'less harsh' than those of other counties, nor even to draw conclusions about whether men of certain ages and certain circumstances were more likely to be given exemptions – often this was decided on wider circumstances of the war and the need of men; agricultural workers were more likely to be given exemptions to finish the harvest, while the government would exert greater pressure on tribunals before a major offensive such as the spring of 1918. The documents do, however, paint an extraordinary picture of the severe impact that war and conscription was having on Northamptonshire.

This impact can be readily understood by how quickly the tribunals became resented by the public. Newspapers, with a duty foremost to their readers, began criticising the system very early on. For example, on 31st March, despite the tribunals not even being one month old, *The Northampton Mercury* printed a condemning editorial:

> *"Journalists are naturally inclined to favour publicity, but at first it seemed to many ourselves that the business of the tribunals ought to be done behind closed doors. Few of those who professionally attended the meetings are of that opinion to-day. There is so much partiality and prejudice and ill-temper that, unless the reporters were present, the danger of injustice would be greatly increased ... members should remember that they are administering an Act of Parliament, and that it is their bounden duty to pay full respect to the law ... [Their] main duty is to enable the Army to get the men required with the least avoidable interference with trade and commerce."*

Nevertheless, it appears that tribunals never discarded their flippant mannerisms. On 28th July 1917, *The Northampton Independent* reported a tribunal case regarding a man from Wollaston who had already seen two brothers killed in the war, with another two in active service. The man applied for exemption so he could take care of his widowed mother and said if one of his brothers came back he would take his place. One of the tribunalists bluntly asked the man:

"If everyone applied like you, where would the army be?"

The man, infuriated, replied:

"If all families had done as ours had done, there would be no need for such cases as mine to be brought forward."

The tribunals could also be accused of not taking seriously the concerns of Mr Samuel Frank Cockerhill. As late in the war as 29th July 1918, 36-year-old Northampton butcher Mr Cockerhill appeared before the tribunal seeking exemption on the grounds that his work was a certified occupation of national importance. In a response to a question, he said he sometimes worked from 6am to midnight. It can be assumed Cockerhill didn't find the reply, published in *The Northampton Mercury*, from Alderman Campion too amusing:

"This man ought to go into the Army to have his labour lightened."

——— CONSCIENTIOUS OBJECTORS ———

The subject of conscientious objection has received extensive attention and is often used as evidence to show the cruel nature of tribunals. In the Northamptonshire Appeal Tribunal, only 106 out of 6,801 cases were made on the ground of conscience, yet they attracted far greater coverage than their small numbers would ordinarily warrant. Thousands of families had seen their sons killed, and both the tribunals and newspapers were increasingly concerned that conscientious objectors were undermining the whole concept of the nation's shared sacrifice.

Serving soldiers sometimes had strong views on those deemed to not be pulling their weight. Sergeant H. Mitchell, while recovering in Weston Favell Hospital, Northampton, drew an image in a book that was created by convalescing soldiers as a memory book for one of the nurses. Titled "The Voluntary System", the cartoon portrays a well-dressed man, complete with a sharp suit and bow tie, slouched against a pole, seemingly without a care in the world. This man, called

THE VOLUNTARY SYSTEM.

THE SLACKER: "Feelin' pretty fit again? When are you going back?"

SERGT H. MITCHELL WESTON FAVELL JANY 1918.

Figure 5.4: Soldiers held differing opinions about the war and those who did not fight. Some, like Sergeant H. Mitchell, the soldier behind this drawing, felt aggrieved by what he saw as 'slackers' – men who could but didn't join the military. So strong was this feeling that Mitchell made this drawing in a memory book for Nurse Alice Robbins, organised by convalescing soldiers as a token of their appreciation for the care they received. Most soldiers wrote a short poem, told a joke or wrote a simple thank you note.

The Slacker, asks a soldier with a bandaged arm: "Feelin' pretty fit again? When are you going back?" This drawing, from January 1918, shows how some serving soldiers truly felt. While not aimed specifically at conscientious objectors, the same sentiments were felt towards them by many in society.

A tribunal's decision to refuse an exemption certificate, regardless of morally difficult family circumstances, could be seen to condemn the man to potential death on the battlefield. The pressure to refuse exemptions on conscientious objection grounds is therefore clear. One can only imagine the resentment felt when a case of conscientious objection arose. Indeed, Beatrice Cartwright, on the appeal tribunal, admitted after the war she had "little forbearance" with conscientious objectors as a "species".

On 8th March 1916, the Northampton Rural District Tribunal heard the first conscientious objection case in Northamptonshire. His name does not appear in *The Northampton Mercury*'s report – perhaps to preserve his anonymity – but the man in question is likely to have been Samuel Ventham Green, a 34-year-old agricultural worker from Thrapston. During his hearing, he had the following dialogue with the tribunal judge, Mr Crockett:

> *Crockett*: "If a man hit you, you would hit him back, would you not?"
> *Green*: "No, sir; it is not the right thing. When they went to attack Jesus Christ, what did He do? One of His servants cut off the ear of one of the High Priest's servants, and He stopped His disciples and healed the man's ear. His was a pure life: an example for us to live up to as near as we can."
> *Crockett*: "You have no desire to protect the women of this country?"
> *Green*: "This is my case. If the women of this country were all true Christians, before they would see a man hit another man in cold blood they would object to it."
> *Crockett*: "That is not an answer to my question."
> *Green*: "When I protect the women of this country, sir, I protect them by prayer. That is 'the' greatest weapon. It is better than all shells, cannons and rifles."

Unimpressed by this pacifist lecture, the tribunal did not issue an exemption certificate. Appealing the local tribunal's decision, Green had more luck at the appeal tribunal, which issued a temporary exemption.

This line of questioning – what would you do if the Germans attacked women in your country? – was very common towards conscientious objectors, with the intention to humiliate them. Today there is a certain, quiet admiration for the men who stood up and declared they did not want to fight. These men did so with the full understanding they would become social pariahs in their communities, who had watched their sons go and fight. Despite all these social pressures, they stood up for their beliefs in public.

Newspapers gleefully covered cases where conscientious objectors almost seemed to take great joy in mocking the tribunals. Such reports helped to achieve two ends: firstly they exposed men who were widely viewed as shirking their duty to King and country; secondly they showed contempt for the tribunals, to the enjoyment of readers.

On 7th April 1916, *The Northampton Mercury* reported the novel case of two brothers, John Reginald Hornsby and Thomas Vincent Hornsby, both of whom claimed exemptions on the ground of conscience at the Towcester Tribunal:

> *Reginald Hornsby*: "I am prepared to fight in my own country, but not in any other country."
> *Councillor Beattie*: "I thought your objection was to fight at all."
> *Reginald Hornsby*: "I should be prepared to fight to defend my own

home in my own country."
Beattie: *"You mean at Towcester?"*
Chairman: *"I suppose you would defend your 34 acres, but not anybody else's."*
Reginald Hornsby: *"I don't think England ought to have come in the war at all. Those that pick the quarrel should fight … Germany did not make any quarrel with England; England declared war on Germany."*

The tribunal rejected Reginald Hornsby's appeal, although did give his brother a two-month exemption. At hearing the decision, a defiant Reginald Hornsby exclaimed:

"Then you will have to carry me there, that's all. I would sooner be shot than fight."

Another example of a conscientious objector arguing his case forcefully is Claude Cunnington's. This case is memorable because Cunnington had already obtained an exemption on the basis he served the military in a non-combat role. He went to the appeal tribunal to contest this exemption because he was doing "my busy duty in protesting against war, as I did before it broke out". A station manager at Thrapston, Cunnington was accused of picking up "the profits which remain after other men go to war and get killed". After being told by a tribunal judge that there would be no England for Cunnington to live in if all men behaved like him, Cunnington resolutely replied, "There would be no fighting if everyone believed like I do." The Chairman then told him to go "preach to the Germans" and dismissed Cunnington's appeal.

On 12th May 1916, *The Northampton Mercury* printed a short summary of 23-year-old William Leonard King's appeal at the Northampton appeal tribunal. Discussing how his education influenced his conscientious objection, one of the judges, Sir Ryland Adkins, had an amusing conversation with Mr King:

Adkins: *"You remember that Tolstoy and his family helped the wounded all they could in the Russo-Japanese War?"*
King: *"But he regretted it afterwards, I think."*
Adkins: *"When his mind was failing?"*
King: *"You may think so: I should say it was improving."*

The paper does not reveal the tribunal's decision, but King was granted a temporary exemption on the condition he was employed in agriculture. It appears King successfully extended his application over the course of the war, but in August 1918 his application for further renewal was dismissed. His case was one of the rare ones sent to the Central tribunal in Westminster, which upheld the appeal tribunal's decision. King still refused to join the military and was subsequently court-martialled and sentenced to imprisonment.

In situations that appear to be clear-cut, tribunals had the potential to surprise. For example, George Robert Wade, a market gardener in Kettering, applied for absolute exemption after his temporary exemption expired on 1st August 1916. *The Northampton Mercury* reported that Wade had caused "considerable dissatisfaction" to the people of Kettering after proudly bragging over the success he had achieved with the tribunals. Additionally, the tribunal was told that Wade had "ostentatiously" remained seated after a church service while the National Anthem was sung. Wade then admitted that he had never sung "God Save the King", nor had he ever believed in monarchy. The Chairman of the Northampton tribunal, Mr S. G. Stopford-Sackville, was noticeably angered with Wade, declaring he could not remain in Kettering with his "poisonous opinions". Wade was lucky enough to have found the rest of the tribunal in a good mood, as they gave the appellant an extension on the condition he found work of national importance. This was perhaps all the more surprising as William Leonard King had his appeal rejected in August 1918, while Wade was successful in the middle of the war, August 1916.

——— MEDICAL EXAMINATIONS ———

Men could also avoid conscription if they obtained a medical certificate. The medical examinations, however, were performed by military doctors under the supervision of the Medical Boards. As the war progressed, the standards of the Medical Boards became pathetically low, and they were held in universal contempt by both the public and tribunals. A large proportion of the bitterness was directed at Colonel Thompson, who controlled the operation at Northampton Barracks.

Matters were made worse when new legislation was introduced in May 1917 aimed at increasing enlistment, which meant the Medical Boards could re-examine men who had already been issued with a medical exemption. On 8th June 1917, *The Northampton Mercury* reported there was some "very plain speaking" at the Northampton tribunal. A solicitor, representing several clients, argued one man, a 31-year-old gardener and greengrocer, had a medical certificate proving he suffered from epilepsy. Despite this, the man was passed as Class A (accepted for service to start in the future) and the solicitor argued his clients were "treated like dogs". One of the tribunal judges, Mr Gribble, agreed with the solicitor, citing several cases he had heard of men who worked in the shoe trade and who suffered from "consumption" (tuberculosis) but had been called up regardless. Their training was soon cut short after the men were admitted to hospital. Gribble had also told the tribunal of two cases where the men had died after being discharged. An indication of the anger felt by the public and the tribunals is revealed in the following quote which was printed in the paper, as Gribble concluded by saying:

"If half I hear is true, Colonel Thompson ought to be sent to Germany."

The same page purposely reports a case that shows Colonel Thompson's flagrant neglect of protocol. A 26-year-old tram driver, who had just had an operation at Northampton General Hospital after being unable to work for the last six months, had been reassessed by the Medical Board to be Class A. As the man sought exemption at the tribunal, he claimed to have shown his medical evidence to Colonel Thompson, who replied, "Certificate be hanged; do you think I am blind? Are you a tribunal Case? You are A1 and you can put some grease on your boots," before scrawling "incorrect" over the medical evidence.

The public trust in the Medical Boards had collapsed and Colonel Thompson was widely disliked across Northamptonshire. Tribunal panels began to ignore Medical Board diagnosis in favour of civilian diagnosis. The huge public backlash eventually resulted in the responsibility for medical examinations being removed from the War Office and conducted by civilian doctors under the supervision of local government boards. Unfortunately, reform took a long time and it wasn't until November 1917 that the new system was active. As part of the changes, doctors would be paid five guineas per session plus expenses, and a man would be examined by four doctors; this was a departure from the old system whereby doctors were paid for each man they approved fit for service. A new grading system was introduced too. Doctors would make a collective decision based on roman numerals (I to IV – where 'I' was the grade for a perfectly fit man).

The tribunals could certainly claim some credit for forcing some of these reforms. Their open defiance of the Medical Boards, their sympathetic ear to public grievances and their formal position ensured that, as McDermott says, "private injustices should not disappear within the vast anonymity of the recruitment process". Ironically, the government had inadvertently created a formal institution which could criticise the implementation of conscription – without fear of censor – that served to hinder enlistment.

However, the system was far from faultless. It appeared too many men were still being approved for the army, despite a sharp drop in men being rated as 'I' compared to the old system of 'A'. On 26th June 1918, the editor of *The Northampton Independent*, W. H. Holloway, criticised the doctors conducting examinations, prompting a reply from Dr A. W. Cooke, the secretary of the Local Medical War Committee, which appeared in the following week's paper:

"Sir, I have always regarded the 'Independent' as a model of fairness, but I feel that some protest should be made against the article in last Friday's issue … It is very trying, very difficult and very thankless

work ... You condemn these men as ignorant of their profession because a few recruits have been re-graded on appeal. If you or the Chairman of the tribunal had any idea of the difficulties presented by the work of examining and grading new recruits, many of them unwilling recruits, and a few, a very few malingerers, you would rather wonder that such incidents do not happen more often."

The demands placed on the medical services during the war on the home front are often overlooked and require more research. In 1917 the Northamptonshire Red Cross fleet of just 18 ambulances covered 73,000 miles to move almost 25,000 patients; doctors in fifteen hospitals located across the county, from the hospital in the village of Blakesley with seventeen beds to Barry Road Hospital in Northampton with 250 beds, treated 8,605 patients. Doctors were also urgently required in army camps across France, while demand for medical services from the same doctors among the civilian population did not cease during wartime. With the pressures placed on these doctors by the War Office, it is unsurprising that there were clear failings in the Medical Boards that led to public distrust and resentment in the system.

Holloway replied to the Local Medical War Committee claiming he did realise that doctors had "a most unenviable task" and that it was "inevitable" that mistakes would occur, but still contended that "too many have been thrust into army life who were obviously unfit".

COMMUNITIES - INDUSTRY

Tribunals also had to consider the substantial effects of conscription on communities. The dearth of young men on the streets led to severe skills shortages in industry. The case of Arthur Hugh Touch, a 39-year-old gents' outfitter from Thrapston, shows two opposing reactions that resulted from tribunals. Mr Touch had been working in Thrapston for 13 years and supplied 20 villages with clothes required for men in industries of national importance such as agriculture and ironstone mines. Appearing in front of the tribunals in May 1918, he presented a petition signed by his neighbours that reads:

"We, the undersigned residents of Thrapston and District, customers of Mr A. H. Touch Outfitter and Clothier, beg to ask the County Appeal Tribunal to reconsider their decision with respect to his exemption from Military Service. The business conducted by Mr Touch is purely a 'one man business' and if he is sent into the Army it must be closed down. We have no other Outfitter in the

District confining himself sorely to our needs and as we live in an Agricultural District and owing to advanced Railway Fares and alterations in the train service, it is practically impossible to go out of town … We therefore respectfully ask you to remove the finality attached to his certificate and allow him to remain to carry on the business that is so necessary to us."

Attached were hundreds of signatures, and while this case may be unique, it certainly echoes the feelings of thousands in Northamptonshire when faced with more of their young men going to war. Far from the scenes of jubilation witnessed in the early weeks of war, public appetite for continued conflict had long faded.

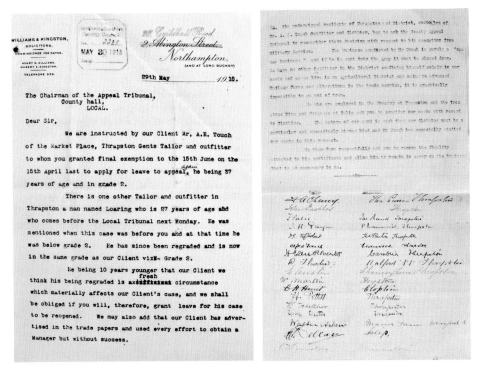

Figure 5.5: Extracts from Arthur Touch's appeal. The images show (left) his lawyer's letter to the Appeal Tribunal and (right) a remarkable petition signed by people in Thrapston pleading with the authorities to give Touch exemption from military service. Touch's case reveals a darker side to Tribunals as his legal representation works to divert attention to a younger man in the town.

Arthur Touch's tribunal papers also reveal a more sinister consequence of conscription. Apart from neighbours supporting each other, the tribunals and conscription served to undermine community relations, pitting young men against each other in a bid to stay at home. Not only had Touch's solicitor submitted a letter explaining his client's indispensability to his community – a typical argument made by those seeking exemption – he also attempts, in great detail, to divert attention onto another man living in the village:

> *"There is one other Tailor and Outfitter in Thrapston a man named Loaring who is 27 years of age and who comes before the local tribunal next Monday. He was mentioned when this case was before you and at that time he was below grade 2. He has since been regraded and is now in the same grade as our client viz – Grade 2. He being 10 years younger that [sic] our Client we think his being regraded is a fresh circumstance which materially affects our Client's case, and we shall be obliged if you will, therefore, grant leave for his case to be reopened."*

Touch had visited the tribunals on at least eight occasions since 1st June 1917 obtaining temporary extensions to his exemption; once again, the tribunals agreed to another extension. Mr Ernest Wilfred Loaring, however, was less fortunate. The military sent an appeal to the tribunal to get Loaring into service in June 1918. He was given a final six-week exemption. He appealed this decision on 19th July in front of the tribunal but had his application refused. Loaring was sent to join the army.

If the impact of a man like Arthur Touch leaving for war could have such a large effect on a village, the consequences for a family could be even greater. On 26th October 1917, seventeen-year-old Tom Chapman of 54 Bath Street, Northampton, appeared in front of the appeals tribunal after the military had objected to his exemption. On Chapman's application form, his mother lists reasons why her son should stay. It is a haunting look into how the war affected individual families – perhaps even poignant due to the unemotional, matter-of-fact language used:

> *"I am claiming exemption for my son, as he is the only one now remaining at Home, except a little boy, aged 9. I have already given three sons to the army, two of whom have been killed in action. The other one, having been out since the war started, being wounded on two separate occasions in France, then preceding [sic] to Salonika where he contracted enteric fever, and after recovering has been out again at Salonika for the past twelve months."*

The military appeal was dismissed, and Chapman was granted an exemption. Cases similar to Chapman's were common; applicants would often state the number of their immediate family who had already served and stress the hardship that would result if they too left home. The tribunals, under pressure from the government, could not exempt all such cases, but it does appear they were sympathetic to cases like Tom Chapman's.

For example, another youngster, Arthur Partridge of Earls Barton, had his application refused at the local tribunal. Darnell & Price Solicitors stated, in a supporting letter, that the "family history is an excellent one" and that the father "has no desire to keep his last boy out of the Army". Indeed, Partridge's four elder brothers were already serving in the army. Partridge, a door machinist, was helping out on his father's farm of 50 acres with 4 horses, 8 cows, 25 pigs and 30 sheep. This appears to have worked against him, as the local tribunal stated its reasons for rejecting an exemption were because "this man is only 18 years of age and single and qualified for general service and only assists in farm work during his spare time which is very limited". Partridge was somewhat fortunate as he was briefly reprieved by the appeal tribunal on 26th November 1917, which granted him a temporary extension until 1st April 1918 on the condition that he spends all his time on the farm. In March of 1918, Partridge once again appeared at the tribunals to further his exemption, but on this occasion was rejected.

In a county like Northamptonshire with its pre-eminent boot and shoe industry – the 1911 census showed 37% of the working-age population were shoemakers – responsible for supplying millions of pairs of boots for the Allied armies, it is no surprise that many applications for exemption were made by employers in the industry. For example, W. J. Brookes, a boot manufacturer based in Earls Barton, appealed to the Wellingborough Rural Tribunal on 25th June 1917 to extend an exemption for their employee Harold Cox, a 22-year-old foreman and mechanical engineer. The firm explained that if Cox was taken by the military they would have no one with the required skills to work their machine and should be "compelled to close" – a situation that both the military and tribunal would want to avoid, as the firm produced 500 pairs of boots for the British Army each week. The firm explained they were "not doing this with a view to keep him [Cox] out of the Army" but because they needed him for "one month for him to teach one of our lads". Cox was duly given an exemption until 12th August.

Despite the strong lobbying efforts of the industry and having the president of the local boot and shoe manufacturers' association, A. E. Marlow, and the president of the incorporated association of boot and shoe manufacturers, Owen Parker, on the tribunal committee, the industry lost many skilled men to the army. It is not unusual to find factories losing between 50 and 100 men, and in some cases up to 300. Anecdotal reports suggest that the quality of boots suffered so much that experienced Northampton bootmakers on the front would re-stitch and mend defects!

While industry bosses protested that they had given their fair share of men to the army while other businesses were less affected, McDermott speculates there might be another reason for their strong efforts against the tribunals. In the late 19th century, the industry had successfully fought off American competition. However, as Northampton shifted resources towards war production, American importers filled the gap in the domestic market. By 1915, American imports reached a record high of 1.4 million pairs of shoes. Manufacturing bosses, with one eye on the future of their businesses after the war, would be keen to retain their highly skilled employees.

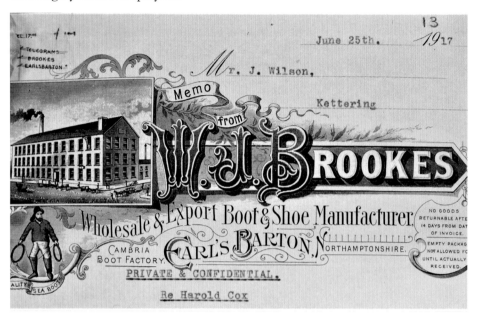

Figure 5.6: A letter sent to the Tribunals by boot and shoe firm W. J. Brookes of Earls Barton, in support of their employee Harold Cox. Note the elaborate design on the letter header.

Other commercial tensions also combined with the slowly increasing societal tensions resulting from tribunals deciding the fates of men. It is clear how such tensions could play out within small communities, as evidenced by the Touch–Loaring case, but it also affected whole industries and towns. In late 1916, Kettering shoe factories accused their Northampton counterparts of appealing conscription deadlines for their staff on spurious grounds, which meant extra work went to Northampton factories while more Kettering men were conscripted. Northampton industry bosses robustly denied this, claiming they had lost £1m of orders from America due to labour shortages. The rift calmed down as the winter progressed, but it was yet another sign of growing tensions within the country.

GOING TO WAR
PRIVATE MORLEY'S DIARY

The tribunals, for all their ills, provide us with a record of the human cost entailed by the war. While newspapers contained, at least in the early years of war, patriotic reports of multiple sons fighting in France, the tribunals present contrasting views such as mothers desperately pleading to the authorities to allow her last living son to stay at home. With many men repeatedly applying for extensions, they also present us with a picture, although incomplete, of a county where thousands of men did not want to fight. It will never be known how many tribunal applications were made as a result of a fear of war and death but which used occupation or family circumstance to conceal the real reasons. It would be reasonable to assume there were several such cases, and, by mid-1916, many men did not share that same patriotic fervour that swept the nation in the early months of the war.

Descendants of Northamptonshire soldiers who fought in the Great War quite often recollect that their relatives barely uttered a word on what they had experienced between 1914 and 1918, aside from a momentary look at war medals shown to grandchildren. Many men wanted to protect their families from the truth; many did not want to relive it, and possibly all of them wanted to leave the war firmly behind. With a lack of primary information from relatives of those who fought, this leaves the lingering question as to what these men thought and felt as they were sent to war in 1916, with the foreboding sense that they might never see their home or loved ones again.

The personal diary of Private Alexander Morley of the 7th Northamptonshire Battalion provides a rare glimpse of army life both at home and at the front with the associated struggles, fear and anxieties of a soldier all laid bare. Personal diaries were banned in the army, lest they fell into enemy hands. However, Morley, as evident from his writing, was highly educated and managed to keep his diary secret.

Private Morley, initially with the 3rd Battalion, begins his daily training at Chatham, Kent, in February 1916. Morley describes the varied and exhausting training activities performed on one day: parading; rifle shooting; carrying coal supplies; trench drills and even gymnastics. Almost immediately the reader is provided with a glimpse of the hardships experienced in army life. After a month in the army and receiving two vaccinations which had an ill effect, a tired Morley wished "to GOD that I were quit of this business". He ponders his fate that in "two months I should be selected to instant death", before distracting himself from the war with his love of poetry, wondering if he can find a publishing house.

The low standards of doctors working for the Medical Boards seem to have extended into the training camps. Feeling poorly, Morley complains that the doctors "disregard" his problems and asked, "How can I recover if the army doctors, to whom alone I can go, will not take such a case into consideration at all?" Soldiers were expected to perform their training drills no matter what their physical condition was; feeling more ill by the day, Morley had no option but to struggle on. After taking the train home to Althorp Park Station on 19th February 1916 , Morley was coughing violently and wrote, while resting before a warm fire, "I felt as if I did not quite belong to a lower state of animal that inhabits barracks."

His short leave was soon over, and on 22nd February he was back in Chatham, clearly loathing his experience. The following morning, Morley, along with his battalion, lined up in the snow, and they were left marching for over an hour while waiting for an inspection by army seniors. When the military inspectors finally arrived, they walked round a Middlesex battalion (who were also marching with the Northamptons) and dismissed both groups without so much as looking at Morley's battalion. In a rather astonishing tirade, Morley severely chastises his army superiors:

> *"But from what I have gleaned about British generals I should think they were the most foolish incompetent of men, if only utterly unfit for their position by the state of their minds which are probably filled up with society languor or sporting inclinations. So much for them. They are nothing but jacks in office and they are aware they can do just as they please. Being in the army under such men makes me feel in a hopeless prison: as if no daylight could ever fall upon me."*

The resentment is palpable when a few days later Morley had to cook for the officers:

> *"The next twelve hours saw us ensconced in the sergeants mess kitchens, the minions of the wants of a hundred and eight sergeants. We saw little of them, but we washed their plates and cups, peeled their potatoes, cleaned their teapots, cooked their peas, scrubbed their floors, brought their coal, lit their fires, and a good many other things."*

From these short passages, the beginnings of the common perception of incompetent generals and with it the immortalised phrase 'lions led by donkeys' begin to appear. However, it was not only his superiors Morley took a dislike to. After a tiring day, he walked solemnly through Chatham to the YMCA hall for some warmth but also to "get away from some of my comrades of the barrack room whose acquaintance I do not precisely relish".

The mental exertion, as well as the physical, took its toll on soldiers. It is hard to imagine just how difficult army life was in 1916, as the urgent need for men meant new recruits were rushed through with very short intense courses. However, as Morley's cold started to clear up, a very curious thing occurs. Morley begins to enjoy army life! On 27th March, he describes a rifle drill in which he came joint third in great detail, concluding that "nothing is more delicious than to see the white marker on the end of its long pole arising out of the trench and flopping down on the hill. It is a thing I could never get tired of." Then, on 6th

April, he writes an exciting entry where he describes a German Zeppelin being shot down, with the pilot captured. For many of the British soldiers in Chatham, this would have been the first glimpse of the enemy they had been fighting for 18 long months. For Morley, the size of the Germans struck out:

> "So we had the pleasure of seeing some of our boys sling down the hill in company of the Germans & very well they marched & very well they looked. Only they looked much slighter & smaller than the German who were hulking big men, nearly corpulent & of much stature ... they were fine naval looking men."

As Morley approaches his last days at home before he will join the 7th Battalion in France, the diary entries become noticeably darker and gloomier; there is a distinct sadness which permeates the page with bleak but poignant prose. On 17th May 1916, Morley spent his last day at home, and like many before and after him, thought about what awaits. It is not the soldier Alexander Morley that confronts the prospect of death, but the poet Alexander Morley:

> "Sat in the garden all the morning looking through my poems & diaries for the last time, conscious that I was, perhaps, bidding them farewell forever. Their keeping & the fruits of theirs may pass into other hands. But in death shall I care? Heaven & earth at their most glorious this day. Foliage & flowers at their best and I destined to make a long farewell to my home & journey away from it, perhaps forever. All the goodbyes said at last ... saw my mother standing alone in the porch, a black solitary figure, very forlorn, & growing old & I thought, one who was feeling the bitterness of this life in that another of her sons was leaving her for war ... And so I have forsaken my home & pass into military life, either until my life ends or the war finishes. And GOD grant me a good ending to the business. Amen."

After leaving home, it is the soldier writing once more. War had been lurking in the distance, its spectre teasing Morley with the prospect of death. After suffering through his vigorous training, pushing himself physically and mentally further than ever before, war is not coming to Morley. Instead, Private Morley is going to war:

> "And I am happy that I can devote my life & all its honour down into the dust for the name of Britain. And I am happy that it is mine to perish with the flower of the English boys, in the very emblem of human beauty & wish them to unite the great triumph

shall reawaken us to our glory. And so tomorrow I leave my native country, in great content, ready to lay down my life, trusting to GOD, & thrilled to fight."

Private Morley's diary illustrates many of the harsh realities of army life. While Morley's attitude may not be representative, his diary provides a rare insight into the raw emotions of soldiers being sent to war, and also offers an understanding of some of the issues that would weigh heavily on men appearing before the tribunals.

When one considers these sentiments and how families were destroyed by war, it is not entirely surprising that the public loathing of tribunals continued not only to the end of the war, but beyond it too. In the Christmas edition of *The Northampton Independent* on 14th December 1918, a feature about the tribunals is printed with the headline, "Most Maligned of Men". Writing with great sympathy and in the Christmas spirit, both of which were less commonly observed during the war, Holloway – the editor who had several public spats with tribunalists – said members of the tribunal had become so detested that it had:

> *"left them without a shred of character, and no hope of peace in this world or the next! To sit on the tribunal has demanded moral courage of no mean order, in fact, several of the members have received letters, one being warned that a bomb would be thrown at him. Someone had to do the work, and probably most people will now admit that the Northampton Tribunal carried a difficult and thankless task with a courtesy and fairness which could not very well have been improved upon."*

Against this background , it is not surprising that the government ordered the destruction of all official records relating to the tribunals after the war. Although no official reason has been given for this, McDermott suggests it is because they wanted "to expunge the legacy of a politically troubled process and a symbolic repudiation of the process itself".

However, the Northamptonshire tribunal papers only tell a small fraction of the overall story. Records reveal that the tribunals sat for 200 days hearing 25,591 applications in total, with 6,801 original appeals. The typical sitting time was five hours, with around twenty-five cases heard each hour. This meant, on average, tribunals would have around only two and a half minutes to hear all evidence and decide the fate of a man. However, a single case on behalf of an employer might include groups of several men, giving tribunals even less time to fully assess each individual man. The pressures on them from the War Office were tremendous and it is no surprise erroneous decisions were made, or that these men and women, with no legal training, did not always meet the high expectations required of them.

Most Maligned of Men.

Conditional Exemption for Tribunal.

Photo, Cooper & Son.

Reading ...   THE MEMBERS OF THE NORTHAMPTON TRIBUNAL.   ... Gribble ... Mr. Herbert Hankinson (Hon. Sec.),

Figure 5.7: An article in The Northampton Independent on 14th December 1918 displays some Christmas spirit by remarking Tribunalists had a difficult job and, in a tongue-in-cheek manner, providing them with a 'Conditional Exemption'.

While much remains unknown about the inner workings of tribunals across the country, statistical analysis of the Northamptonshire tribunal records finds the average age of a man who appeared before a tribunal was 34 years old. As would be expected, the average age of men also went up in each year of the war as fewer young men remained. In 1916, the average age was 29; in 1917 this had increased to 34, before reaching 36 in 1918. Interestingly, the average age of a conscientious objector was 27 – significantly below the average age of men who appeared before tribunals[1].

A snapshot of the national picture published after the war reveals that 779,936 men, aged 41 or under, held exemption certificates issued by tribunals on 30th April 1917; 45% were under 30 years old. It is worth stating that only 5.5% of men aged 30 or under were given absolute exemptions and 22% were on temporary exemptions. The majority were likely to have joined the army at some point. Half (51%) of men aged 30 or under who possessed an exemption certificate worked in occupations listed to be of national importance.

---

1   Average age calculations include men who appeared at Tribunal multiple times. Ages have been rounded up.

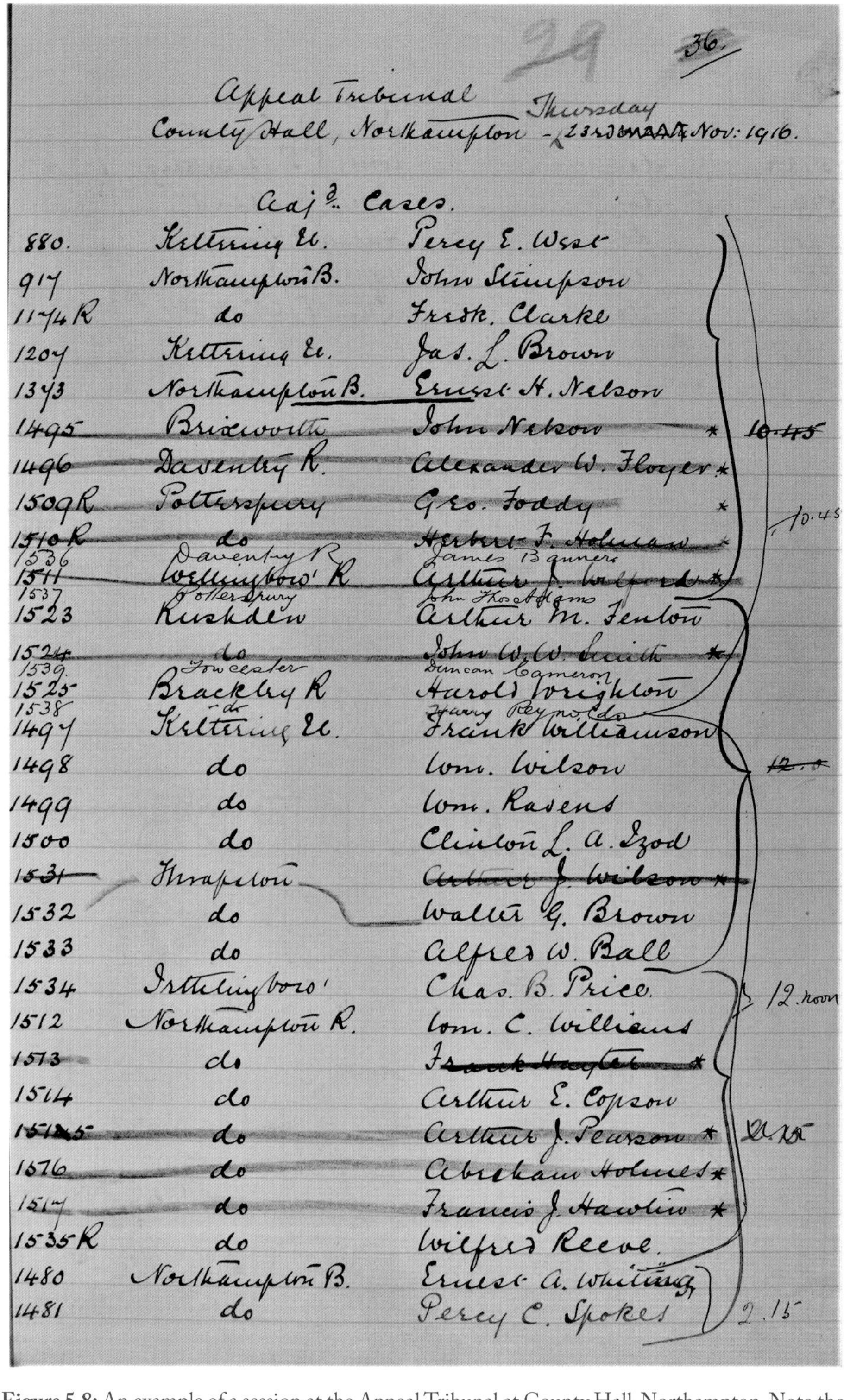

29 36.

Appeal Tribunal
County Hall, Northampton – Thursday 23rd Nov: 1916.

Adjd. Cases.

880.	Kettering U.	Percy E. West	
917	Northampton B.	John Stimpson	
1174R	do	Fredk. Clarke	
1207	Kettering U.	Jas. L. Brown	
1343	Northampton B.	Ernest H. Nelson	
~~1495~~	~~Brixworth~~	~~John Nelson~~ *	~~10.45~~
~~1496~~	~~Daventry R.~~	~~Alexander W. Floyer~~ *	
~~1509R~~	~~Potterspury~~	~~Geo. Foddy~~ *	10.45
~~1510R~~	~~do~~	~~Herbert F. Holman~~ *	
1536	Daventry R	James Banners	
~~1511~~	~~Wellingboro' R~~	~~Arthur J. Wilford~~ *	
1537	Potterspury	John Thos Adams	
1523	Rushden	Arthur M. Fenton	
~~1524~~	~~do~~	~~John W. W. Smith~~ *	
1539.	Towcester	Duncan Cameron	
1525	Brackley R	Harold Wrighton	
1538	do	Harry Reynolds	
1497	Kettering U.	Frank Williamson	
1498	do	Wm. Wilson	~~12.0~~
1499	do	Wm. Rasens	
1500	do	Clinton L. A. Izod	
~~1531~~	Thrapston	~~Arthur J. Wilson~~ *	
1532	do	Walter G. Brown	
1533	do	Alfred W. Ball	
1534	Irthlingboro'	Chas. B. Price.	12. noon
1512	Northampton R.	Wm. C. Williams	
~~1513~~	do	~~Frank Hagler~~ *	
1514	do	Arthur E. Copson	
~~1515~~	~~do~~	~~Arthur J. Pearson~~ *	~~2.15~~
~~1516~~	~~do~~	~~Abraham Holmes~~ *	
~~1517~~	~~do~~	~~Francis J. Hawtin~~ *	
1535R	do	Wilfred Reeve.	
1480	Northampton B.	Ernest A. Whiting	
1481	do	Percy C. Spokes	2.15

Figure 5.8: An example of a session at the Appeal Tribunal at County Hall, Northampton. Note the number of names and the scribbled times indicating the tight schedule the Tribunal ran to.

The Northampton tribunal papers also reveal some of the more obscure aspects about a society at war, such as the strong effect local circumstances could have on national decision making; the influence of big employers, such as the boot and shoe industry, which had a hand over decisions; conscientious objectors, who were treated with strong disdain yet granted exemptions in some cases; tribunals, for all the criticism of them, defending the public from unscrupulous army and medical officers; newspapers, absorbing all the controversy invoked by the rich tapestry of society, their editors struggling to obey censorship laws as they sided and sympathised with their readers.

Indeed, if the tribunal papers expose anything, they explicitly capture the individual human story behind the war – for both tribunalist and appellant alike. Unlike most First World War historical sources, they portray men as individuals rather than as numbers, as men who had a life before the war; they reveal a man's family, the type of work he was engaged in and the community he belonged to. It is through these documents that the men who fought are given a voice in history to tell their story, rather than just a grave.

The information contained in these records provides several faces of the tribunals; some serve to humanise the tribunals; some shatter myths that the tribunalists were autocratic bureaucrats drunk on power; some reinforce such views; some show tribunals to be kind and understanding in even the most difficult of cases. Moreover, the records show that individual tribunalists might act compassionately one day, yet cruelly the next. This presents a blurred view with no firm conclusions, but it is perhaps a blurred view that is needed to understand the societal impact of war. People strove for fairness, equality and justice, but in a time of severe shortage, constant dreariness and painful death, dark forces found strong breeding grounds to weaken common humanity. Tribunalists, just like the men whose fate they would decide, were capable of mistakes, capable of anger, but also capable of love.

Tribunal documents ultimately reveal a tired, exhausted country. Deep divisions had appeared in both society and the British Army, within which different microcosms had their own ill-perceived treatment by tribunals: members of tribunals pitted against conscripts , conscientious objectors against the army, neighbours against each other, generals against their troops, towns resentful of other towns, whole industries envying other industries.

The home front was now at breaking point, and large sections of the British public were war-weary. The mass arrival of American troops, the subsequent breakthrough on the Western Front and a series of victories in the Holy Land in 1918 provided a timely antidote to the continued scourge of war and conscription. Society had been truly on the brink.

Figure 6.1: This stunning image appears to show the 1st Northamptons along with the King's Royal Rifles walking on the Kapellestraat, the main retail district in Ostend, a Belgian city on the coast captured by the Germans. The soldiers were taken prisoner after their disastrous losses on the beaches near Nieuwpoort.

CHAPTER SIX

DUNES DISASTER
10TH JULY 1917

On 10th July 1917, in the late afternoon under a waning sun, the normally quaint and beautiful Belgian coast around Nieuwpoort found its golden sands coloured red with blood. Hundreds of bodies lay still, slowly being engulfed by the soft sand. As a soldier rests near his machine gun, unable to stand, another man rushes to him and attempts to drag him out. The gunner protest, adamantly telling the soldier: "Don't mind about me, smash my gun and get back." There is not enough time to save both the man and to destroy the machine gun. The soldier obeys and sets about disabling the machine gun. Time is running out as he dashes to the River Yser and dives in. He frantically swims across to where the remnants of the 1st Northamptons are located. Trapped, beaten-up and surrounded, these men were in the middle of what would later become known as the 'Dunes Disaster'.

SINCE THE EARLY MONTHS OF THE WAR, the Germans had captured the majority of the Belgian coast in the 'race to the sea' as both sides hastened to envelop the northern flank of their enemy; several key towns were taken and used for German naval exercises. Soon after the Battle of the Somme ended, the Allies decided that an amphibious landing should be undertaken on the Belgian coast. Combined with a supporting attack on Nieuwpoort, the aim was to eventually liberate Ypres from the German forces. Plans for this attack were soon crafted and it was given the codename Operation Hush.

Figure 6.2: As the Northamptons travelled across Flanders, they would witness sights of destruction and rubble, like the city of Nieuwpoort pictured here in January 1915, with its Grande Palace reduced to ruins.

In preparation for the landing, the British XV Corps took over the French sector of the Belgian coast. After receiving reports from his coastal troops, the German commander, Admiral von Schröder, cleverly deduced that the British were preparing for an attack. He urgently started planning a pre-emptive strike to destroy the Yser bridgehead, codenamed Operation Strandfest.

By the time Operation Strandfest began with a German bombardment on 6th July 1917, British defences had not been completed and only 176 of their planned 583 artillery guns were available. The German barrage was rather aimless; its real objective was to conjure up a smokescreen hiding troop movements. Thus, on 10th July, a large German artillery force, supported by masses of naval troops, opened fire on the British positions on the bridgehead. All but one of the bridges over the River Yser were destroyed. Two British battalions were trapped in the middle of the onslaught: the 2nd King's Royal Rifle Corps and the 1st Northamptons. Death surrounded these men as the German artillery nearly wiped out the two battalions, inflicting a 70–80% casualty rate. At 1900, the German artillery finally fell silent. Suddenly, German stormtroopers rushed in to finish off the survivors; specialist flamethrower teams even supported them to flush out troops in the more protected dugouts. Operation Hush was over before it had even begun.

Figure 6.3: This photograph, taken by a German war photographer near Nieuwpoort, shows the considerable trench defensives the Germans had built along the dunes leaving them well prepared to make a ruthless offensive against the Northamptons.

Before the day of the Dunes Disaster, most of 1917 had been relatively quiet for the 1st Battalion as they journeyed towards the coast. On 23rd June, the men had reached the most extreme point of the Western Front, located three miles behind the trenches at Nieuwpoort. A curious mix of golden sands, quaint beach huts and barbed wire made the environment a marked change from what the troops had previously experienced.

On 4th July, around 400 Northampton men had gone into the front line with the King's Royal Rifles. The area was a wedge-shaped tract of land only 600 yards wide. Many of these men were new recruits who had not been under fire before. Senior officers said this would be a good opportunity for the men to gain some familiarity with trench warfare; this most northerly part of the Western Front was relatively quiet, and it was thought the soft sand would prevent many German shells from exploding.

On 10th July, the day started calmly enough, with no incident of note. The British soldiers in the line would have had no idea of the impending slaughter that awaited them just hours later. In the Regimental History, the authors dubbed this battle as the 'dies irae, dies illa', a line from a medieval Latin poem describing the Day of Judgement, wrath and doom.

At 0645, the quiet seaside landscape was set ablaze by the powerful German bombardment. For around an hour, its focus was on the reserve line and bridges over the canal. As each hour passed, the bombardment grew in intensity as the German 5.9-inch howitzers created a "tornado of fire". There was scarcely any shelter amidst the sand dunes for men to protect themselves from the carnage dealt out by the German shells. To make matters worse, German aeroplanes dropped bombs over the British trenches in areas untouched by the shelling. Nowhere was safe in this so-called "quiet sector". It was clear that the Germans had amassed vast numbers of their most powerful guns, with senior British soldiers heard muttering that they had never witnessed such a heavy bombardment. Von Schröder's careful preparations were paying off at severe cost to the Northamptons and King's Royal Rifles.

By late morning, the Germans had succeeded in completely isolating the British soldiers. The communication wires had all been destroyed, thus preventing calls for reinforcements. Far more alarming was that, after being hit by German shells, the bridges over the River Yser lay in rubble, and with them their only escape path. To make matters worse, the German artillery had also knocked out the British artillery. In a war epitomised by trench warfare and endless shelling, the German strategy, preparation and execution had worked perfectly and to devastating effect.

The Northamptons and the King's Royal Rifles were trapped with little means to put up effective resistance against the overwhelming German forces. The Regimental History describes the scene on the dunes: "The earth was rocking; the smoke and sand were so dense that one could hardly see a yard in front. Hell was let loose with a vengeance. We were like a lot of stupid beings as we were helpless to do anything but wait till the end." Men were frantically digging out those who had been buried under the masses of sand that were lifted each time a shell exploded. Moreover, the survivors faced a hail of gas shells and the danger of being burnt to death by petrol bombs.

The bombardment lasted throughout the afternoon, with no drop in its ferocity. At around 1900, the German artillery finally stopped. Soon, a German marine division appeared. Those Northampton soldiers who were still standing hopelessly tried to fight back with whatever firepower they could muster after their artillery was rendered useless, having been wrecked by the German bombs. The Germans had surrounded the Northamptons and launched a surprise attack on the battalion headquarters from behind. As soon as they realised what was happening, the officers destroyed as many documents as they could lay their hands on. Lieutenant Colonel Tollemache, leading the Northamptons, was intent on fighting with only his revolver, despite the odds. The Regimental History describes Tollemache and his adjutant, Captain Chisholm, fighting "back to back with their revolvers" until Tollemache's gun broke, and he had no option but to surrender. Both the lieutenant colonel and the captain were subsequently taken prisoner.

Figure 6.4: German soldiers peer above their dune trenches near Nieuwpoort; unbeknown to the British troops, the Germans had planned to trap them, forcing them back to the River Yser.

In the middle of the torrent of fire, it appears that Sergeant Mansfield volunteered to swim the River Yser to warn the King's Royal Rifles of the impending danger, an act a fellow soldier described as being worthy of the Victoria Cross. The Regimental History suggests the sergeant's intervention was essential in preventing further deaths. As Mansfield left his battalion, he glimpsed a small group of surrounded Northamptons "fighting to the end with their revolvers".

One of the men Mansfield would have seen was 20-year-old Sergeant Benjamin Cope of 77 Eastgate, Peterborough. Recounting the incident, Cope said: "We stuck it till there were only seven of us left, the Germans outnumbering us by about twenty to one." He then decided to try and lead his remaining men to safety by swimming across the river: "I dashed into the canal and got safely to the other side although the Germans were still having a splosh at me." Once he reached the division headquarters, he was given a whisky and allowed ten days' leave.

Although he was unaware it was Sergeant Cope and his men fighting to the very end, the famous war reporter Sir Philip Gibbs wrote of the heroic scene in *The Daily Chronicle*:

> *"The picture of these six heroes out there in the sand, with their dead lying around them, refusing to yield, and fighting on to a certain death, is one of the memories of the war that should not be allowed to die."*

The Man who Swam the Yser.

A Wounded Man's Warning.

Figure 6.5: In a war epitomised by monotonous trench warfare, the horrors of the Dunes Disaster spurred tales of heroic actions that were enthusiastically reported in the local press; 28th July 1917, The Northampton Independent.

Elsewhere on the battlefield, the Northamptons also put up a valiant fight but were simply delaying the inevitable. The German march continued relentlessly, and with nowhere to go, the men were faced with a tough choice: fight on until death or surrender. Many did the former, even fighting the German troops with their bare fists once their ammunition had been depleted. However, in a move more suited to a Hollywood epic, around a dozen men decided to evade capture by frantically sprinting across the loose sand, in which they "sank up to their ankles", to swim across the Yser, desperately hoping the whole time that they would not be struck by the German fire.

Around 2100, the German victory was complete. The Northamptons and the King's Royal Rifles had been annihilated. Almost 1,000 men were thought to have been killed, wounded or captured, although officers were cut off from the battlefield and could not obtain more precise numbers of casualties. According to the Regimental History, those who escaped were unable to give a coherent account of the day's events, such was the horror of what they experienced. Indeed, the battalion's war diary paints a chaotic picture, with the diarist seemingly struggling to record an accurate chronicle of the day, using short sentences, time estimations and uncertain phrases:

"The Bosch shelled very heavily, starting at 6.45 am on front line, with 5.9's. 7.45 am barrage lifted to support line. 8.45 am barrage lifted

to SW side of Yser. 9.45 am – 9.50 Pause. 9.50 Barrage on support line. 10.50 am barrage lifted to SW side of Yser. 11.50 am Barrage lifted to front line … The enemy appears to have made his main attack, at the point where the two battalions touched, the left of the 48th and the right of the 60th. He advanced to this point in 3 waves and on reaching it split up into 2 parties, one going to the left, and the other to the right towards Bat. Hqrs."

So shocking were the day's casualties that it attracted attention from senior officers of the 1st Division, who demanded a report from the 2nd Infantry Brigade, to which the 1st Northampton and King's Royal Rifles belonged. Found at the end of July's war diary are two typed reports, both remarkable for their content. The first presents an account of the intelligence gathered in the days before the German attack on the 10th. Details about the number of patrols sent and their findings are summarised. It appears one of the patrol team had engaged in a skirmish with German soldiers on the enemy's side of the wire. A second patrol unit later found "the ground between the ditch and enemy wire is very marshy with a good many either ponds or shell holes filled with water". Crucially, however, their intelligence report also said that the ground is "passable", although a crossing "would be rather slow". Information on the structure of enemy wire, trench mortar locations and enemy movements was provided. The report states that in the 48 hours before the main thrust of the German assault, the Northampton trenches had been shelled. After three years of warfare, this would not signal anything out of the ordinary, but the report also states that "several direct hits were made on the bridges", which in hindsight was a consequential piece of information.

The second report, an account of the operations on 10th July signed four days later by Brigadier General G. C. Kemp of the 2nd Infantry Brigade, attempts to provide a factual record of what actually happened, although it was still not clear four days on how the German attack materialised. The report states that "the enemy infantry carried out their assault under a creeping barrage", that the Germans were "believed to have reached the Battalion Headquarters in about an hour" and that "the enemy is believed to have attacked in groups over the top and to have had a particularly large working party along the coast". Further into the report, a rundown of tactics employed by the German soldiers is detailed, including the use of flamethrowers and smoke bombs to force men out of dugouts, and having German soldiers lined along the banks of the River Yser armed with light machine guns aimed at retreating British soldiers. It hauntingly reports that while a few men from C Company were able to swim across the river, there were "no survivors from the other companies".

The conclusion of Kemp's report makes for striking reading. Kemp lists factors that contributed to the disaster, such as that dugouts were not shell-proof and the trenches they inherited were in an already poor state. He explicitly

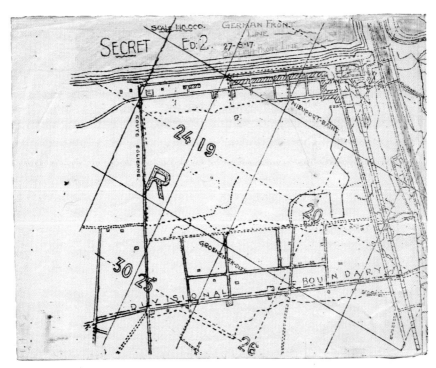

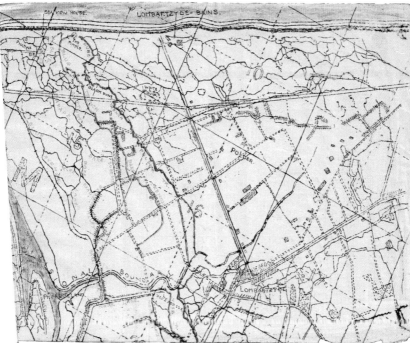

Figure 6.6: Attached to Brigadier General G. C. Kemp's report into the events of 10th July is this 'Secret' map showing the British and German positions on 27th June. The River Yser is coloured blue running down the middle of the map, while the North Sea runs across the top. This map shows the close proximity of the British and German trenches.

attributes blame to the Royal Flying Corps (RFC), claiming "our aeroplane arrangements were so incomplete that the enemy were at entire liberty in the air" and "we obtained no information of any value from our own Air Service". The lack of air support meant all technical communications were disabled early in the morning, so the troops had to rely almost exclusively on pigeons to carry messages to nearby battalions, hampering efforts to send support.

Back in Northampton, just two days after the dunes battle, the town held a baby show in Sheep Street. Completely unaware of the events near Nieuwpoort involving the 1st Northamptons, the show was a rare spot of jolly news after three years of war. The coverage of the baby show merited three pages in *The Northampton Independent* with a "bonny pair" of 11-month-old twins, the children of Mrs Farrar of Havelock Street, Kettering, winning first prize out of 97 entries. Elsewhere in the paper is a full-page advert for seaside swimwear. Both examples provide a glimpse of how normal life carried on in wartime despite the growing shortages at home and the bloodshed abroad.

Figure 6.7: In the midst of war, normal daily life tried to carry on. A baby show held in Sheep Street, Northampton, provided the town with a bit of much-needed amusement; 14th July 1917, *The Northampton Independent.*

Rather surprisingly, the papers were allowed to report on the Dunes Disaster. On previous occasions, battle details could not be reported until months later, if at all. However, a mere eleven days after the battle on the dunes, a dramatic leader in *The Northampton Independent* titled "The Noble Northamptons. LEFT TO DIE" was published. The short passage reported the location of the battle quite accurately, although no precise details on casualties were given, nor was the exact Northamptonshire battalion reported. However, most people would have quickly realised that the account referred to the 1st Battalion since they had been in the same division as the King's Royal Rifles since the start of the war. The lead article contained a stinging attack on the government by the editor, Mr Holloway, for the disaster:

> "We have been told over and over again that we are superior in guns and have an ascendancy in the air. If so, how is it that our splendid lads were left to die without help from land, air or sea? Will not our Members of Parliament demand an explanation of why such disasters are possible after three years? It is all very well to soothe us with assurances that this is an empty success for the Germans. That is no consolation to the hundreds of darkened homes in Northamptonshire, especially when it follows so closely upon the almost equally serious calamity for our other County Battalion at Gaza."

On this occasion, it appears that history can partially exonerate military commanders for the huge losses. Operation Strandfest had taken the British completely by surprise. Early newspaper reports feared that most men had been killed. Indeed, *The Northampton Independent* said on 21st July that there was "little doubt" that Lieutenant Colonel Tollemache and Captain Chisholm were killed. A week later the paper reported a German claim that over 1,000 prisoners were taken on 10th July, although no official confirmation was provided. Later, on 11th August, the paper ran a lead article titled "Survivors of the Dunes Disaster," which added that there was a "strong probability" that a "considerable number" of soldiers, including Lieutenant Colonel Tollemache, had been taken prisoner and were being held at Karlsruhe.

Figure 6.8: Lieutenant Colonel D. P. Tollemache.

While men of the Northamptonshire Regiment being held prisoner would be of the greatest concern to those at home, occasionally the issue of the German prisoners being held at the Pattishall Camp would command attention. Renamed Pattishall from Eastcote in December 1916, the camp had undergone several changes since coming under the control of the War Office in October 1915. The most noticeable, for both prisoners and local villagers alike, was the 2,600 feet of 8 ft fencing, protected with 66 tonnes of barbed wire, that now surrounded the camp. By September 1916, Pattishall exclusively held military prisoners of war, with civilian detainees relocated. The camp was still allowed to run itself internally, but certain luxuries were curtailed; in May 1917, all alcohol was banned within the camp, a far cry from the early days when each man was provided with three bottles of beer a week.

It was perhaps this change that finally led a German trio to break out of the camp. Lieutenant Gustav Lutz, Sergeant Major Wilhelm Landes and Corporal Walter Rivera used forked sticks to create an opening between the fence and barbed wire. Amazingly, the trio managed to board a train full of British soldiers and remained undetected, despite Rivera wearing his German military clothes. The escapees arrived at Cambridge, where Lutz used his English skills to purchase items at a local shop. After boarding another train, they went to Ipswich and walked to Southwold on Saturday night. On Sunday morning, they walked to Wrentham. A local policeman, dressed in plain clothes, saw the men and approached them after noticing their unusual appearance. The men were arrested without resistance and sent back to Pattishall, where they were court-martialled. Of all the attempts at escape from Pattishall, this incident gathered the most media attention as the men got further than in any other jail break attempt.

The story highlighted the relative ease of travelling across the country but also shone a spotlight on the camp's security. With manpower low and women considered unsuitable for guard roles, keeping watch over 3,000 men was a difficult task. The real question, perhaps, is why there were not more escape attempts. In their history of the camp, Chapman and Moss speculate that despite the relatively basic conditions and cramped living quarters, the camp was far preferable to the war. The men could organise their own activities, had a nine-acre sports field, were allowed to work on nearby farms, had a basic hospital on-site, and even had electricity, a convenience that Eastcote village wouldn't benefit from until 1930.

While the treatment of prisoners at Pattishall was reasonably good considering the shortage of food and other materials, reports circulating from the early months of the war regarding the treatment of British prisoners of war by the German army would have caused great worry to family members back home. Luckily, the Regimental History suggests that by all accounts the treatment of the prisoners from the Dunes Disaster was "humane and generous". Finally, on 1st September, the paper reports that letters sent by the prisoners to their relatives had started to arrive and that around 269 prisoners were already on the Northamptonshire Regimental Prisoners of War Fund's list to support.

Figure 6.9: These rare photographs show German prisoners at the Pattishall POW camp, posing in front of a water mill they had built and in a carpentry workshop. Life for prisoners was cramped, but with several activities available, it was preferable to life in the army; c1915-1916.

Although this was probably welcome news after the hopeless situation of the troops, it did come with its own challenges. As the editor of *The Northampton Independent* promptly reminded readers, "an immense amount of extra labour and expense will be imposed upon the Northamptonshire Regimental Prisoners of War Fund in keeping the poor boys well supplied with parcels". With a weekly cost for food alone at 12 shillings for each man at the camp, this amounted to a serious financial burden.

It probably came as a relief that 'The Great Red Cross Fair' was an outstanding fundraising success. In response to the growing demand for war funds, the local Red Cross organised a magnificent fair held in Market Square on Thursday, 27th September 1917. The fair was adorned with draped Venetian masts, striped awnings and streams of flags, and the decorations were crowned off with an elaborate, realistic replica of the old town gates, which *The Northampton Independent* said: "transformed [the square] as though by magic". After an opening ceremony featuring the political and social leaders of Northampton, including Earl Spencer and Field Marshal Lord Grenfell, the fair was officially opened and was so successful it did not close until after dark, a rarity in wartime.

By 1917, extravagant events such as the one witnessed by Northampton were exceedingly rare. It is difficult for us to imagine the delight created by the fair, but the excitement generated from the event is palpable from reviewing old newspaper articles. Several news pages were devoted to covering the fair in the weeks after, with the editor of *The Northampton Independent* claiming that "the talk of the town is still the triumph of the Old English Fair", before adding that it surpassed "anything of the kind ever attempted before". In mid-November, it was announced the Red Cross had raised £30,711 from the fair, or around £1.6 million at present value. This was a remarkable and timely success after the huge extra burden placed on the prisoners' fund after the Dunes Disaster.

The fair was a brief respite for a town and county that had seen their way of life utterly transformed by three hard years of warfare. Food rationing had been established, with local food control committees formed to combat shortages, prevent hoarding and impose price stability to prevent inflation skyrocketing. In fixing prices, the Northampton Food Control Committee had reasonable success, with meeting minutes showing meat prices barely changed in the second half of 1917. However, the food price the consumer paid masked the serious difficulties businesses faced getting hold of stock and also making a profit to survive. One Northampton butcher, Joseph Pitts in Bridge Street, for example, saw the cost of obtaining pigs rise by a third since before the war. Some basic staples saw exponential rises, with the same butcher seeing his flour costs double from 1913 to 1917.

These rising costs and fixed prices caused serious pressure on businesses, some of which can be witnessed in the cases presented to the Northampton Food Control Committee. Made up of sixteen local people, the Northampton branch contained members from all backgrounds, including four women, six councillors and representatives from industry. The committee decided on 17th August they would "not at the present juncture, allow members of the press" to attend their meetings. This was highly unusual, considering reporters had previously been allowed to cover meetings, and no reason was provided for this change of policy. Aware of the growing critical reporting in local news, as evidenced by the immediate reaction to the massacre of the county regiment on Belgian beaches, the committee decided to operate without much press attention. Perhaps wary of the controversial decisions that lay ahead, such as the creation and appointment of a 'chief inspector of nuisances', a position that would be responsible for investigating and punishing individuals and businesses whose practices were contrary to the rules of the food committee, the committee wanted less public scrutiny.

In the following week, the Northampton Trade Representation Council protested against the new post. Their objection was due to the role carrying with it a tribunal exemption from military service, while businesses faced losing essential staff. The Food Control Committee decided to remove this exemption and advertise this position with a requirement that applicants be classed ineligible for military service. This only temporarily placated industry before tempers flared up in December.

The Northampton Master Butchers' Association had formally complained against the decisions of the Food Control Committee, making negative statements in the press accusing the committee of forcing butchers to work at a loss by fixing the price of meats across the county. In response, the food committee issued a remarkable rebuttal at their meeting on 12th December:

> *"The Committee wishes the public to understand they have no animus against the butchers or any other trading concern.*
>
> *They [Inspector for Nuisances] were appointed for the specific purpose of protecting the consumer against the profiteering element which had largely entered trading since the beginning of the war, while at the same time endeavouring to act fairly by the honest dealer.*
>
> *The Meat Order allows a profit to the butcher of 2.5d per lb, or 20% (whichever is less), as a maximum, and with this regulation before them the Committee fixed certain retail prices.*
>
> *The claim by Councillor Fox, a member of both the Food Control Committee and the Northampton Master Butchers' Association, that butchers were asked to trade for less than nothing – presumably meaning they were forced to work at a loss – is not borne out by facts.*

This is proved by the statistics which are laid before the Meat Sub-Committee each fortnight, when the butchers' trading returns are submitted. From these returns we gather that the butchers' profits vary up to as high as 18%, according to the skill and capacity of the butcher in cutting up the carcase.

Thus it will be seen that butchers are not trading at a loss; they are simply not making so much profit – a very different thing."

In this instance, somewhat unsurprisingly, the committee was keen to have the press's help in reporting the statement to the public. Significant for several reasons, this statement firstly shows the strain war placed on society, as food shortages became ever more serious and as prices were held artificially lower than the market equilibrium. It is, however, the level of detail the committee provides to dismiss the Butchers' Association's accusations that is especially revealing. Aware of the public antipathy to tribunals, the food committee was alert to the possibility of public opinion turning on them as food prices rose and quantities became scarce. By explicitly providing details such as precise profit margins, this was a statement aimed to divert blame towards the producers.

The impetus to win public approval was growing in urgency as the food supply become ever more squeezed and rations tightened, which the committee viewed with "considerable anxiety". As queues for food increased in Northampton in the run-up to Christmas, the committee wrote to the Ministry of Food in London claiming that there was enough product, such as butter, arriving in the town, but that it was being unequally distributed, with one firm receiving the bulk. The committee suggested a system whereby each firm would receive products in the proportion to their number of customers. More radically, the committee floated the idea of 'food tickets' that could be traded for specific items such as sugar to "prevent persons from purchasing more than a fair proportion of the essential articles of food". While the critical moment for this radical change had not arrived in December 1917, that it was being discussed by the local food committee illustrates how desperate the situation was getting. In January 1918, as sugar shortages became even more acute, the Ministry of Food prohibited the production of ice cream; a gesture that would have little impact in the winter months, it nevertheless revealed the authorities thought the war would carry on at least until that summer. Preparatory measures were therefore being put in place to ensure basic food staples were not wasted on unnecessary foodstuffs.

If the war, the tribunals and the food shortages hadn't put enough strain on society, it was around summer 1917, the same time as reports of the Dunes Disaster filtered through to the local press, that what became known as the Spanish flu began to appear around the county. Although the start date of the epidemic has traditionally been given as January 1918, there is some evidence that the strain

appeared in 1917. The headmaster of Campbell Square School in Northampton closed his school early in July for the summer holidays due to the "influenza epidemic", the name initially given to this deadly virus. It is a curious detail that the word 'epidemic' is used; schools being seriously affected by flu strains were not a rare incident in this period, and normally 'epidemic' would not be used to describe several children being afflicted by the virus.

Nothing else was heard that year regarding the 'dunes prisoners' in the local press. However, on 5th January 1918, a small article appeared in *The Northampton Independent* stating that little information had been forthcoming because the men were working many miles from their camp and so it was difficult to send letters and parcels to them. However, after the truly desperate situation in July when hundreds of the battalion were feared dead, many of the survivors were known to still be alive. In early 1918, with no end to the war in sight, little else mattered for the relatives of the 1st Northamptonshire Battalion.

THE CIVIC PROCESSION ENTERING THE OLD TOWN GATE.

Figure 6.10: The Great Fair held in Northampton to raise funds for the Red Cross was heralded as a great success and gave the town some much-missed entertainment after three years of heavy warfare and struggle. The Northampton Independent dedicated several pages of coverage to the big event.

Figure 6.11: The depraved humanity of war: the men of the 1st Northamptonshire Battalion and the 2nd King's Royal Rifles lie vacantly on a rubble floor in Ostend, Belgium after being captured near Nieuwpoort on 10th July 1917.

Figure 7.1: The Yeomanry in Italy, 1917.

Figure 7.2: The Yeomanry's regimental crest.

CHAPTER SEVEN

THE NORTHAMPTONSHIRE YEOMANRY

THE WAR

WARNING TO THE YEOMANRY

"The members of the Northants Yeomanry have received a notice from headquarters giving instructions as to procedure on mobilisation. This warns them that in the event of mobilisation they must rejoin the regiment if medically fit, or be treated as deserters. They will be required to parade in full marching order, and be in possession of arms, clothing, and necessaries. Horses will be provided by the regiment."

The Northampton Independent – 1st August 1914

"Sought the Lord earnestly that we might not have to fight that day, being Sunday."

Diary of Cyril Day – 30th October 1918

In a war characterised by stagnant trench warfare, with men slowly clambering over the parapets only to be mechanically mowed down by machine guns in cold sodden fields, the cavalry is something of an oddity. The image of the proud cavalry soldier, upright on his horse, charging bravely towards the enemy, perhaps epitomises the notion of pointless sacrifice like no other. Horse and lance were no match for tanks and heavy artillery.

Brave and daring as these men were, no longer were their actions immortalised and venerated in poetic epics such as Lord Tennyson's '*Charge of the Light Brigade*', which commemorated the infamous British charge in the Crimean War. Instead, the First World War is often seen through the lens of technological change, with the continued use of horses embodying the anachronistic British command unable or unwilling to adapt to the new rules of warfare, resulting in senseless numbers of casualties. Nonetheless, yeomanry troops played an important role in critical moments of the war; the British cavalry charge at the Battle of Mons is credited with being successful in holding off the advancing Germans.

The fifty-four yeomanry regiments were the mounted troops of the Territorial Force formed in 1908 after a major structural reform of the army. Recruitment of Territorial Force units, composed of part-time volunteers whose main role was home defence, was very localised compared to the main army; the Northamptonshire Yeomanry would contain more local men than the Northamptonshire Regiment.

At the start of the war, the Northamptonshire Yeomanry was sent to Derby and Luton for training, which was completed at Hursley Park near Winchester. The mobilisation was swift, with each man knowing his role once called. The procedure was strict and those who did not inform their headquarters of a change of address, and therefore did not receive a 'Notice to Join', would be treated as deserters. Simply turning up was not adequate for a yeoman; the soldier was responsible for bringing a host of items, including his own soap and cutlery.

The regiment left Southampton on 5th November 1914 and was sent to the Neuve Chapelle sector, where they busied themselves with defensive work. The New Year brought with it the stark realities of warfare on the Western Front. On 2nd January 1915, Private Fred Sumner, 26, was assisting work to improve defences by digging trenches in the rear of the main line when a bullet pierced his body below the ribs. Sumner, who had only joined the Yeomanry at the outbreak of war, became the first Northamptonshire Yeoman to be killed. Lieutenant Wartnaby wrote home to Sumner's father in Desborough:

> "*He was one of the best of chaps, and if I had been asked to pick out a man I would sooner almost have lost anyone but him. He was a good horseman, good shot, always smart, and as good a soldier in every way as there is in the troop … May your sadness be mingled with the proud thought that he gave up his life for his country.*"

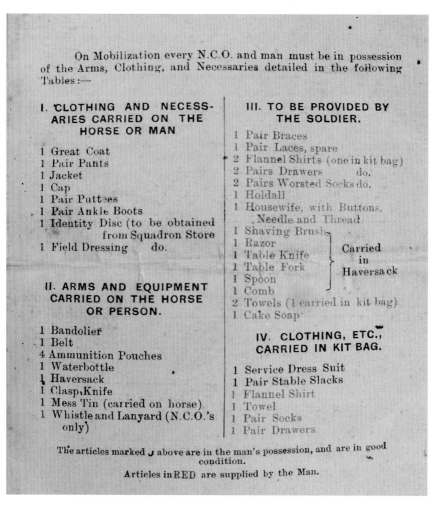

On Mobilization every N.C.O. and man must be in possession of the Arms, Clothing, and Necessaries detailed in the following Tables:—

I. CLOTHING AND NECESSARIES CARRIED ON THE HORSE OR MAN

1 Great Coat
1 Pair Pants
1 Jacket
1 Cap
1 Pair Puttees
1 Pair Ankle Boots
1 Identity Disc (to be obtained from Squadron Store
1 Field Dressing do.

II. ARMS AND EQUIPMENT CARRIED ON THE HORSE OR PERSON.

1 Bandolier
1 Belt
4 Ammunition Pouches
1 Waterbottle
1 Haversack
1 Clasp Knife
1 Mess Tin (carried on horse)
1 Whistle and Lanyard (N.C.O.'s only)

III. TO BE PROVIDED BY THE SOLDIER.

1 Pair Braces
1 Pair Laces, spare
2 Flannel Shirts (one in kit bag)
2 Pairs Drawers do.
2 Pairs Worsted Socks do.
1 Holdall
1 Housewife, with Buttons, Needle and Thread
1 Shaving Brush
1 Razor
1 Table Knife } Carried
1 Table Fork   } in
1 Spoon   } Haversack
1 Comb
2 Towels (1 carried in kit bag)
1 Cake Soap

IV. CLOTHING, ETC., CARRIED IN KIT BAG.

1 Service Dress Suit
1 Pair Stable Slacks
1 Flannel Shirt
1 Towel
1 Pair Socks
1 Pair Drawers

The articles marked ↙ above are in the man's possession, and are in good condition.

Articles in RED are supplied by the Man.

Figure 7.3: A pamphlet issued to all Yeomanry members contained instructions on what men should bring and what would be provided.

More casualties were to follow as the Yeomanry were sent into their first major battle at Neuve Chapelle on 10th March 1915. Trooper Donald Siddons said the opening bombardment was so ferocious that those "who have been through Mons, Aisne and Ypres say that they were absolutely child's play [compared] to it".

Two days later the men were disturbed during breakfast and sent into the trenches. The Germans had launched a terrific artillery assault on the British lines and the Yeomanry suffered their heaviest casualties of the war so far. Eleven men were killed in the battle, with a further eighteen wounded. One of the men killed was Private John Edwin Brown of Gloucester Place, Wellingborough. Casualties would have been higher, but the Northamptons were partially saved after another division's attack had been delayed. As a result, the men were stuck in the trenches for three days, unable to make a charge that would surely have proved fatal.

Figure 7.4: Private John Edwin Brown; note his regimental cap badge is facing the wrong way – the horse should face the opposite direction. This was "typical" of Brown according to his family.

After the action at Neuve Chapelle, the battalion was split, with A Squadron joining the 4th Division on the Somme, B Squadron moving to Ypres with the 6th Division, and C Squadron joining the 5th Division on the Somme. All squadrons were mainly engaged in defensive work for the following year, haunted by the presence of the German artillery. A squadron was sent to Ypres in April and contributed to the construction of new defences and clearing of the battlefield. The war diary says that the men encountered poison gas but were not equipped with gas masks: "there was only one thing to do, re: – get out of the danger area as quickly as possible". The regiment was eventually re-formed on 10th May 1916 and sent to Arras to join the 6th Corps. Again, the men were put to work improving defence structures, digging tunnels and fortifying trenches.

After an extended period of hard labour, the men were grateful for their happiest Christmas in France so far. One can imagine how grateful the soldiers, normally living on rations such as 1 lb of meat, 1 lb of bread and 10 oz of biscuits a day, would have been when they saw the wide selection of foods available for their Christmas lunch. Sergeant Cyril Day of B Squadron wrote the men feasted on "geese, roast beef & plum pudding … all those who had come out with us agreed it was the happiest X-Mas we had spent in France".

Meanwhile, considerable preparations were being made in anticipation of a spring offensive at Arras. After the miserable failures on the Somme the previous year, where both the 1st and 2nd Battalions had suffered gravely, Arras had become a key target for the new commander-in-chief on the Western Front, Robert Nivelle. A complex tunnel system had been constructed around the area and was capable of concealing 24,000 men and supplies. A preliminary bombardment had begun in late March 1917, and on 9th April, the British troops launched their assault, with the ground covered by snow.

The Yeomanry was left with no misapprehension about how important this battle was for the Allies, and that it were to make a decisive charge. On the eve of battle, Colonel Seymour delivered a final rallying cry, telling his men they were about to "take part in one of the biggest battles history will ever know". As evening set in, the night sky began to illuminate the horizon towards Arras with the continuous flash of guns. The yeomen shared a drink of rum with their superior officers before heading to a barn for one final rest before the action that awaited them the next day.

One soldier who tried to sleep in the barn was J. A. Townsend. Writing in 1940, he remembered sleeping that night:

> *"the waxing and waning, the quivering of the earth under the discharge of the giant Howitzers, the wonderful heavy of stars above when the full flurry of the fire world was awakened."*

By noon, the regiment was prepared for the charge where it would enter Arras and seek to push forward towards Scarpe Alley. Around 1400, Colonel Seymour shouted "Mount!" The Yeomanry, after close to three years of warfare, was about to embark on its most daring charge. Townsend, understandably nervous, said he began to recall "memories of stories and pictures of the cavalry charges at the beginning of this war, and of past history".

The order to charge was given and the regiment moved off at once. Hundreds of horses, hundreds of men, the gallop in unison creating an amazing crescendo – this was a magnificent sight. It was moments like these, not endless digging and defence work, that the Yeomanry was renowned for. Townsend was extremely proud:

> *"As we climbed the hill leading out of the village, I had a good view of practically the whole of the regiment ... A well turned out cavalry unit on the line of march is always an impressive sight ... Good horses well ridden – every man's equipment worn to a certain uniform order – and every saddle packed alike, with rifle-bucket on the off-side, and sword on the rear, nose-bags, canvas water buckets, picketing pegs, all in position – not even a strap out of place."*

The event, however, was something of an anticlimax. As the cavalry entered Arras, they were shocked at the devastation. Buildings in all directions were crumbling, the city little more than a collection of ruins. The sight of wounded British soldiers walking side by side with Germans troops, even sharing cigarettes as they left the battlefield, added to the surreal atmosphere that greeted the Yeomanry.

Figure 7.5: This photograph of the Northamptonshire Yeomanry hurtling down a steep slope in Italy is similar to the sight that the Germans would have seen as Townsend and his comrades carried out a daring charge in Arras.

Figure 7.6: As the Northamptons entered Arras, they were shocked at the endless wreckage that now made up the city. This photograph, taken on 30th April 1917, shows the gouged buildings on the town square barely standing, as a British military band performs an ensemble.

On 11th April 1917, they prepared to move once more. The unpleasant mixture of snow and mud meant fitting out their horses was a much more arduous task than usual. Moreover, the men found the horses to be restless after the previous day's excitement and after the unrelenting explosions during the night. Townsend's horse, Fan Tail, was particularly suffering, although the plucky animal "rose to the occasion" when it was time to go. As the regiment moved towards Orange Hill, they were suddenly attacked from the skies by a German aeroplane. This was one of the few aerial encounters the Yeomanry would have faced and they were not able to muster any defence; instead, men and horses chaotically dispersed to avoid the hail of bullets. Eventually, the plane left and the Northamptons were fortunate to come out unscathed.

The Northamptons soon arrived at Orange Hill, where they were to provide cover to the 45th Infantry Brigade, who were trying to take Monchy-le-Preux after several failed attempts. The Yeomanry went through Feuchy and onto Grange Hill, where they once again encountered more heavy shelling before they were ordered to move towards Monchy-le-Preux, a small village on a hill. The Yeomanry was tasked with going through the village and clearing two wooded areas. As the men approached on their horses, they found British infantry soldiers still inside the village. They were meant to be clear of the village by now but had been held up by strong German resistance. Once more, the Northamptons readied for action.

Cyril Day describes the dramatic charge:

> "We went up at a gallop, the enemy simply pouring shells at us. The cavalry-led horses came into the village & blocked the streets ... Field guns & machine guns were sweeping the country & cutting horses & men down everywhere. It was like being shot in a trap, everyone wanting to go on but finding it absolutely impossible to get through, [so] we had orders to retire."

Private Townsend describes a similarly hectic and chaotic spectacle:

> "That ride from Orange Hill will never be forgotten by the men that took part in it. To run the gauntlet of the German shell fire, especially now that the enemy was so aware of our intentions, made one wonder how many would reach the village. As the danger increased, the way seemed longer ... The explosion of a shell bursting quite near to [Private] Becklake appeared to lift him and his beautiful bay mare and throw them a yard or two sideways ... Big Harry Smith lost his steel helmet, and he galloped along with his right hand on his bare head, – just as if a hand could offer any protection! We thought it very funny – afterwards."

The charge was far from straightforward, with riders wary of shell holes and trenches. Apart from acting as testing obstacles, they gave the men a cause for

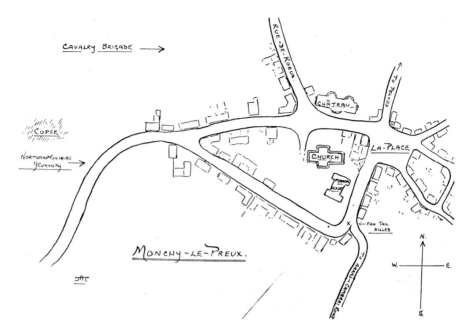

Figure 7.7: This map of Monchy-le-Preux, penned by Townsend, shows the Yeomanry's position as well as Fan Tail's final resting place.

cheer each time they successfully cleared one. More worryingly, a wounded British soldier lay in the gutter, causing the yeomen to suddenly steer clear. Adding to this chaotic scene, the Germans were unleashing heavy shellfire on the Yeomanry as they galloped at extraordinary speed down the hill. With the bursts of flashes from the guns, the vicious roar of the artillery and the adrenaline pumping hard, it is easy to understand why Townsend described this moment "the most thrilling of the war".

Astoundingly, the regiment did not suffer any serious casualties. Townsend remarked, "No wonder the regiment sometimes called itself 'God's own!'" Day was somewhat more measured when he wrote, "how thankful I felt to God for bringing us through. I couldn't understand this or see why we came off so much lighter than the others except that it was an answer to my prayers." In war, however, much can change in little time. While both these men had been lucky so far, the cruel pain and loss dealt out by the Great War would soon be coming for them and their regiment.

The Northamptonshire Yeomanry had reached Monchy-le-Preux. As a result of the collapsed buildings, movement became less fluid; the enemy was suspected to be hiding in several vantage points, covered by thick dust from the debris, patiently waiting for the men to walk right into their rifle sights. Townsend, still mounted on Fan Tail, rushed to his next checkpoint and reached a spot where the road veered sharply to the left. On the inner side of the turn, a high brick wall marking the grounds of the local manor house obscured the view. The outer side of the turn offered a house for some protection. Townsend and some other yeomen approached the turn and they crept past the house. As they emerged from the smoky dust cloud, they realised they had walked straight into a trap. A large party of Germans, including machine gunners occupying a concealed trench, had been patiently waiting for them. The guns fired before Townsend had a chance to realise his mistake:

> *"I must have been about half-way past this exposed turn when I felt, and heard, something strike the inner side of the leg of my left field boots, and I looked down expecting that I had been wounded. While I was looking down, Fan Tail suddenly collapsed on to his knees and his hind legs bent under him."*

Fan Tail had been riddled with machine-gun bullets. This loyal animal, however, was not done just yet. The impact of the bullet Townsend felt on his boot had been softened after piercing Fan Tail's stomach. Fan Tail, in obvious agony, did not collapse to the ground, exposing Townsend to the mercy of the German guns. With blood splattering several feet from his nostrils, the brave horse continued his stride until he had cleared the exposed area before finally succumbing. In death, he had saved his master.

Townsend, his shirt drenched in Fan Tail's blood, now found himself without his trusty charge. From behind, a rush of men and horses, some with no riders, swept past him, trying to escape the German fire. The private noticed one of his officers, Sergeant Hamilton, and shouted out to him. Sergeant Hamilton shouted out, "It's every man for himself now!" leaving Townsend isolated and unprotected. Despite bolting past Townsend, Hamilton could not escape death. He soon died in Monchy-le-Preux after having one of his arms severed by the blast of a shell. Townsend recalled men who witnessed Hamilton's final moments said he died bravely. Townsend eventually managed to grab a large black horse and rode off to safety. A short while later, Monchy-le-Preux finally fell to the British after a small German resistance force abandoned their positions.

Other British troops suffered gravely during this attack, with Day suggesting 100 men and 140 horses were either wounded or killed. Townsend, reminiscing about the attack 23 years later, said there is a "useless slaughter" in almost every battle, but "sometimes the sacrifice of one day means the saving of even greater carnage spread over weeks and months". Remarkably, the Northamptonshire Yeomanry were more fortunate with only three casualties, two of them minor.

The men, nevertheless, were exhausted after intense fighting in freezing conditions. Life was not much better at the billets, with supplies so scarce that Townsend did not change into his spare pair of socks, preserving them for later after his friend alluded that the regiment would soon be in action again.

On 9th May, Cyril Day took a working party out in the middle of the night to clear some trench holes filled with German corpses. Venturing out into No Man's Land in the chilling dark for such a task was dangerous, with enemy artillery periodically firing their ammo. Day was working with one other man to clear a trench hole when a trench mortar exploded a few yards from their spot, injuring the other soldier in the knee.

Shocked and scared at this awful sight, with the thundering sound of shells exploding all around him, Day began to panic as he called for a stretcher:

> "I had asked the Lord to protect us & was afraid He was leaving us. This made me cry mightily unto the Lord for help … Our enemy, the devil seemed to whisper 'Where is your God now? He has left you & you are responsible for this fellow being wounded.'"

The soldier soon died from his wounds.

This episode had a profound effect on Day. He was a devout Christian and his faith, like that of so many others, had been rocked by the harshness of this war. Over the next few days, out of battle and relaxed, Day read his Bible with more confidence and reflected on the past events:

> "The Lord appeared unto me & blessed me with his presence. Something seemed to tell me that what I had been through had been for the trial of my faith."

In his thesis, *British Cavalry on the Western Front 1916-1918*, David Kenyon singles out the Northamptonshire Yeomanry's charge at Monchy-le-Preux as one of the rare examples of a successful cavalry charge during the First World War, despite lacking resources and the overly ambitious targets set by demanding generals. Kenyon argues that the subsequent carnage at the hands of the Germans has led historians to overlook the effectiveness of the cavalry in favour of a narrative of "mass casualties" and "pointless sacrifice" that fulfils popular expectations of a Great War cavalry battle.

Over on the Arras front, the Allies pushed on and captured the German strong point of Vimy Ridge. Sixty metres high, the area provided a good view of the German activities behind the front line. The French had unsuccessfully attempted to secure this area in 1915 but had suffered severe casualties. This turned out to be the last of the major gains; like so many battles before it, Arras became a war of attrition once the Germans brought in reserves and launched some successful counter-attacks. Fighting laboured on until 23rd May 1917, when the offensive ended with 158,000 Allied casualties and a similar number of German casualties. Monchy-le-Preux actually fell to the Germans once more during their spring offensive in March 1918 but was soon captured by the Canadians as part of the Allies' decisive offensive later that August.

The Northamptonshire Yeomanry were now given an opportunity to rest, although even in these moments, soldiers were never truly safe. On 26th May 1917, a few weeks after the intense period of fighting, Private Frank King found his limbs seizing from cramps as he bathed. Unable to call for help, King drowned, aged just 22. His former school, Guilsborough C of E, received news of King's death on 1st June. Ceremonies were held in honour of fallen former pupils, ensuring the seriousness of the war was not lost amongst the children. Indeed, Guilsborough had received similar news two years previously with the death of another former student, George Ward, with the school flag positioned at half-mast as prayers and patriotic songs were sung.

A few weeks after receiving the news about Private King, the headmaster of Guilsborough wrote in his diary that for the "first time for over two years" he caned two girls for being "very unkind" to a Belgian girl. Notable for the specific detail in an otherwise mundane and matter-of-fact diary, this entry neatly illustrates a wider trend of schools across Northamptonshire becoming more forgiving of their students during the war years. At the girls' department at the Far Cotton School in Northampton, punishments were issued with the same regularity in the early months of the war, with young Doris Church, 12, receiving two lashes from the cane for the "wilful disturbance" of other children in September 1914, and Ruth Coleman, 13, also receiving the same punishment a month later for "continual disobedience" and "open defiance" towards teachers. After June 1916, however, only five girls had their names entered into the punishment book. Even after the war, there was a lull in punishments handed out which abruptly ended in November 1919 when five girls, all aged 11, were rewarded with two strokes on the hand for "insubordination" towards the cookery teacher. However, as normality slowly returned to society, so did the functioning of schools. In January 1922 alone, seventeen girls were on the punishment log, more than the number of girls during the entire war. Punishments were also handed out more liberally; poor Doris Street, 12, received two strokes from the cane for "carelessness" in exams in April 1922, and in October the girl was caught eating during class, which warranted smacks to both her hands.

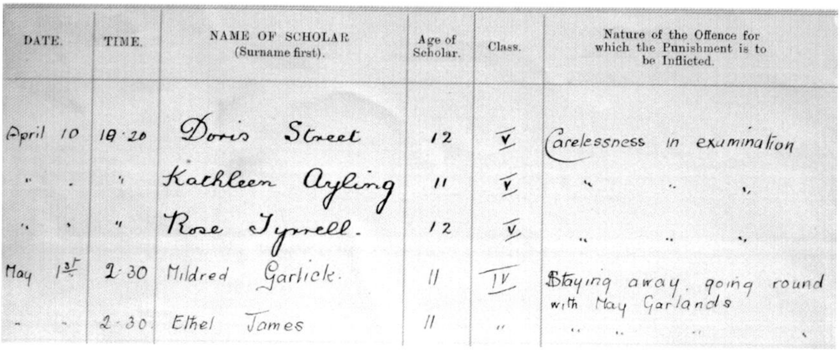

DATE.	TIME.	NAME OF SCHOLAR (Surname first).	Age of Scholar.	Class.	Nature of the Offence for which the Punishment is to be Inflicted.
April 10	10·20	Doris Street	12	V	Carelessness in examination
"	"	Kathleen Ayling	11	V	" " "
"	"	Rose Tyrrell.	12	V	" " "
May 1st	2·30	Mildred Garlick.	11	IV	Staying away, going round with May Garlands
"	2·30	Ethel James	11	"	" " " "

Figure 7.8: The Punishment Log Book in Far Cotton School for Girls, showing Miss Doris Street's punishment for "carelessness" in her exams.

Despite their most testing period of the war, the Northamptonshire Yeomanry had not mellowed. Some of the few positive features of the war were the friendships, camaraderie and humour shared between soldiers. This was no less true for the Northamptonshire Yeomanry, who displayed these sentiments in abundance. In the middle of August 1917, after months of testing battles and several fearless charges, the regiment attended a concert hosted by the Royal Flying Corps. The night's programme took full opportunity to gently rib superior officers and satirise features of army life through answering some of the most asked questions in the camp.

CAMP QUERIES.	CAMP ANSWERS.
How does porridge become pudding?	We have porridge for pudding.
Why the Orderly Officer allows vegetables to grow in buckets.	Grass is growing in the fire buckets that have sand in them.
Why men wear "gas" masks on Church Parade?	The men wear their Masks on Church Parade which is held in the mess tent.
Does the preacher wear one? If not, why not?	The Preacher don't wear one.
Why the "dug-out" was a "wash-out"?	The Dug-out is one an officer was building and which, when it got deep, was not supported round the sides so it fell in and is now all filled up.
Why they call it a "Mess" Tent?	The mess tent is also the canteen.
If the heavenly name of a certain dashing young Pilot resembles his reputation?	The officer's name is Angell.
If it is a purely technical interest that attracts Officers to the pea factory?	There are two or three girls at the pea factory.
If the "Pride of the Park" mistook a "P & M" for a moto plough?	The "Pride of the Park" is the Sgt. Major and he rode a motor cycle into a corn field while practising.
If the young lady who lives not a hundred miles from DUNKERQUE knows the Flt. Sergeant is married?	The Flt. Sergt. Is not me, but one who goes with a very nice young lady. His name is Calam.
Why the chocolates purchased by an Officer were never delivered?	Lt. Angell bought some chocs for a girl he wanted to talk to, but when he went to find her, found she was sitting by the canal bank with some of the men so he had the chocs himself.

Figure 7.9: A selection of humorous questions and answers found in the programme of a concert the Yeomanry held during a rest period.

In a 'little manual' of French-English translations, the Yeomanry was equipped with common phrases needed for simple conversations such as "Quel villain temps!" ("What bad weather!"), "Combien vendez-vous?" ("At how much do you sell it?") and "Donnez-moi du tabac" ("Give me some tobacco"). Some of the other phrases are of a more particular nature: "Vous êtes une charmante jeune fille!" ("You are a lovely girl!"), "Je vous offre ces fleurs" ("I offer you these flowers") and "Êtes-vous marié?" ("Are you married?"). Curiously, the next translation is "C'est dommage" ("It is a pity").

FRENCH	ENGLISH
Je vous attends	I wait for you
Cela me fera plaisir	That will please me
Quand vous reverrai-je !	When shall I see you again !
Vous êtes un charmant garçon !	You are one nice fellow
Vous êtes une charmante jeune fille!	You are a nice girl
Je vous aime beaucoup	I like you very much
Je vous offre ces fleurs	I offer you this flower
Je viendrai vous revoir	I shall come to see you again
J'espère toujours	I hope always
Je partirai bientôt	I shall go away soon
Je m'ennuie beaucoup	i am very weary of it
Je suis sûr	I am sure
Quel âge avez vous	How old are you
Etes-vous marié ?	Are you married ?
C'est dommage	It is a pity
Je suis heureux de vous voir	I am pleased to see you

Figure 7.10: The Yeomanry were provided with a handy translation guide.

The regiment's time in France soon came to an end as they were sent to Italy in November 1917. Reinforcements were being sent to Italy to support the British and Italian armies against the Austrians, who had made steady progress and were nearing Venice as the Italians retreated from the Isonzo River. To the soldiers taking the train to Ventimiglia, near Monte Carlo, and riding through the Italian Riviera while being enthusiastically greeted by cheering locals, the sunlit Italian landscape, full of vivid greenery and rosy vineyards, was a marked change from the cold, muddy, waterlogged trenches of the Western Front. A minor setback occurred after several horses were poisoned at Noli, delaying their journey to the battleground. The war diary says milk was "used to counteract the effect of the poison" as the regiment reached Savona on 19th November.

By the 25th, the Yeomanry had reached Brocon, located near the Piave River, where the Austrian advance had come to a halt. The men now settled down for a "very severe" winter living in "very poor" accommodation, spending the months training and keeping their horses fit, routines men would be all too familiar with after their time on the Western Front. Figure 7.11 shows Private Frederick Jarett engaged in woodwork. The group had seemingly adopted a young Italian boy into their number, who is also engaged in his share of the work, perhaps for his share of cigarettes. Jarett, from Wootton, joined the Yeomanry during the war and served in the Italian campaign.

Much of 1918 was spent travelling across the mountainous areas and valleys to seek out the enemy. In June the Yeomanry were billeted at Sarcedo, at the foot of the Alps, and one can imagine the astonishment and wonder many in the regiment would have felt at this dramatic backdrop, the gentle, rolling fields of Northampton replaced with towering, snowclad mountains. The regiment was in reserve during the Austrians' failed attack at the Battle of Asiago Plateau in the middle of June. The next months, like the previous ones, were spent performing route marches and general training. The regiment would have to wait until late October for their defining action of the Italian campaign.

In October, the Allies were planning their final offensive to overawe the struggling Austrian army. Between 15th and 23rd October, the Yeomanry was patiently awaiting orders at Mirano ready to attack. These were cold, long nights with a downpour of rain that flooded the River Piave. On 26th October, the regiment crossed the Piave and pushed forward to the Monticano River on flooded, broken roads, the result of the preliminary bombardment. The Austrians were putting up a resolute final stand, but they could only delay the inevitable. On the 27th, B Squadron captured a key bridge near Vazzola and took a haul of 600 prisoners plus their machine guns.

The Austrians were now chaotically retreating from the Northamptonshire Yeomanry under the command of Sir Charles Lowther in conjunction with a cyclist battalion, a memorable sight at the end of the regiment's war. Cyril Day described the epic scene:

> "We galloped across into some maize & fired from our horses backs, [illegible] rifles, drew swords and galloped at their positions & to our great surprise the whole line to the next bend in the river surrendered to about 10 of us. We then went to the next bend and the same thing occurred although the bank was swarmed with machine guns. One or two fellows took each batch back to our infantry who were then at the ford. We cleared nearly a mile this way."

The charge was so rapid that the Austrians did not even have time to destroy bridges, although their field battalions did put up some resistance by shelling the

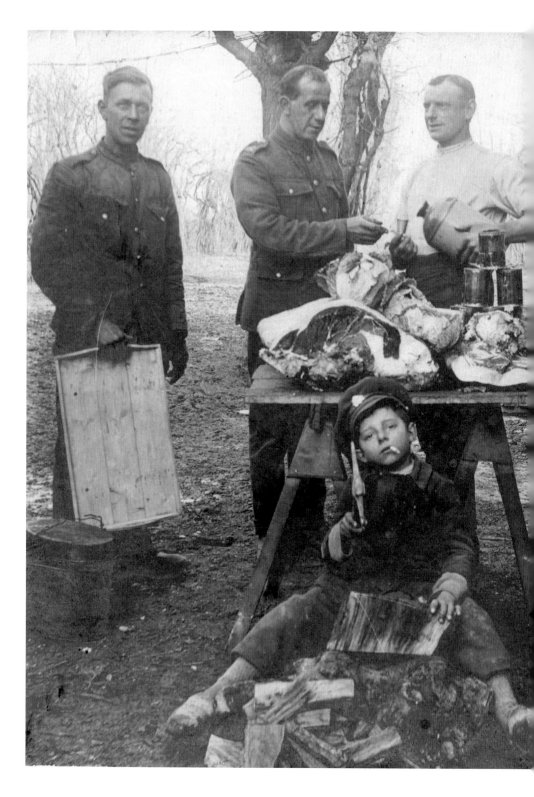

Figure 7.11: Private Frederick Jarett, top middle, posing with his crew in Italy, including a young Italian boy, with a penchant for cigarettes, they have seemingly adopted.

advancing British troops. Cyril Day was knocked off his horse from one of the blasts and, not for the first time, received a "good soaking".

Figure 7.12: Lieutenant Colonel Charles Bingham Lowther (front, centre) seated with the officers of the Northamptonshire Yeomanry in Italy; Lowther was bestowed with several Italian honours for his role in helping defeat and free Italy from the Central Powers.

The pursuit was successful as the British caught the Austrians by surprise and took 1,000 of their men as prisoners. Over the next few days, thousands more Austrian soldiers were taken prisoner as the British captured several villages and towns, such as Cimetta, Codogné, Bibano and Orsago   , as the Austrians chaotically fled. In each liberated town and village, the locals joyfully welcomed the British troops, and a jubilant atmosphere infected the camp, a marked change from the rough years on the Western Front.

Austrian reinforcements eventually arrived to put up a frantic last stand and succeeded in forcing the Northamptonshire Yeomanry to retreat from Sacile. Day noted, "Bullets were hitting & flying all around; but only one of our Squad was killed. He was my batman & very good fellow." However, the weary Austrian army could not hold the tide any longer: on Sunday, 3rd November, the Austrians signed the Armistice of Villa Giusti, thus ending hostilities. The Northamptonshire Yeomanry's journey, which had begun in training camps in England and seen action in some of the most difficult positions along the Western Front in France, had ended in victorious glory against the Austrian army amidst the soaring mountains in north-east Italy.

The official war diary shows no sign of joy when recording the signing of the armistice, while Cyril Day's diary ends abruptly. On the back page of Day's diary, there is an assortment of names of other soldiers' names, numbers and addresses;

it was common for soldiers to provide contact details to each other in case of their death. Day, who was awarded the 1914 Star, a Territorial Efficiency Medal, and received a Distinguished Conduct Medal (DCM) for gallantry in Italy in 1919, became a Baptist preacher and farmer after the war, spending his retirement in Willingham, Cambridgeshire. He passed away on 17th November 1974 at the age of 82.

A host of honours were conferred on the regiment in recognition of their role in liberating Italy, with Lowther awarded the Freedom of the Town of Sacile and given the Croce di Guerra, one of Italy's highest military honours. However, the success late in the war had not come without cost; five yeomen were killed, with an additional nine wounded during the action in October. In total, 1,750 men had served with the Northamptonshire Yeomanry, of whom fifty-seven had lost their lives: twenty-five were killed in action, fourteen died from their wounds and eighteen died as a result of accident or disease. An additional 116 men were wounded. The editor of *The Northampton Independent* wrote that the casualties were "much lighter than might be supposed considering the severity of their engagements".

The regiment remained in Italy after the peace settlement, and they began the slow process of demobilisation. On 10th April 1919, the final eighty-four yeomen to leave Italy arrived in Northampton in the middle of the night. There was no parade, no celebrations and little recognition. Indeed, the Northampton Regiment quickly disappeared into the annals of history when the War Office disbanded all but ten yeomanry units, with the Northamptons not spared the axe. The regiment was converted into an armoured car company with only 192 men. Lieutenant Sergeant Henry Simmonds, who had served with the regiment at La Basse, Neuve Chappelle, Ypres and Arras, was given £12 16s 10d as leaving pay (around £370 in 2015). Demobilisation pay for privates would have been less.

Often sent into dangerous trenches for mundane cleaning and defence work, these local Northamptonshire men (and their horses) who made up the Yeomanry, in the rare moments they were able to charge, performed splendidly

Figure 7.13: The Italian government showed its gratitude to the British military by bestowing several honours on its officers and celebrating their efforts with parades. This photograph shows the Northamptonshire Yeomanry marching past a saluting Victor Emmanuel III, King of Italy, in Castelgomberto on 27th November 1918.

with great valour and bravery. The historian David Kenyon argues in his thesis that the contribution of cavalry on the Western Front has been "consistently underestimated by historians". The Northamptons' actions at Monchy during the Battle of Arras and later on in Italy act as strong evidence to support that statement. Kenyon states that the reasons for the overall ineffectiveness of the cavalry were not structural but rather operational. Senior commanders often denied the cavalry the necessary firepower and heavy artillery needed to take full advantage of their superior mobility.

The depiction of a soldier on his horse, with cold steel in one hand, charging in No Man's Land and faced with barbed wire and bombs, remains a potent image of the bravery, sacrifice and valour displayed by British troops during the First World War. The Northamptonshire Yeomanry served their King and country; they had done their duty.

Figure 7.14: The dashing Northamptonshire Yeomanry, crossing a river in Italy, 1917.

Figure 8.1: Photographed is a soldier of the 4th Northamptons receiving treatment in front of a first-aid post in Gaza in early 1917.

Figure 8.2: Men from the Northamptonshire Regiment travel to Egypt by train; c1916. The image provides a glimpse of the conditions soldiers faced when travelling in cramped carriages and sweltering temperatures.

CHAPTER EIGHT

Gallipoli Palestine

"Of the dead heroes – they are with God…
They lost their lives for the cause of their country, but in losing their lives
they have found them, according to the promise of the Old Redeemer'.

Reverend Walkey in *The Northampton Independent*

ACCOUNTS OF THE WAR TEND to focus strongly on the horrors and hardships of the Western Front while battles in the Middle East feature only as mere historical footnotes, albeit with the occasional anecdote about Lawrence of Arabia. While the Western Front deserves no less attention, events in the Middle East were no less dramatic, violent or important. Indeed, the resounding failure of the Gallipoli campaign and the subsequent retreat in early 1916 both paved the way for the Bolshevik Revolution of 1917, and with it the birth of the world's first communist state. Therefore, it is imperative that students of the war are not only aware of the disastrous outcome of the Gallipoli campaign but also understand the reasons behind its conception and its far-reaching consequences. Some 480,000 Allied soldiers were involved in the campaign, of whom 46,000 were killed and a further 214,000 wounded. The Turks also suffered horrendous casualties, seeing 65,000 of their troops killed and an additional 185,000 wounded. The sacrifices made by these men warrant that adequate attention be given to this bloody campaign.

Three months into the war, the Ottoman Empire was the sole remaining world power that had yet to declare its allegiance. The war did not come at a good time for the Ottoman Empire; its industries and economy were faltering, and its army was still humiliated after losing most of its European territories in the First Balkan War two years earlier. In the first few months of the Great War, it appeared that there would be little stopping the German war machine after a series of stunning victories and the sheer amount of territory invaded in such a short period. After months of Ottoman officials debating their next move, the Sultan was won over by German promises of extra land and the attractive prospect of ending British influence in the Middle East. On 11th November 1914, the Sultan made his decision: he declared a military jihad against the Allies. This single decision would ultimately lead to the end of four centuries of direct rule and the ruin of his empire.

By early 1915, Russia's Grand Duke Nicholas, with his country now reeling after desperately fighting Germany on the Eastern Front, appealed to Britain to send basic goods and military help. 'Grain and guns' were the necessary combination, but there existed no suitable supply lines. The North Sea was guarded by the Germans and, in any case, was too often frozen, while the Far East route was too distant. Western powers began to investigate the feasibility and benefits of opening another front along a narrow sea passage from the Mediterranean, the Dardanelles, which connected the Aegean Sea to the Sea of Marmara in north-western Turkey. It was in the midst of this geopolitical situation that the now infamous Gallipoli campaign (also known as the Dardanelles campaign) was born.

Once the Dardanelles Straits were under control, the Allies would move to force their way through to the Black Sea, thus providing a sea route to supply Russia and a platform to launch joint attacks on Turkey. The plans were vociferously championed by Winston Churchill, the First Lord of the British Admiralty.

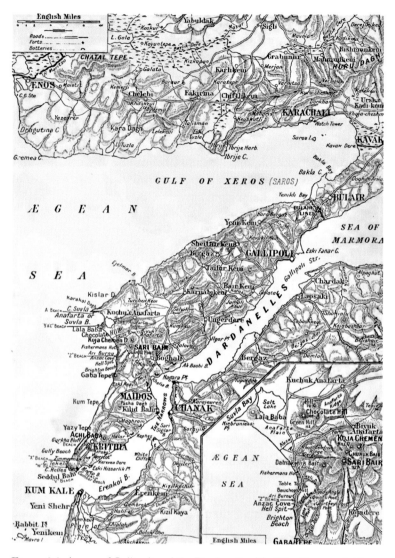

Figure 8.3: A map of Gallipoli and the Dardanelles; The War Illustrated Album de Luxe, volume IV, published 1916

However, he encountered strong opposition from the British cabinet and naval commanders, first and foremost from the head of the Navy, Admiral John Fisher. With the Germans just one breakthrough from reaching Paris, the Allies on the Western Front could not afford to have any men diverted to open a new front. Several senior naval commanders were also concerned at the rapid haste with which Churchill was pushing his plan, seeming to ignore the long-term planning that would be necessary. From Churchill's perspective, he sympathised with the Tsar's position; if Russia fell, Churchill thought the entirety of the German war effort would be directed upon the Western Front. Additionally, he thought the Germans would have to split their army to support a poorly organised, poorly trained, weak Turkish army after their failures in the Balkans.

On 29th July 1915, the Northampton Territorials embarked at Devonport for the Dardanelles. Shortly after their ship had left England, they encountered a vessel full of Canadian soldiers who loudly cheered them off to war. A glimpse of the emotion felt that day by each man is revealed in Captain Pemberton's account:

> *"We didn't utter a sound in reply. The fact was just beginning to dawn on us that we were leaving our dear ones for an indefinite period, and, like schoolboys spending their first night at boarding school, we had big lumps in our throats at this seemingly ironical burst of cheers."*

On Sunday, 15th August, the 4th Battalion of the Northamptonshire Regiment sailed to Suvla Bay on the Aegean coast as part of a new wave of Allied reinforcements that would attempt to bring an end to the deadlock at the Battle of Gallipoli. The campaign had begun in February 1915 with a failed naval attack by the British and French ships on the Dardanelles Straits. The British and French battleships launched long-range artillery bombardments on Turkish positions, which Churchill and others thought would be enough to dislodge the Turks, much to the dismay of Fisher, who claimed that naval gunfire alone could not bring victory. Fisher's view was soon proven correct with the huge number of casualties that followed.

The Turks exploited several advantages to wreak havoc upon the British battleships; namely, they were attacking from a position of height with land-based artillery that fired with greater precision. By the time the Northamptons arrived, a land invasion had been launched on 25th April 1915[1]. This too was a failure. The troops had suffered from a lack of intelligence and poor knowledge of the terrain and had severely underestimated the Turkish Army. On 6th August, the Allies attempted another troop landing at Suvla Bay. On this occasion, the British found little opposition, but indecision and delay stalled progress. As the Northamptons landed a few weeks later, the battalion of 941 men were greeted with the sights and sounds of shells falling near them amidst the swarms of flies buzzing feverishly in the extreme heat, a grim combination that they would experience many times in the following years. After meeting with the rest of the 162nd Brigade of the 54th Division, the men were sent into the trenches on 17th August.

In a sign of the bloodiness of the battle and the fierce rearguard action launched by the Turkish artillery, the Northampton Territorials, despite not being

---

1   Coincidentally, this is the same date that the systematic massacre of Armenians living in Turkey began as Turkish officials rounded up hundreds of Armenian intellectuals. An estimated 1.5 million Turkish Armenians were killed in what is now referred to, by most historians, as the Armenian Genocide.

Figure 8.4: The image shows a member of the Territorials preparing a quick meal in the desert. Cooking in desert conditions with little equipment was tough and meals were kept simple; *The Northampton Independent,* 28th April 1917.

involved in a major operation, had nevertheless incurred 66 casualties, 10 of whom were killed by the end of August. One Northampton soldier later wrote:

> *"After my nervy and trying time I almost envy the poor fellows who have been done in."*

September was spent in various reserve positions, but the battalion continued to suffer casualties as they were still within reach of the Turkish guns. One such casualty in this period was Corporal Albert Charles Thompson. A Northampton boy who had grown up in Kingsthorpe, he arrived in Gallipoli fully aware of the brutality of war after his brother, Henry Thompson, had been killed earlier that year in January. Albert Thompson was wounded in September 1915 and was evacuated from the Gallipoli Peninsula on a ship called the El Kantara. Grateful that this ship had delivered him to relative safety, Thompson renamed his house in Adnitt Place, Northampton, El Kantara when back from war. Like many veterans, Thompson barely uttered a word about the war. He never stopped serving his country; leaving his home on a motorbike at random times in the middle of the night during WW2, Thompson was suspected of being a dispatch rider at Bletchley Park.

The environment was proving as much of a fearsome enemy as the Turks; soldiers had to survive on small amounts of water despite the soaring temperatures, suffered from several foul diseases and shared cramped living quarters with flies, lice and even corpses. Amongst the rank and file, the Gallipoli campaign became synonymous with stories of personal degradation. Private Harold Boughton of the 1st London Regiment said: "One of the biggest curses was flies … the whole side of the trench used to be one black swarming mass … they were all around your mouth and on any cuts or sores that you'd got, which then turned septic."

Figure 8.6: Albert Thompson with his wife, Edith, and their children Norman and Dora. The photo was taken on Knightley Road, Northampton.

Dysentery was all too common, a disease that one soldier said would "rob a man of the last vestiges of human dignity before it killed him".

By early December, a bitterly cold snap had descended upon the region, a marked contrast to the intense August heat the battalion experienced when they first arrived. It is often forgotten that the men of the Gallipoli theatre also had to contend with freezing temperatures and snow like their countrymen on the Western Front. After no progress and mass casualties, it was soon decided to proceed with evacuation plans, starting on 7th December 1915. The Gallipoli campaign had been a personal humiliation for Churchill. Now deeply unpopular in Westminster, he spent the remainder of the war trying to make amends, leading an infantry brigade near the front line in France.

Figure 8.5: This stunning panoramic photograph shows a section of Suvla Bay as the Allied forces prepare to depart as part of the evacuation operation; 18th December 1915.

The Ottoman Army had proven its worth by staving off sustained attacks by the Allies for almost a year. Its victory meant Russia's main trade routes had been effectively cut off. In February 1917, economic crisis, military weariness and large public demonstrations led to the collapse of Tsar Nicholas II's regime. After months of instability and political manoeuvring, the radical Bolsheviks seized power in October. Their leader, Vladimir Lenin, almost immediately issued a decree declaring Russia would exit hostilities. After months of negotiations, Russia was humiliated into accepting extremely punitive terms whereby it lost huge swathes of territory, including most of modern-day Ukraine and parts of Latvia, Estonia, Lithuania, Poland and Finland. In total, Russia lost the governance of around 50 million inhabitants.

The Northampton Territorials, now transferred to the 163rd Brigade, embarked for Alexandria, Egypt, where they landed on 18th December. The successful defence of the Suez Canal has received less than its fair share of attention in history. If control of this important trade channel had been lost, it would have been practically impossible to supply large parts of the Western Front, and the whole war effort would soon have faltered. The canal provided a route both to supply the British Empire with goods and to provide the Western Front with soldiers from Australia, New Zealand and India.

Despite not participating in any major offensives, with disease and sickness rife, the 4th Northamptons was at little over half its full strength: only around 450 to 550 soldiers were fit to fight. Reinforcements were brought in to shore up the battalion, and by the middle of March the battalion was 900 strong once again. The recruits contained not only men from Kitchener's Army but soldiers who had been fighting on the Western Front. The fact that these soldiers were diverted gives an indication of just how important the Suez Canal was to the Allies.

In April 1916, the 54th Division moved to defensive desert positions around the Suez Canal. Here the men spent the rest of the summer toiling in extreme temperatures improving fortifications. One day in June, a record 50.56°C was recorded in the shade. Their reward, however, was on occasion to be in the shadows of the ancient Pyramids of Giza. For long periods of the summer, the Northamptons were primarily engaged in defensive fighting in the mountainous deserts of Sinai (north-eastern Egypt), where, 2,000 feet high in the glaring sun, the men fought off advances from the Ottoman troops who then staged a successful retreat 130 miles across the desert to Beersheba.

The battalion saw little action during the remainder of the year, spending its time at El Kubri, where they did little else but dig defences. On 30th January 1917, a full-strength 4th Northamptons entrained for Kantara (modern-day Al Qantarah El Sharqiyya, on the eastern side of the Suez Canal). Compared to the last year of relative quiet, what was to come would push the men to the limits of human courage, endurance and ability. The affair would be bloody, agonising, yet also heroic: the Palestinian campaign was about to begin.

Figure 8.7: This grainy image shows the 4th Northamptons resting in the shadow of the Pyramids in Cairo, Egypt; c1916.

The British soldiers who fought in the Middle East were largely brought up on a diet of military heroism in building the largest empire the world had ever known. Stories of the dashing Clive of India; the victorious Captain Wolfe, the 'hero of Quebec'; the valiant Admiral Nelson, whose eternal quote that "England Expects" was surely remembered as millions of young men marched off to war; and the 'Iron' Duke of Wellington, conqueror of Napoleon and his army, were all absorbed by boys at an early age with epic battles, acts of courage and imperial wonder published in titles such as *The Boy's Own Paper* and *Chums*. The Palestine campaign had a strong hint of the romanticism that burned strongly in pride for the empire; soldiers in this campaign found themselves in a hostile environment as they trekked across the desert under a blazing sun, touring ancient biblical sights.

By early 1917, the Turkish Army had been forced out of the Sinai Peninsula and had retreated to its Palestinian strongholds. The War Office, aware that they had the enemy on run, instructed Sir Archibald Murray, the commander of the British-led forces, to prepare for an attack on Palestine. The Turkish troops here were under the command of the German General Kress von Kressenstein. The overall aim was to take Gaza, but they first had to break through a series of well-guarded ridges between Gaza and Beersheba, along with other Turkish bases scattered around villages and towns.

First, however, the troops had to make their way to Palestine. The Northamptons left Kantara and began their epic 120-mile march across the Sinai Peninsula. In the stuff of legends, the men would march 10 miles a day across the heavy dunes for weeks on end. Despite the heat, lack of water and absence of any luxuries, remarkably few Northampton men were taken ill through exhaustion. Finally, the men reached Rafah, a small city on the Sinai–Palestine frontier that had been captured by the British forces in early January that year. From there, the men would launch their efforts as part of a wider attack to take Gaza.

At 0400 on 25th March 1917, the men marched out of Rafah in darkness to Khān Yūnus, the second-largest city in the Gaza Strip, occasionally pausing to conceal themselves under the cactus hedges to prevent detection by enemy aeroplanes. After spending much of the previous twelve months in barren desert landscapes, the sight of Khān Yūnus was a joy to behold for the soldiers. The battalion's chaplain, Reverend Frank John Walkey, described the rejuvenating scene:

> "The fresh green of the lovely gardens and surroundings brought before our eyes visions of old England that has never been loved so much by us all as during these long days of separation from her shores."

The battalion would have precious little time to admire its new environment, for at 1600 it was rushed to Seirat, five miles south of Gaza, in readiness for a major attack the following day now known as the First Battle of Gaza. The 4th Northamptons were to take up key support positions along the Gaza road to cover the charge of the mounted division.

At 0600 on the 26th, the 4th Northamptons left their base under a cloud of thick fog. They safely reached their positions at 0900, by which time the artillery battle had already begun. Here they waited for further orders with only the sound of guns firing in and around Gaza breaking the anxious silence. The men sat in reserve for most of the day but then embarked on a long march to a new position, where they arrived at 0400 on the 27th in preparation for an attack that morning; there would be little time for rest as the attack was planned for 0530. From 0600 to noon, the Northamptons were under a "furious" shelling but were lucky to suffer no fatalities, with only one man wounded. During the night, the men received a message that the battle had been called off and to withdraw immediately. The battle had been a horrible disaster for the British.

It was later found that the early stages of the battle had been going very well for the British-led forces. At one stage, victory even seemed possible. With the British-led forces outnumbering the Turks by a ratio of 2:1, Kressenstein thought Gaza was lost and had cancelled his request for reserves to be brought in. However, Sir Charles Dobell, Murray's subordinate on the field, ordered Sir Philip Chetwode to withdraw his cavalry forces from the battle. Dobell was under the impression that the infantry charge had failed and thought it pointless to involve the cavalry in further action. By the time Dobell had realised his error, Kressenstein had reversed his premature decision to abandon Gaza and had brought in heavy reinforcements during the night. In the morning of the 28th, a combination of determined Turkish counter-attacks and a lack of water forced Dobell to call off the whole attack.

Over the course of the following weeks, generals made plans to renew the attack at the earliest opportunity. It was decided to make another attempt to take Gaza on 17th April. The 4th Northamptons were to support the 5th Bedfordshires and the 11th London Regiment, both of whom had taken up positions on a hill range some fifty feet high called Sheikh Abbas Ridge. Their task was to attack a village called Ali Muntar and take the Old Beersheba Road located a mile south of Gaza. Orders arrived informing the battalions that the attack would resume on 19th April, a day that was later dubbed "the day of destiny" by Reverend Walkey. The Northamptons were likely to be in a buoyant mood for the battle after receiving a package of cigarettes from readers of *The Northampton Independent*. Lieutenant Colonel John Brown wrote appreciatively to the readers of the paper, "I am sure the Turk was able to taste the aroma and envied us."

At daybreak, the Northamptons advanced through the Bedfordshires. Ahead of them lay 3,500 yards of flat, empty, barren land and a heavily fortified enemy with artillery and machine gun support. At 0800, as the Turkish and Northampton artilleries rained shells upon each other, the men climbed out of the ridge and faced two miles of open country before they could invade the enemy-held ridge. It was a desperate task as the Turkish guns went to work on the advancing Northampton soldiers, cutting them down one by one. Lieutenant Colonel John Brown was shot in the arm in these early moments, but, rallying his men, stood up and pressed forward.

Captain Dudley R. Church, leading the charge, was shot in his wrist and shoulder. Valiantly trying to fight on, he looked around and saw a trail of bodies behind him. Realising the hopeless situation, he turned to the few men that had managed to reach the Turkish trenches and ordered them to retreat 1,000 yards to a makeshift defensive line that had been scrambled together.

Church, however, was wounded gravely. He could not stand and lay there waiting for the inevitable. Beside him was Private Charles H. Horton. Instinctively, Horton stabbed the ground repeatedly with his knife and used his bayonet to dig a small hole for his captain. As Church was placed in this with little hope of survival, Horton risked his life running manically across the fight to relay messages to headquarters. Miraculously, Horton survived the ordeal. As he took off his helmet, he noticed a large penetrating hole. If he had placed one foot differently, the bullet would have penetrated his skull. Both Church and Horton had their courageous actions formally recognised after the battle; Church received the Distinguished Service Order (DSO) while Horton was awarded the Military Medal.

Military Items.

D.S.O. FOR CAPT. CHURCH.

Capt. Dudley Church.

The many friends of Capt. Dudley R. Church, of the Northampton Territorials will hear with pleasure that his gallant services in the battle of Gaza have been recognised by the award of the Distinguished Service Order. This gallant young officer, who is the son of Mr. and Mrs. T. D. Church, of Cliftonville, was severely wounded in the desperate battle in which the Northamptons fought so courageously and suffered so heavily. In the magnificent story of the battle we published exclusively last week the Chaplain of the regiment wrote: "Capt. Church set another example of great heroism by leading his men in attack although wounded three times, and only sheer exhaustion caused him to hand over his command to a junior officer." No finer tribute could be paid to an officer than this.

THE SOLDIER WHO SAVED CAPT. CHURCH, D.S.O.

Pte. C. H. Norton.

The Military Medal has been awarded to Pte. C. H. Norton, Northamptonshire Regt. for his bravery at the battle of Gaza. After Capt. Church had been wounded three times he helped him into a hole which he dug with his knife and bayonet and ran the gauntlet of a terrific Turkish fire to convey an important message from the Captain to headquarters. As he sped across the open, bullets flew thick and fast around him, and one penetrated his helmet, but he managed to get the message through safely and to return to Capt. Church, whom he helped back at night. Pte. Norton is the son of Mr. and Mrs. T. Norton, of Old, and has three other brothers serving, Alfred, of the 4th Batt.,

Figure 8.8: Both Church and Horton had their brave deeds recognised in the local press; The Northampton Independent, 26th May 1917.

For three long hours, the Northamptons held out as long as they could against the shrapnel, high explosives and rifle fire being thrown at them from several Turkish positions. Facing obliteration, the Territorials were saved by timely and accurate artillery fire from British warships on the Turkish positions at Ali Muntar. They were finally relieved by the Bedfordshires. The battalion's supply of officers had been exhausted: 20 out of 21 officers were either killed or wounded. In addition, 366 non-officer ranks were either killed, wounded or missing. Almost half the battalion had been wiped out in a single day's fighting, and Walkey described the majority of men as being "more fit for hospitals and convalescent homes than for trench making and defensive works".

After this loss, the battalion spent the following weeks in trenches and even caves, where they were slowly rebuilt with new recruits. While life in the trenches may have been preferable to actual combat, it was by no means easy. The trenches in Palestine had few comforts and men had to struggle against various diseases and terrible living conditions in cramped, sweaty surroundings. Walkey described the conditions as being the "life of animals rather than that of free men". As the battalion was strengthened, the survivors of this battle slowly healed their wounds. They did so knowing that they had unfinished business. Another attack on Gaza beckoned on the bloody horizon.

The embarrassment felt by the British Army from this defeat can be gleaned from the fact that it was many months before the full details of what had transpired at Gaza were published in the local press. The first mention of the

Second Battle of Gaza came surprisingly quickly, on 28th April, as *The Northampton Independent* reported the battalion had been in action under the dramatic headline: "Northampton Territorial Suffer Severely." It was also reported that Lieutenant Colonel Brown had been wounded "but not very seriously", as Brown was still on duty with his battalion. Two weeks later, the paper reports that Brown had been sent home at the insistence of the doctors, as his wound was "more serious" than first thought. No details on Brown's wound – being shot in the arm – were given in the reporting.

Figure 8.9: Desert warfare: this image shows the 4th Northamptons in the Sinai region with trench lines as far as the eye can see in a barren, arid landscape.

Figure 8.10: This striking photograph taken by Rev Walkey shows a wounded Colonel Brown being rescued, his hands resting on his forehand and grasping in pain.

Finally, on 19th May, weeks after both of the failed attempts to take Gaza, the paper was able to print a long letter from Reverend Walkey describing the action in both March and April. However, the extract is noteworthy for its lack of content about the overall result. While certainly not wishing to portray the battles as a major success or breakthrough for the British Army, nor wishing to distract from the major losses suffered, Walkey does not mention the lack of progress made or the failure to take Gaza. Instead, he simply writes about the men consolidating newly won positions and that they were "waiting only for the day when the toils and sacrifices of our men shall be rewarded". It is perhaps this absence of clear information that led the editor of *The Northampton Independent* to issue a lead article complaining that despite the second battle having occurred over a month previously, there was still no official account of the incident or explanation for the "deadlock which appears to have been reached". The article continues: "the official silence over the position has naturally created an impression that the staff work was at fault and that our objectives, despite the great sacrifices, were not attained … The time has passed to treat Britishers like children." This statement is yet another example that the press did have a certain element of leeway to be critical of the government and its managing of the war.

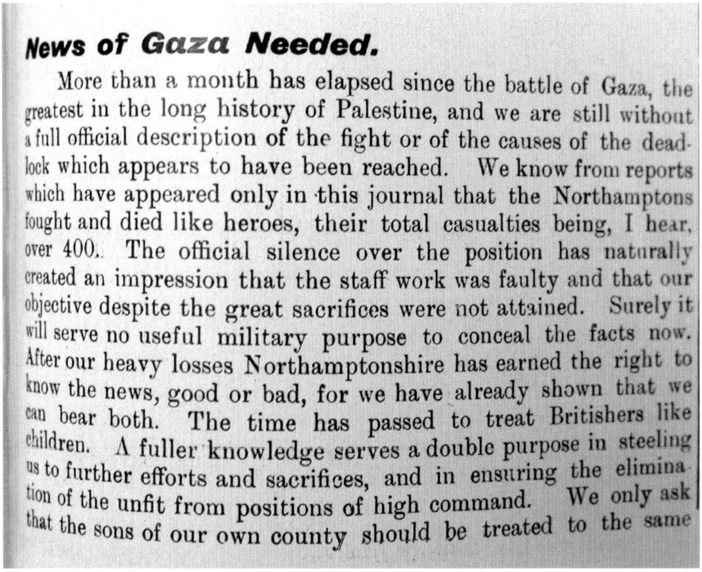

News of Gaza Needed.

More than a month has elapsed since the battle of Gaza, the greatest in the long history of Palestine, and we are still without a full official description of the fight or of the causes of the deadlock which appears to have been reached. We know from reports which have appeared only in this journal that the Northamptons fought and died like heroes, their total casualties being, I hear, over 400. The official silence over the position has naturally created an impression that the staff work was faulty and that our objective despite the great sacrifices were not attained. Surely it will serve no useful military purpose to conceal the facts now. After our heavy losses Northamptonshire has earned the right to know the news, good or bad, for we have already shown that we can bear both. The time has passed to treat Britishers like children. A fuller knowledge serves a double purpose in steeling us to further efforts and sacrifices, and in ensuring the elimination of the unfit from positions of high command. We only ask that the sons of our own county should be treated to the same

Figure 8.11: A stinging editorial reprimanding the authorities for the lack of information about the 4th Northamptons in Gaza; The Northampton Independent, 2nd June 1917.

Hidden from the public eye, the War Office in London had received an extremely misleading letter from Sir Archibald Murray claiming that his forces had won a clear victory in the raid on Gaza in March, stating that the Turkish losses had been extremely high, three times as large as they actually were. London, encouraged by Murray's report, ordered him to attack at the earliest opportunity. On this occasion, Jerusalem was the ultimate target, as officials believed it would not take long to capture Gaza, a city believed to be on its last legs. It was this chain of events that led to the Second Battle of Gaza on 17th April, an attack which the soldiers did not have adequate time to prepare for after their exertions only three weeks previous. The Turks, on the other hand, built up their complex defences on the Beersheba line with renewed vigour after holding Gaza in the first battle.

Throughout the second battle in April, British forces were struggling not only against a well-defended enemy but also with chaotic transportation logistics, as their headquarters were located 20 miles south at Rafah, causing numerous problems in replenishing depleted stocks of ammunition. This time, there would be no hiding the catastrophic loss from London. Murray, perhaps anticipating the reaction from London, relieved Sir Charles Dobell of his command. However, this did not quell London's fury at the events. Murray himself was soon relieved of his duties and recalled to London. Murray's replacement was Sir Edmund Allenby. Allenby was a veteran of the Boer War and had been commanding the Third Army on the Western Front. He was sent to Palestine after a disagreement with Field Marshal Haig over his tactics used during the Battle of Arras. It was during this Middle Eastern campaign that Allenby would cement his reputation as a national hero with a series of stunning victories.

The British realised their venture into Palestine was reaching a critical point. There would be no room for error lest it give the Ottomans and Germans a strategic advantage and morale-boosting victory. Allenby immediately set to work, ordering both a railroad to be built running from Egypt to supply his troops and even a pipeline across the Sinai Desert to bring water from Egypt to his troops in Palestine. Trenches were improved, new tanks brought in and thousands of gas shells stockpiled. Nothing was being left to chance, and in October 1917, Allenby had almost 90,000 men under his command, with the 4th Northamptons once again built up to full strength. In late October , the men were ordered a week's rest, sports and relaxation. During this period, the Northamptons enjoyed football competitions, concerts, a debate and even a cinema show. It would have dawned on the men, after seeing hundreds of their comrades fall in previous attempts to take Gaza, that these might be their last moments of happiness. The attack was imminent.

On 2nd November, after months of meticulous preparation, an attack was launched from Beersheba, which had just been captured two days earlier by the Allies, with the Australian 4th and 12th Light Horse Regiments performing a brilliant cavalry charge. The main push would occur to the east of Gaza, aiming to penetrate the city. A second force would engage the enemy on the seafront, seeking to prevent Turkish troops from being transported into Gaza. As part of the 54th Division, the Northamptons were stationed by the seafront. In the depth of the night, as the evening's bright moon rippled across the sea, the attack began. By 0630, the 161st and 163rd Infantry Brigades had taken the enemy posts and the village of Sheikh Hassan. D Company was sent forward to occupy several defensive positions in Sheikh Hassan, by which time the Turkish troops were forced to retreat to their second line of defence.

Meanwhile, in the dusty light of daybreak, A Company advanced under the command of Captain Marriott. They were dealt an early setback after the tanks supporting them broke down. In the thick mist, visibility was very poor and the Northamptons were marching right into the fiery battle. Undeterred by this twist of fate, the men courageously advanced, reaching their target as planned. After this checkpoint, progress began to stall as the enemy, better defended by three whole battalions, provided stiffer resistance, with Marriott being shot in the hand. Nonetheless, the men bravely carried on with their orders and managed to clear the Turkish barbed wire, despite coming under heavy rifle and machine gun fire. This selfless act was critically important, for it allowed the cavalry a route into the battle.

A Company's gallant actions had opened up a large distance between them and the rest of their battalion and brigade. The vast, open landscape offered little natural protection. The Turks, intending to take advantage, attempted a counter-attack around 0800 with the aim of surrounding the Northamptons. Initially, A Company held their positions but soon began to suffer serious casualties. Captain Marriott, in charge of A Company, ordered a retreat back to Sheikh Hassan. C and D Companies also played an important role as they were sent to help take 'Tortoise Hill', an area that British troops had been struggling with. Their arrival was credited as helping swing the fight in their comrades' favour as their artillery halted the Turkish counter-attack.

Figure 8.12: This photograph shows the Turkish cavalry galloping in front of Gaza in April 1917, a scene similar to what the Northamptons faced during the Third Battle of Gaza in November 1917.

The morning's action had proved intensely bloody. Already, 50 men had been killed, while 133 were wounded with a further 33 missing. In such a short period these numbers appear very high. However, when one considers the unfriendly environment, the limited support for the isolated A Company, and the heavily armed and prepared Turkish troops, it seems almost miraculous that there were not more casualties. The low casualty rate was partly because of the actions of the soldiers. Displaying scant regard for their own personal safety in favour of the strong, unrelenting bonds of camaraderie, the men selflessly carried scores of their own wounded across the dusty plains when retreating to their base, despite the persistent fire and shelling from the Turkish line. It would have been far easier and quicker to simply run back 'every man for himself'.

Over at the main thrust of the battle at the Beersheba sector, the British attack was progressing very well, overwhelming the Turkish troops through sheer force. Chaos and confusion ran amok in the Turkish lines, and they were hastily ordered to abandon their positions and evacuate, with the triumphant British forces hot on their tails.

After the battle, men from the Territorials were sent to the battlefield where A Company had fought valiantly to gather their fallen. In the absence of constant shelling, the area was eerily quiet compared to the scene just a few days previous. The men built a small cemetery on the side of a hill along the cliff facing the battlefield. Reverend Walkey witnessed the kind act and said, "under the star-lit heaven of Southern Palestine we committed our dead to the grave and to the God of Heroes". The site is the final resting place for sixteen men from the 4th Battalion.

When the Northamptons finally entered Gaza, they found a city of ruin and rubble after months of constant warfare. The Great Mosque of Gaza, situated on a holy site used for worship for more than a millennium, was severely damaged by British bombs after intelligence established it was being used as an ammunition store. However, it was not only the British bombs that had caused the wreckage; every building that had survived the British shelling had been destroyed by the Turkish in a typical scorched earth tactic. If they could not inhabit the city, they would make sure no one else could either. Carcases of camels and horses littered the streets. This ancient city, according to Reverend Walkey, was said to be "only a fit haunt for owls and the prowling hyenas".

Walkey's articulate accounts never mentioned his personal actions in the combat, only reserving praise for the whole battalion. Despite his humbleness, Walkey displayed great courage throughout his service to the Northampton Territorials. Indeed, it was in this Third Battle of Gaza that Walkey was awarded the Military Cross for:

> *"conspicuous gallantry and devotion to duty. He was most untiring in his efforts throughout the day in bringing in the wounded under heavy shell fire, and his courage and perseverance inspired all ranks."*

Figure 8.13: (Left) A British solider inspects the crumbled interior of the historic mosque which was hit by British artillery after intelligence confirmed it was being used as a munition store by the Turks. (Right) The pulpit in the Great Mosque of Gaza stands alone surrounded by masses of rubble.

In early 1918, Walkey left the 4th Battalion to assume a military chaplain position in the Middle East. While he left the regiment, Northamptonshire never left him. After being further recognised with the Order of the British Empire (OBE) in 1919, Walkey moved with his family to Northampton in the early 1920s. Residing first at 47 Hazelwood Road and later at 15 Woodland Avenue in Abington, he spent ten years in the town working as an area superintendent for the Baptist Union. Later in life, the reverend spent his final years in Chesham, passing away in 1949.

The year 1917 had tested the Northamptons' fortitude to the limit. It began with a grand march across the desert, followed by several grim defeats and then ending with a wounding victory. In October, Colonel John Brown rode with a few of his men to the site where the Northamptons had fought during the Second Battle of Gaza in April. Here they found a group of clothed skeletons lying right in front of the Turkish wire. One of the bodies was identified as Lieutenant Stanley Marlow. Brown's party also found something else. The Turks, in accordance with their religious beliefs, had respected the corpses by making a slight detour of their transportation route to avoid trampling over the fallen. One wonders about the thoughts of Colonel Brown and his men, struck by this simple act of humanity from an enemy they had been in brutal combat with for the last three years. The site where the men fell is now known as 'Northampton Mound'.

The victory in the Third Battle of Gaza was initially given a low-key mention in *The Northampton Independent*. Three weeks after the victory on 24th November, the paper simply reported that the troops had captured "Beersheba, Gaza and Jaffa" and were now marching to Jerusalem, with the editor adding a small complaint that the Northampton Battalion that had borne the "brunt of so much hard fighting" had not been mentioned in any of the war dispatches.

Figure 8.14: In a show of strength, Turkish soldiers march through Jerusalem carrying a religious banner. Soon these soldiers would be involved in a desperate struggle to defend the Holy City from British forces.

Two weeks later on 8th December, the paper was able to print a letter from Reverend Walkey. It is a wonderful, detailed account describing events of the battle; readers would be transported to the sandy landscapes of Palestine and learn what life was like for their territorial battalion. The account would take an increasingly war-weary yet still patriotic public through a series of exotic-sounding, biblical villages and towns where they would be allowed a glimpse of what a hard-fought victory ed like; for several months all they had heard about the Palestine campaign was military failings, casualties and setbacks.

While Gaza had fallen, the Ottoman Army had not. Therefore, the battalion spent the weeks following its victory in pursuit of the Turks. Prime Minister David Lloyd George, always supportive of Allenby, ordered him to capture Jerusalem by Christmas and promised extra troops if needed. On 25th November, they reached the outskirts of Jaffa (the oldest part of Tel-Aviv, Israel). As part of the wider attack to take Jerusalem, the Northamptons were assigned the Mezerieh-Yehudieh sector, which was around two miles long. B Company was handed a trench defending Wilhelma (now Bnei Atarot, Israel), one of the many German Templar colonies in Palestine, which was now under British control. In the Regimental History, the authors write of the strange sight witnessed in this village, with children running around speaking German and wearing German-style clothes in the Holy Land.

Figure 8.15: A map showing General Allenby's illustrious advance, highlighting key towns and cities that were captured; The War Illustrated Album de Luxe, volume IX, published 1918.

The following day, on the 26th, British observation posts detected significant enemy movement on a range of hills to the east. A patrol party was rushed out in the small hours of the morning to investigate. They discovered that the Turks had dug new trenches and were starting to dig in around Rantieh. As the battalion settled down for the evening, the officers knew something was afoot.

Suddenly, at 0615 the next morning, the enemy's plans were revealed. The sky erupted with a shock bombardment by the Turkish artillery. At 0800, the Turkish troops began advancing in considerable numbers towards the startled Northamptons, but instead of attempting an invasion, they began to dig themselves in around one mile from the Northampton trenches. The numerical advantage of the Turks became immediately apparent: the Northamptons had only 400 men against an invading force of 3,000 Turks. Meanwhile, the artillery bombardment was continuing to pound the British line. At around 1140, the battalion headquarters was destroyed by a direct hit and with it, their communications system. Colonel Brown was blown through the window of the headquarters, but, proving a gallant example to his men, rose to his feet and carried on fighting.

Figure 8.16: The photograph shows the 4th Northamptons' gouged headquarters after it was struck by a Turkish bomb. The ferociousness of the blasts sent Colonel Brown hurtling out of a window.

Eventually, the shelling came to a stop. As the sand filling the air dispersed into the dry atmosphere, the enemy soldiers crossing the open plain were a menacing sight to behold. There was little time to stand looking as the Northamptons gripped their rifles tightly and began firing. Men working the machine gun also quickly got into the thick of the action. What followed was horrific carnage, the flesh of the Turkish soldiers being little match for the Northampton guns. The Turks had experienced appalling losses; hundreds of their men lay motionless on the sandy plain, the ground now a shade of dirty crimson as the blood from the fallen was absorbed into the dusty earth.

The Turkish commanders, alarmed at their situation, redirected their heavy artillery from Wilhelma to once again focus on the Northamptons' line. At 1600, a second attempt to advance was staged by the Turkish command. The outcome was the same violent one that had befallen their comrades a few hours earlier. An hour later, at 1700, after the Turkish artillery launched an extremely powerful bombing on the Northamptons' trenches, the Turkish troops attempted yet another advance. On this occasion, the advancing soldiers, benefiting from the cover provided by their men left stranded in the middle by earlier advances, were able to reach a wādī (an Arabic term referring to a valley in dry ground) located 400 yards from Wilhelma. Lieutenant Colonel Brown realised the vastly superior numbers of the Turks would render their advance unstoppable unless something drastic was done. He ordered two platoons in the front line and two reserve platoons to counter-attack the exposed enemy flanks to enfilade fire. The attack was made at once and was a massive success, avoiding almost certain annihilation for the Northamptons.

Figure 8.17: Wilhelma: the German colony in Palestine. The sight of towering avenues of eucalyptus trees was foreign to the natural landscape; c1914-18.

Brown was later presented with the DSO for his actions at Wilhelma by the Duke of Connaught (Queen Victoria's third son, Prince Arthur) in March 1918; his medal was one of a total haul of thirty-one awards given to the battalion, the high number signalling the importance and intensity of the fighting. After a long day of vicious fighting with nothing to show for it, the dejected Turks retreated toward Rantieh.

The Northamptons could count their day of action as a resounding success. Not only had they held their position, but they had also forced an enemy of vast numerical superiority into a hurried retreat as other British forces had won a victory in Jerusalem. The battle at Wilhelma was not simply a sideshow to the main event in Jerusalem; the Northamptons' efforts were essential in safeguarding the lines of communication for victory in the Holy City. Compared to other battles fought by the Northampton Regiment during the war, the 4th Battalion suffered relatively few casualties on this occasion despite the intensity of the fighting: twenty-five of its ranks had been killed, with a further sixty wounded. The Turkish Army, however, had suffered far more casualties, as an estimated 400 of their men lay still on the windswept plains.

The following spring and summer of 1918 were split between marching, periods in the trenches and capturing several small villages. The Northamptons, like other battalions who had fought victoriously at Gaza, were exhausted. So too were the Turks; despite receiving German reinforcements from Syria to help stem the flow of desertions which now numbered thousands, they could offer no serious resistance against the British after losing Gaza and Jerusalem in the space of a few weeks. Demanding more troops from London, Allenby was forced to pause his advance for several months while he began preparations for a final major offensive designed to land the decisive blow.

Figure 8.18: This image shows the final resting place for over 500 men of the 4th Northamptons. The graveyard, in Gaza, contains bodies collected from several battlefields; The Northampton Independent, 7th June, 1919.

The offensive was set for 19th September 1918 and is known as the Battle of Megiddo. The Northamptons were to take the surrounding town of Medjal Yaba. At 0530, the men of the 162nd Brigade left their bivouac and marched northwards, with the 4th Northamptons leading the formation. The Turkish knew their fate would soon be decided and began desperately firing their machine guns at the advancing British troops. The men gave it their all and finally finished at 0500 the following day after fighting for over 22 hours; this was a truly remarkable feat of human endurance, with an eleven-mile march over hard desert ground, a lack of water and an enemy frantically fighting for its very survival. Already exhausted from their exertions during the battle, the men were ordered to march a further five miles to help cut off the Turkish retreat.

For their part in leading the march during the battle, perhaps one of the hardest tasks of the war, Major H. St. John Browne and Lieutenant Haptie were both decorated with the Military Cross. Initially, it seemed that the men's work was not done as they were ordered to be ready for another battle. However, it soon transpired that Turkish morale had collapsed; after a series of vicious defeats, their armies had no will to continue fighting. The Northamptons reached Kurawa Hasam (now Qarawat Bani Hassan), where they found the Turkish ranks retreating in a state of mindless anarchy. At the end of this offensive, the battalion had eight men killed in action with sixty-seven wounded. However, despite the losses, the survivors had a huge cause for celebration: the whole British operation was a resounding success. The Turkish troops were in complete disorder and were chaotically fleeing their posts, attempting to run from the pursuing British cavalry. The men pushed on to the seaport town of Haifa, where they indulged in various recreational activities, the jubilant atmosphere perhaps aided by a piano the Northamptons managed to sneak on their transport train, despite such items being officially forbidden!

Figure 8.19: The Territorials' victory at Gaza is commemorated on the Regimental WW1 memorial flag. This flag is displayed in the Church of the Holy Sepulchre, Northampton.

Figure 8.20: This image appeared in The Northampton Independent on 21st April 1917 with the title 'History Repeated After 800 Years'.

The remainder of the war was spent continuing the march northwards with their brigade. Along the way, they stopped in many towns and villages. On the day of the armistice with Turkey, 31st October 1918, the 4th Battalion had reached as far as Beirut (the city was part of Ottoman Syria, modern-day Lebanon). The war had taken them on a long and difficult journey across the Holy Land that their forebears would have been familiar with. Indeed, the editor of *The Northampton Independent* remarked that it was a "romantic coincidence" that Northampton men found themselves fighting the Turks in the Holy Land, 821 years after their ancestors in the First Crusade had travelled to the same region to fight. On that occasion, Simon de Senlis, the first Earl of Northampton, captured Jerusalem from Turkish hands. At Jerusalem, de Senlis would have seen the Church of the Holy Sepulchre. On his return to Northampton, de Senlis commemorated his victory by building St Sepulchre's Church in 1100, a smaller replica of the original. The church is extremely rare, being one of only four round churches still standing in England, an image of Jerusalem on Northampton's green and pleasant land.

Although the war had ended, the 4th Northamptons were not immediately able to go home. They would spend another full year abroad before finally returning to Northampton on 4th November 1919. The 4th Northamptons of the 162nd Brigade had suffered gravely over the course of the Palestine campaign. They had seen defeat, stalemate and, ultimately, victory. The only constant, regardless of the battle outcome, was the high number of sacrifices that fell upon the battalion. If further evidence of the battalion's courageousness is required, it should be noted that the battalion won more honours than any other unit during the Palestine campaign.

Figure 8.21: The 4th Battalion return home; Captain R. A. Marriott is seen shaking hands with Mayor J. J. Martin. On the right are Lieutenant Colonel John Brown and Major H. St. John Browne.

Figure 9.1: A cartoon from the 1917 Christmas edition of The Northampton Independent making light of premature predictions of the end of war.

CHAPTER NINE

THE END OF THE GREAT WAR

Shall we speak of peace with liars,
Looters, murderers, tyrants, ghouls?
Shall we seek of baby-killers
A coward's peace, and lose our souls?

Would the ask for peace terms
If he saw a chance to win?
Belgium, France and Serbia witness
To the fate we'd get from him

Justice call aloud for vengeance,
Freedom asks that tyrants' might
Shall be vanquished, so that nations
May be free to do the right.

13th July 1918 – *The Northampton Independent*

"*Theers sich a lot o fooaks as caent see as th gret wors med a lot of difrens in th world. They tihnk as they can tek an start wi politiks agen jist weer they dropped orf in noineteen forteen, but they never med a bigger mistacke in ther loives. Nothins th saeme, an it neer will be th saeme in our toime.*"

29th November 1918 – Village Talks by Ole Tom – *The Northampton Mercury*

There was yet more bloody trench warfare in 1917 for the British Army with major battles at Arras, Ypres and Gaza. As the year came to an end, little did the troops know that this would be their last Christmas spent in the trenches. Indeed, the bloodshed in late 1917 continued apace; December 1917 was one of the worst months of the whole war for hospital admissions in Northampton, with nine train convoys arriving in the town full of wounded men.

The Northamptonshire Red Cross Committee, to help meet the growing demand for their services, opened three new hospitals in 1917. Such was the need for medical facilities that they increased the number of beds across their sites from 881 at the start of the year to 1,325 by the end. The Northamptonshire Red Cross treated 8,605 patients in 1917, with hundreds of men from as far as Canada and Australia arriving in the county for treatment.

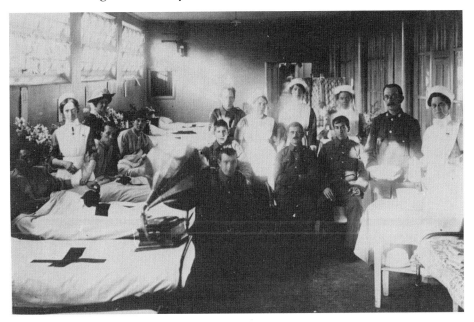

Figure 9.2: Convalescing soldiers with nurses in Kettering VAD hospital; July 1915.

With hindsight, we might assume the four years of warfare were a slow, measured defeat of a mighty enemy; year by year, blow by blow, the Allied forces gradually gained victory over Germany. In actuality, it was no such thing. As the world entered 1918, there were few signs that victory would come that year, despite all the optimistic predictions for peace; such mantras had been uttered repeatedly since August 1914, but all had proved futile.

A cartoon printed in the 1917 Christmas edition of *The Northampton Independent* presents a humorous take on such predictions. The cartoon itself is a rare attempt at humour; unlike previous Christmas specials, the 1917 edition is reduced to a small 16-page supplement with few cartoons, special features or jokes. After three years of war , the belligerent attitude in the face of adversity that Northampton displayed was fading. The editor of *The Northampton Independent* commented that "Never has Northampton looked less Christmassy". With the price of a turkey rising to 2s 6d a pound, few would enjoy a traditional Christmas dinner. Holloway did, however, express the hopes of many in the town:

> *"It is a hard task to feel like a Christian when one contemplates the savagery of this horrible war against an enemy that wantonly murders innocent women and children, but yet these outrages should serve to stimulate us all in striving to achieve the Christian ideal of making the angels' anthem on that first Christmas morn at Bethlehem, a blessed reality until the world rejoices in the restoration for ever of 'Peace on earth goodwill to men'."*

It was not victory that people wanted. It was simply peace.

This peace, however, did not seem to be on the horizon as the war continued in 1918. After seizing power and toppling the Tsar in October 1917, one of the first acts of the Bolshevik government was effectively to end Russia's involvement in the war and surrender to Germany. While the United States had entered the war in April 1917, there was still no sizeable American contingent on the Western Front. If anything, as the world entered 1918, it was Germany and the Central Powers that were more likely to emerge victorious.

Both the Allies and the Central Powers were feeling the severe strains from three years of war. Millions of men lay dead, and millions back home in all the countries involved were living on meagre rations. If hopes of a German victory were to be realised, a decisive move had to be made quickly before American reinforcements started to arrive en masse. German generals planned for a spring offensive codenamed Operation Michael.

Circumstances were in Germany's favour; the absence of an enemy on the Eastern Front, once Russia submitted to humiliating peace terms in the Treaty of Brest-Litovsk, allowed Germany to send thirty-three divisions to the Western Front. On the other side, Britain was facing a severe manpower shortage, with most divisions having fewer battalions.

Erich Ludendorff, the German military leader who had won international fame for his role in Germany's victories against Russia in the early months of the war, had been awarded control over the strategic plan on the Western Front. General Ludendorff produced grand plans to unleash the 'Kaiserschlacht' (Kaiser's Battle): coordinated interrelated attacks in quick succession that would destroy the structure of the Allied armies. The brunt of the attack would focus on the British Army between Arras and St Quentin, on battlefields already scarred from the Battle of the Somme in 1916.

Figure 9.3: The famous Soviet revolutionary and communist theorist, Leon Trotsky, arrives for the peace negotiations at Brest-Litovsk. Trotsky had a tumultuous 1917 which saw him begin the year in New York, being captured by the British and sent to a Canadian POW camp, before arriving in Russia and cementing his position as the second highest ranking officer in the country after Lenin; circa December 1917.

At 0440 on 21st March 1918, 10,000 heavy artillery guns opened fire on Allied positions as 74 toughened German divisions awaited their signal to charge. British communications were soon knocked out, and elite stormtroopers were sent deep into the action to break through weak points along the line. The attack was a stunning success. The British positions were crumbling, although the German progress was not replicated along the whole line. The British Fifth Army had retreated 12 miles in certain areas in just two days; such was the German success that the Kaiser announced 24th March to be a national holiday.

In early April, the Germans had advanced a staggering 40 miles – movement not seen since August 1914 – but were utterly exhausted. Ludendorff had overestimated the strength of his armies, and eventually the Allies began to push back. Both the Germans and the Allies had suffered around 200,000 casualties. However, Americans were now arriving in their hundreds of thousands, bolstering weakened Allied lines. The Germans had no such reinforcements, and their leaders would have realised the harsh reality: their gamble had not paid off; Germany could not win.

Despite this, the tribunals at home continued apace, with a steady stream of men being handed final postponements for military service. Arthur Dryden wrote that "Pipps, the gardener of the age of 45" was called for military service and passed medically fit at his examination in late May. Pipps had his appeal rejected by the Daventry Tribunal, despite the support of his titled employer, his relatively old age, and the six children he cared for. The promise of victory in the near future had been prophesied too many times before to act prematurely, and so the government provided no signal to the tribunals to slow down recruitment.

Northampton too felt the growing American presence in the war as US troops arrived in the town. The belief and appreciation that American military power would propel the Allies to victory were palpable. In an amusing lead article in *The Northampton Independent* on 13th July, the editor, William Holloway, reminds readers that Northamptonshire was the ancestral home of the first American president, George Washington, and that barriers between the two countries only arose due to the "stupidity" of George III and his ministers. Holloway also prints a very tongue-in-cheek historical account:

> *"There happened to be on the English throne a German gentleman named George. Over in Virginia there was an English gentleman named George. Now the German George started to deny the rights of the English George. Being an English gentleman of course he would not stand that. So he went to war and defeated the German George."*

Despite the realisation that Germany could not be victorious, Ludendorff ordered yet another push along the Western Front on 15th July 1918. It would be his and Germany's last. General Foch, now given full control over the British troops along the front, cunningly let the Germans advance up to the Marne, knowing that their over-stretched supply chains would break. A massive French counter-attack wreaked devastation on the poor, weary German soldiers.

Figure 9.4: As General Ludendorff prepared to rally his men for what would be their final offensive, the 1st Northamptons were visited by Prince Arthur, Duke of Connaught; 1st July 1918.

The British media rejoiced at these new developments. In Northampton, however, Holloway, in his capacity as the honorary treasurer of the Northamptonshire Prisoners of War Fund, gave a speech titled 'When Will the War End?' at Kettering's Victory Hall on Sunday, 6th July 1918. Holloway told his audience that reports the war would end in one hundred days were optimistic, and the plan was to defend their lines until American forces "came in full force next spring". Holloway might have been somewhat off the mark in this prediction, but he reasoned that the Allies "had not only to beat the Germans but to conquer war and teach the world that war is a crime that can be suppressed like slavery". In other words, Germany must be taught a lesson; it would not suffice to accept surrender when they were still on French soil. On this point Holloway's discerning rationale is uncanny. There was a resurgence of German nationalism in the 1920s founded on myths that Germany had been 'stabbed in the back' by traitors who signed the armistice. A chief proponent of this view was Adolf Hitler, but interestingly Ludendorff, too, was a key advocate.

Meanwhile, the Northampton Food Control Committee was still engaged in ensuring the food supply remained robust. While public spats between producers and the press had quietened after 1917, there were a series of running issues with some traders. A. F. Liddington, a local Northampton trader, had his government butter allocation withdrawn at a committee meeting on 31st July. His customers were in the process of being transferred to other shops. Liddington's meat business had also drawn the "deep resentment" of the committee, who threatened "if any further complaint is made … we shall have no option but to withdraw his trading certificate".

On 14th August, Liddington is once again under the ire of the committee. Liddington had been found submitting incorrect fortnightly returns to prove his sales. These returns determined the level of public payments to firms. In essence, Liddington was being accused of trying to defraud the committee, a highly sensitive issue in a country in the midst of war. Consequently, the committee voted to withdraw Liddington's trading licence and prosecute him, sending his case to the Ministry of Food for review. Liddington was also fined £14.

In a surprising twist, the committee had a change of heart at Liddington's appeal hearing. On 28th August, the committee wrote:

> "After hearing Mr Liddington's explanation, his expressions of regret, and his promise of strict compliance with the rationing orders in future, it was resolved that the Committee having no desire of recommending closure of the business if it is properly conducted, adjourns the matter for one month."

This was a marked departure in the committee's approach and tone to not just Liddington, but other tense incidents. Importantly, the committee minute book around these August and September 1918 shows an almost complete absence of discussions on food shortages compared to the start of the year and previous years. In January, Arthur Dryden wrote that food shortages were becoming so critical that orders using powers from the Defence of the Realm Act were issued not to feed the estate's deer, whose food could be used for human consumption. With little choice but to curtail the deer population on his estate, four bucks were shot;

their carcases revealed that it was not only humans that were struggling with food shortages, as each animal weighed 60lb compared to the average 90lb.

By September, however, the situation had witnessed such a vast improvement that the division food commissioner issued a statement to the committee that "it was not desirable to request return of unused sugar" provided the sugar was used for jam. Just a few months prior, surplus food supplied would have been recalled and distributed elsewhere in the country or given to the army.

With the Allied forces in a far better position than at the start of the war with the arrival of American soldiers, the extreme pressures on the food supply had eased, and with it, the committee's appetite for penal measures as public opposition to the war cooled. Indeed, it was not just Liddington that found the food committee in a forgiving mood; in September, the committee had investigated Messrs James Bros of the United Stores, Abington Street, for selling bacon to "a person not registered with them", while Mr Ingman of the Peacock Hotel and Mr Gibson of the Vine Inn were investigated for offences under the Beer Prices and Description Order. In all cases, the committee decided not to take any further action, apart from issuing a warning letter.

In August, the Allied forces launched what was later termed 'The Hundred Days' offensive, during which they made rapid gains on key German positions. The Germans, despite low morale, growing troop disobedience and increasing desertion, fought fiercely to the end, suffering over 700,000 casualties, a similar number to the combined Allied casualties. The Northamptonshire Regiment was not on the front line of these advances but was involved in trench fighting to the very end of the war.

It was not until September that optimism that the war might soon end turned to anticipation and finally expectation. Such were the jubilant scenes in the town in September 1918, a visitor would be forgiven for thinking the war had ended. Abington Park was filled with the sounds of four orchestras, families enjoyed gentle boat rides in the lake and shoppers could feast their eyes on over 100 metres of stalls in the park. However, this was not a premature celebration but purely coincidental timing that Northampton held a three-day carnival. The aim of the carnival, like the previous year's Old English Fair, was to raise donations for the Prisoners of War Fund.

The festivities were certainly more joyful than past events as the press reported the rapid gains being made by Allied troops. For instance, visitors to the carnival took great pleasure in one of the attractions, which involved driving a nail into a wood carving of the Kaiser; even Field Marshal Lord Grenfell got in on the act. Not only were the heavens smiling over the troops in France, but the weather also behaved splendidly during the carnival. The day after the carnival ended, such was the ferocity of the rain that the roofing of stalls collapsed and general wreckage resulted.

The carnival was a great fundraising success for the Prisoners of War Fund, whose members had worked so tirelessly. The fund was established by Holloway after he received numerous letters from local men held in German-controlled prisons after the Battle of Mons. Throughout the war, the local press extensively covered the horrific treatment suffered by prisoners. While some accounts may have been exaggerated, the treatment of prisoners by Germany shocked the town and helped spearhead the successful fundraising campaign. *The Northampton Independent* in October 1918 reported that a former prisoner had died in Northampton after being "literally murdered by the horrors he suffered" in the notorious Wittenberg camp.

By the end of the war, 1,300 men were catered for by the fund, a total of 85,985 parcels were sent to Germany and Turkey, and £75,000 (£4.6 million in 2018) was raised. To organise and distribute this number of parcels required a professional operation and much of the work was done by women. The committee of the fund wrote after the war:

> *"The news which arrived on Wednesday last week that no more parcels need to be sent came as a relief, almost beyond words, to those heroic ladies to whose self-sacrifice and devotion our prisoners owe so much, for they had reached almost the limit of human endurance in their self-imposed task."*

As the town digested the excitement generated by the carnival, events in France moved to a decisive end. On 7th October, *The Northampton Chronicle* announced, "THE GROGGY BOXER SAYS 'STOP' – BUT IS HE READY TO ADMIT DEFEAT AND THAT VICTORY IS OURS?" The new German chancellor, Prince Max of Baden, was reported to have sent a note to the American president, Woodrow Wilson, to discuss terms of peace. The paper wrote that there were further signs that the Germans were preparing to leave the Flanders region, but were burning villages as they retreated:

> *"The Germans are blowing up bridges on the Suippe and the Retourne and burning villages in the rear of the line. Their peace proposals do not mean that useless destruction of French homes is to cease … the Germans, simultaneously with their peace move, are ordering their hordes to kindle conflagrations. Along the vast front the whole horizon is in flames, revealing their hideous work."*

On 11th November 1918, France and Belgium woke to dull grey skies. The 1st Northamptonshire Battalion was billeted in Fresnoy, east France, near the Belgian border. The battalion war diary states, in typically impassive fashion, "Armistice signed". There is no description of men cheering, celebrating or rejoicing.

Nevertheless, these two solemn words are resounding. The 48th, among the first in France, had ended the war in a position further back than when they had arrived four years earlier. The battalion had been annihilated several times, only to be kept alive in name by waves of fresh recruits. The 2nd Battalion was near Mons when the armistice was signed. Like that of their sister battalion, the diarist of the 58th was similarly sombre, only recording the armistice and the weather.

Figure 9.5: Soldiers of the 1st Northamptonshire Battalion are photographed resting in the trenches at Molain, France, on 17th October 1918. The men would have been glad to hear of the Armistice agreed a few weeks later after several exhausting years.

In Northampton, the scene was rather different. The day had been long-awaited and when it finally arrived, it would be one to remember. Schools, factories and offices were all shut, with or without official permission, as people took to the streets in great excitement. The news of the armistice was revealed at the office of *The Daily Echo* just after 1030 and spread rapidly throughout the town.

Strangers shook hands with each other as the town centre was suddenly transformed. Hundreds of buildings proudly flew flags from windows, and a vibrant sea of red, white and blue ribbons decorated the town, vehicles and even dogs. Not only were the Union Jack and the flag of St George to be seen but also French, Belgian and American flags were all displayed. *The Northampton Mercury* jokingly reported that shops even faced a run on flags from eager customers!

The Northampton Chronicle said that the news gave people "an electric thrill – the blood was sent coursing through people's veins, and all idea of further work vanished". Factory workers on hearing the news erupted in cheers, their joy loud enough to drown out the noisy whir of machinery. One manager told *The Northampton Mercury* that his factory "was like a concert hall when the news reached us". Factory workers soon joined the cheering crowds, which were now full of young men and women singing arm in arm, accompanied by a multitude of bands playing the national anthem. School children were dismissed from school, and they too made their way to the euphoric scenes in the town centre. A reporter from *The Northampton Chronicle* noted an amusing incident:

> *"Boys are nothing if not realistic. The surrender of Germany was represented by a number of lads wearing imitation Boche helmets being marched along as prisoners by proud little Tommy Atkinses, followed by cheering crowds of flag-waving youngsters."*

The celebrations grew to a crescendo during the night with "endless processions of men and women and boys and girls" adorned with patriotic decorations. Curfews were lifted, and shops were allowed to keep their lights on – the sight of night lights, rare since the war began, added to the memorable atmosphere. As the Volunteer Band performed on Market Square, men and women danced late into the night.

The sight of wounded soldiers as they emerged onto the streets after hearing the news delighted the crowd but also tempered the celebrations, for they were a stark reminder of the huge price of victory. The soldiers themselves, wrote *The Northampton Independent*, were more subdued than the civilians. The paper also commented that,

> *"The middle-aged, the old, seeing things, perhaps, in a truer perspective, could not forget the agonies of nearly five years of the most terrible war in history now that the mutual slaughter was over. They were subdued and by no means inclined for festivities. Relief and a great thankfulness were in their hearts – just that and nothing more."*

Many on the streets were not celebrating victory but peace, joy bounded with pain.

As the celebratory mood faded, a period of reflection occurred as people turned to the question of what should happen next. In Northampton, like most of the country, there was an understandable wave of anger to make Germany pay for its actions over the last four years. *The Northampton Independent* cried out "Punish the Brutes!" as prisoners of war arrived home fully revealing the scale of their treatment, which would make "even the tepid blood of a conscientious objector boil with indignation". On 15th November, *The Northampton Mercury's* regular 'Village Talks' feature, written in a colloquial manner by Ole Tom, expressed what many in the town were thinking:

> *"Thanks be ter God it looks as if th foitins ooer onyrooad, but oi caent 'elp a feelin as arter old ther wicked docins th Germans look loike getting*

*orf oncom mone chep. Its bin said orl alung as dire as it looked as if theyd
'av th foitin in her ooan country theyd giv up quick."*

Within a matter of days after the armistice had been signed, people were
already recognising issues that might threaten peace in the future: namely the
fact the Germans were not pushed back into their country before surrendering.
As mentioned previously, this simple fact allowed conspiracy theories regarding
Germany's surrender to flourish, sowing the seeds of the Second World War.

However, Ole Tom, always in tune with public opinion, recognised that:

> *"Theyr licked, an badly licked an its no good a kickin on em now
> they down, no matter ow much we may think they deserve it fer ther mean
> wickadness, an if theyre annoind ter set ther oon doorway strait praps its
> jist as well ter nick it as easy can be for em ter get on in it."*

The last four years had ushered in a colossal shift of the social foundations
in British society, and there appeared to be this universal optimism, expectation
even, that things could not, and would not, go back to the old system where the
masses lived in poverty. It was as if the world were entering a new age, decisively
breaking from the old one for the better; with war finally over, the overwhelming
desire for the majority of people was to make sure it stayed over, ensuring the new
world that they were entering would be a peaceful one.

For instance, the labour market had been transformed by the introduction
of thousands of women working in industries traditionally dominated by men.
Fully aware of the magnitude of this change and the role played by women who
"literally came to the rescue of the nation", *The Northampton Mercury* said that no
one should be under any illusions that women will "fall back into the old ruts", and
that women who wish to stay in work "have every right to do so".

For the millions of men who were slowly arriving back in England, things
also had to change. Politicians on all sides began to produce grand plans for housing
and welfare. For example, the local MP, Charles McCurdy, produced a list of
fourteen points (alluding to President Wilson's famous manifesto) which promised
to "rebuild the slums of Great Britain from Land's End to John O'Groats", and
build 250,000 houses to meet immediate demand. McCurdy also vowed to provide
pensions and to ensure a "proper standard of living". Ole Tom in *The Northampton
Mercury* expressed the hopes and aspirations of the working class when he wrote:

> *"Theers no getting away from it; wot 'e laid down theer as wot 'e
> wer out arter wer a wunnerful program, an if we ony get some o th things
> carried out this ole country ul be a new land fer a foine many. Its got ter
> be done an orl. Oim said afoor as th thousans o foine lads as er bin out an*

*fit th devul in 'ell an wuss fer th sacke un England, aent a comin back ter
be content wi wot they 'ad afoor, an if big things aent done fer them, arter
wot theyr done fer England an th world, theer ul be trubbel, an theer ort
ter be trubbel."*

The Northampton Independent put it slightly more eloquently when the editor
wrote that the men had "had the stark facts of life revealed to them" and would
not be "deceived by political clap-trap". The editor goes on to tell readers that
reforms must be implemented quickly as the huge social changes that began with
the war would not end with it, pleading that "all our ideas must be readjusted to
fit the new conditions". For a country epitomised over centuries by careful, slow
and peaceful reform, unlike revolutionary continental Europe, Britain was about to
see its social foundations rapidly and permanently transformed. There is always a
struggle between change and conserving traditions of old, but many felt the ending
of the Great War heralded a transition to a new world. While there were clearly
difficult challenges ahead, so far optimism was triumphing over despair.

As the country began the process to transform an economy geared for war,
the question of jobs was a natural consequence. There were numerous opportunities
for Britain as Belgium, France, Germany and Russia saw their industrial base
weakened in the immediate post-war years. Japan and the United States, on the
other hand, would provide stiff competition to Britain.

During the war, the boot and shoe industry thrived with masses of orders. *The
Northampton Independent* wrote that the industry was "better equipped and better
organised than ever". Over the course of the last four years, Northamptonshire
factories had produced over thirty-two million pairs of boots and by 1918 were
producing over 250,000 boots a week. They were responsible for a third of all
British boots and also produced footwear for all of the Allies apart from Japan.
This stunning achievement came despite the industry having had many of its
skilled workers leave for war. Indeed, the tribunals were inundated with appeals by

Figure 9.6: After
establishing their abilities
in industries where they
were previously barred from
entering, women continued
to work and break further
social barriers after the war
ended. This photograph
shows women working
at the Mounts Factory
Company, Northampton
in 1919.

employers seeking to secure exemptions for their staff. The agricultural industry had also performed exceptionally; by 1918, the total acreage of wheat had risen 33% from its 1916 level. The performances of both the footwear and the agricultural industries were a testament to the many women who laboured in these traditionally male domains, proving their utility in the workplace and helping to usher in new social norms.

As hostilities came to a close, soldiers did not immediately arrive home. For the first time, finally released from the torment of war, soldiers had an opportunity to relax and enjoy another country. The relief even seems to have permeated into the normally expressionless diarist of the 48th, when, in December 1918, he recorded the troops having visited Chevetogne Abbey in south Belgium, which was inhabited by Benedictine monks, commenting, "unfortunately they were unable to produce any liqueur of that ilk".

On 27th January 1919, the 48th travelled to Bonn in Germany. Here they began a brigade inter-company football tournament. Not only were the Northamptons hardy soldiers, but they also proved to be capable footballers, making it to the final of the tournament after winning seven games, drawing two and losing six. On 8th February, the 48th won the brigade cup, beating the Field Ambulance 2-1. Sport was a major part of the recreational activities available to soldiers, and the men also played hockey and even basketball: invented in only 1891, the sport was younger than many men in the battalion.

The 2nd Northamptonshire Battalion was the first to arrive back home on 26th April 1919. Thousands from the town and county lined the streets, cheering and waving handkerchiefs at the troops as they arrived at the old Castle Station at 1715. The county's great and good were all in attendance; on arrival, the troops were greeted by Earl Spencer in his role as lord lieutenant, the mayor, and other dignitaries, while the 1st Northamptonshire Volunteers heartily played 'Home Sweet Home,' a song popularised during the American Civil War. Afterwards, speeches were given and thanks were received at a luncheon hosted by the mayor.

The 6th Battalion arrived home in late July but to a more muted reception by local officials , which drew the ire of the town. The authorities disbanded the 6th Battalion before they were afforded the opportunity to parade in the town and given "the welcome such heroes deserve". The battalion, largely composed of local men from farms and factories, distinguished itself in the war under gruelling conditions, earning four Victoria Crosses.

The 7th Northamptons arrived back in Northampton on 21st June 1919 to cheering crowds. The battalion had been formed in September 1915, with Edgar Mobbs playing a key role in recruiting local sportsmen to the colours. On 31st July 1917, Mobbs was shot when leading his men through a difficult part of the line during the Third Battle of Ypres (also known as the Battle of Passchendaele). For ten minutes, Mobbs fearlessly composed himself to write an update on his battalion's position and handed it to a runner before he died. The battalion was in action until the very end, with its final major battle at Cambrai in early October 1918. Earl Spencer suitably eulogised Colonel Mobbs when he wrote,

> *"The name of the ever-lamented Colonel Mobbs will live in the annals of the County, and the power he showed in imbuing his men with his own gallant spirit is a cherished possession, not only of the battalion, but of the County at large."*

Figure 9.7: Men from the 7th Northamptonshire Battalion are pictured drawing rations from the quartermaster's stores. Near Dikkebus, Belgium; 9th August 1917.

Earl Spencer also donated Dallington House as a facility for disabled soldiers and sailors as an expression of his thankfulness after his two sons returned safely from war.

It wasn't only the British troops who were not home in 1919. Over 4,500 German soldiers were still found to be held at the Pattishall Camp during a Swiss Legation inspection in May 1919. The process of repatriation was a long and prolonged one; the signing of the armistice did not immediately lead to the freeing of prisoners, as both sides still had the final peace to negotiate. When this peace, as represented by the Treaty of Versailles, was signed on 28th June 1919, the process of transferring prisoners of war ought to have become smoother. However, the number of Germans in prisoner of war camps across Britain actually surged after German Admiral Ludwig von Reuter, displeased at the peace terms which he saw as a betrayal, ordered his fleet, which was currently interned at Scapa Flow, Scotland, to be scuttled just three days after the signing of the treaty.

As summer gave way to autumn, the prisoners were sent back home, so that by December 1919, Pattishall was vacant. This vast camp, which had housed over 4,000 men just months before, lay barren. Row upon row of beds lay empty, grey corridors once full of activity were now silent, and hundreds of showers, toilets and sinks were all unoccupied for the first time. As the former occupants left, attention turned to the items inside. On 19th March 1920, an advert in *The Northampton Mercury* publicised the notice for the sales of effects from the camp. This revealed to the public the level of resources that was required to maintain such a vast camp. Among the items available were 4,200 bed boards, a flour store 55 ft x 25 ft, 8 industrial-sized ovens, an electricity generator, two boiler houses, baths, sinks, stoves, miles of electrical wiring and 235 tables. Members of the public were perhaps surprised to learn that the prison camp had its own concrete reservoir, capable of holding over 2.75 million gallons of water, and its own hospital, complete with fitted wards, staff rooms and isolation units. The logistics of prison camps are rarely considered in studies of the war, but they required huge investment and organisation to operate. The men may have been prisoners, but they were first and foremost men who had to eat, sleep and live.

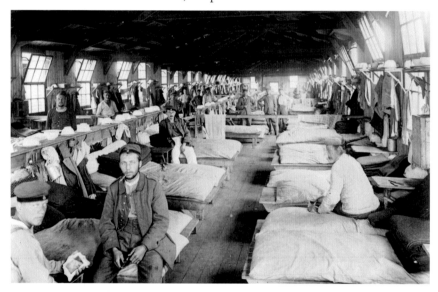

Figure 9.8: German prisoners are photographed in their living quarters in the Pattishall Camp. After the camp closed, items used to house thousands of men during the war were sold by public auction; c1915-1916.

Not all, however, did live. Searching through the dusty burial records for Pattishall that date back centuries reveals a very curious anomaly during the First World War years. Among names like Hart, Jones and Foster, there suddenly start to appear names of a foreign persuasion. On 5th August 1915, one Karl Möller appears on the burial record. This entry has several intriguing aspects. Firstly, and most importantly, Möller's "abode" is listed as "alien from the concentration camp Eastcote". The term 'concentration camp' had not acquired the negative connotations it carries in modern times, hence its usage. Also striking is the use of 'alien' to describe the German Möller rather than 'prisoner of war'. This is perhaps due to Möller's age, which is listed as 64. Möller was not a soldier; therefore, he was not a prisoner of war, but one of the thousands of German civilians who were housed at the Pattishall Camp during the war. Finally, the use of the umlaut in Möller's name is notable; it signifies not only close attention to detail but also the very respectful manner in which Möller's death was treated.

Möller was not the only German who passed away at the Pattishall Camp. In total, thirty-two men died while resident at Pattishall. Three-quarters of the deaths occurred after the signing of the armistice. While this may seem unexpected, it speaks volumes about the devastation the German military suffered in the final battles of the war. These men, unlike Möller, were not old. Their average age at death in 1919 was 29, with five men under 25 years old. These men, who arrived at Pattishall in 1918, were already beaten and broken after fighting a series of losing battles that year. Adding to the desperate situation, the crowded conditions of the camp were the perfect breeding ground for the Spanish flu, which also took hold among the prisoners; Chapman and Moss state that the virus was responsible for half of the camp deaths in 1919.

In a sad twist of fate, the ending of the war coincided with one of the deadliest epidemics in the history of mankind. The first significant wave of the Spanish flu beginning in spring 1918 was relatively mild, and as a result concerns about the virus were lightly dismissed; Ole Tom in *The Northampton Mercury* in July 1918 commented that the town was lucky they only had something like the flu to worry about when there was a war going on, joking "fooaks 'ad ter baeke ther ooan dinners" as the baker and his wife were both stricken with flu. Even when 1 in 3 school children in Northampton was absent from school after contracting the flu in August, the Education Board suspected one-third of cases were an excuse to keep children at home. The same month, *The Northampton Mercury* reported that 14 deaths in Northampton had been recorded. The death toll rapidly increased: in the week before the armistice 55 deaths occurred, and the disease had become so widespread that all schools across the county were closed. The flu would go on to be a deadlier killer than the war, amassing, by some average estimates, 50 million victims compared to around the 18 million that the war claimed.

This viral epidemic was just one of many factors serving to dampen the optimistic mood of victorious Northamptonshire. Signs of the permanent scars war had left on millions of men now returning home soon began to appear. On the evening of Sunday, 13th October 1918, Captain Frank Wood wandered into 35 Billing Road, Northampton. He immediately went upstairs and entered a bedroom, where he met a maid. Wood asked where his former fiancée, Miss Dorman, was. As the maid nervously left the room, Wood pulled out a revolver and fired three shots: one into the ceiling, one into the frieze, and one into the bed. The owner of the house, Mr J. F. Harris, was startled and ushered his household outside. As the captain went downstairs, he was detained by Dorman's two brother officers.

Appearing in court, the captain's defence said that the war had changed him. Woods had been one of the first to volunteer at the outbreak of war and had amassed an excellent record, including being rewarded with a commission. In 1916, he was transferred to the Flying Corps, where he took part in many bombing raids. His defence said three years of consistent warfare had "told upon his nerves" and he was sent to a London hospital. In the week before the incident, Miss Dorman had publicly announced her engagement to Captain Hugh Price Jones, one of the soldiers attached to the Welsh regiment billeted in the town at the start of the war. On hearing news of the engagement, Woods had written to Dorman:

> "When I am more normal I will come down and give it to you, and then go out of our life, taking you with me."

The breaking of his engagement to Dorman and her announcement with Price had apparently caused a "mental disturbance and aberration", leading to the incident. The court sympathised with Captain Woods and let him off without punishment after his defence said Woods would leave Northampton at once.

This incident was an early sign that while the war had ended, and while the men had left the war, the war had not left them. Millions of men returned home bearing deep psychological scars after years of torment. Little was known then about post-traumatic stress disorder (PTSD) or mental health issues, and soldiers often bottled up their experiences of war, saying little about their service. In another letter to his former sweetheart, Captain Woods desolately wrote:

> "I am a murderer."

The war had ended but its harsh realities would last for a long time to come, not only for the men who fought in it. Herbert Smart, born in Kingsthorpe in 1878, volunteered for military service in August 1915. Smart was shot in the leg in October 1917, but on 23rd May 1918, despite being forty years old and despite the arrival of American troops at this late stage of the war, he was sent back to France. Soon after, his daughter Mabel received a postcard from her father that read:

> "Dear Mabel, just a line to let you know that your Dad [sic] is going over the water again xxxxx."

On 20th October 1918, Smart was killed while serving with the Cheshire Battalion near Courtrai. Mabel and her three siblings lost their father just 22 days before the armistice. The kisses on the postcard are smudged; Smart's descendants wonder if they were made by the tears of the sender or the recipient.

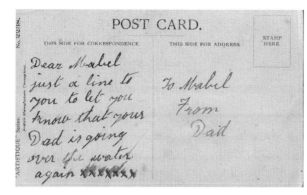

Figure 9.9: (Left) The postcard Herbert Smart sent his daughter, Mabel. Note the kisses on the postcard are smudged; Smart's descendants wonder if they were made by the tears of the sender or recipient.

Figure 9.10: (Below) The Smart family; Mabel, the eldest sister, is standing in the centre.

In 1923, Mabel, now 13, wrote an essay on 'The Privileges and Duties of Citizenship'. Her essay warned against self-righteousness and argued that good deeds should be done without drawing attention to oneself. There is, however, one evocative remark regarding conscientious objectors that suggests the haunting experience of losing her father in the war never left her:

> *"If all men who went to the war followed their [conscientious objectors'] example, the Germans would have been ruling England by now."*

For her entry, Mabel jointly won an essay competition held in Northampton. The other winner, Ray Hulbert, also touched upon the war in his essay when he wrote that military service should be deemed "a matter of honour" by each citizen. Mabel and her siblings were just some of the millions of children who lost their father in the war. While life moved on, there was resentment in society that the

Figure 9.11: After the initial exuberance of victory, feelings of resentment proliferated in society. As part of their victory celebrations, the people of Brackley hung a figure of the Kaiser in the town centre; photograph taken 11th November 1918.

Treaty of Versailles was perceived to be a weak punishment for Germany. With the consequences of the war still very much alive and visible, mainly in the form of a large number of amputees and disabled men around town, the war clearly impacted the next generation of Britons for decades to come.

While men like Herbert Smart perished in the war leading to long-lasting anguish felt by their families, some of the men who did survive carried the same anguish with them for the rest of their lives. Jim Coomes, born in 1888, was by all accounts a happy, lively boy growing up in Northampton. Living in St James, he was a keen supporter of the Saints, the rugby club a stone's throw away from his house, and he would often be found carrying the players' boots from the pub to the pitch. In December 1915, he left his job working in a shoe factory and enlisted for service. In a postcard sent to his wife in August 1916, he wrote:

> *"Just a line to let you know that I are going on all right at present, but it is very hard work, but I shall have to put up with it … we could hear the guns where we are. Sorry I can't tell you more, but you will never know till I come home from war."*

Jim did come back home, but he was severely wounded and lost his leg and several fingers after being struck by a shell. After coming home, he seemingly lost his faith, preferring the bottle to going to church with his wife. In many ways, Jim was typical of many soldiers who did come back: rarely speaking about his experience of war, carrying noticeable physical wounds, losing interest in social life and consuming too much alcohol.

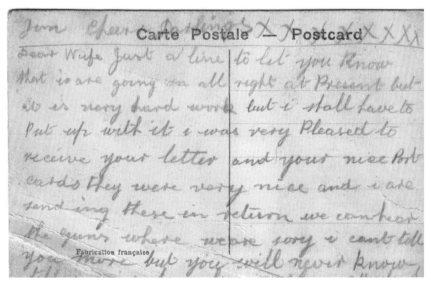

Figure 9.12: The postcard Jim Coomes sent his family which contained veiled descriptions of the war to avoid the censors.

For all the devastation and horrors soldiers and their families had seen, for all the resentment and bitterness aroused by war, and for all the long-lasting mental health issues endured by those who fought, it seems the most common feeling resulting from four years of war was sorrow. One common observation among interviews with descendants of Northamptonshire soldiers reveals that the men who fought rarely spoke about their experiences of war. For men like Arthur James Ette, born in Wilby Street, Northampton, it is unsurprising why he rarely spoke about his war: being gassed several times and wounded on multiple occasions and having to crawl over dead comrades after a shell strike did not make for comforting bedtime stories for his children. Instead, Arthur's experience actually made him kinder. Like many of his fellow soldiers, his family said he held no animosity towards the Germans; after the armistice, while billeted with a German family, he learned some German after striking up a friendly relationship with his hosts. A kind brother, Arthur was spoilt by his five sisters, who fought each other to iron their brother's shirts and cook him meals after his safe return from war.

Figure 9.13: A fresh-faced Arthur Ette poses in his military uniform shortly after enlisting, around 19 years old.

Figure 9.14: Arthur Ette (middle row, second from left) now cutting a more defined figure, with his battalion in a gymnastics session; taken in May 1917.

It was therefore unsurprising that Arthur presented a rejuvenated figure on his wedding day in May 1920, when he married Annie Elizabeth Kinch. A local girl born in St James, Northampton, Annie's life was also turned upside down by the arrival of war. Almost immediately, a soldier from the Welsh battalion that arrived in Northampton in September 1914 was billeted in Annie's family home. Born in 1895, Annie was of age to join the Women's Forage Corps with her friends to support the war effort. For part of her service, Annie was located at Aldwicle Farm, where she stayed with an old lady in her thatched roof cottage. During these years, Annie was engaged in hard farm work previously thought unsuitable for women. The days were long and tiring but provided Annie with fond memories of working outside with her friends, in service of their country.

Memories of the war for Annie, like many other young girls, were also tinged with deep personal sorrow. Annie's boyfriend at the time of war, Harry Rands, was serving in the Royal Navy and was killed when his ship was sunk. Annie's daughter and granddaughter recalled she never spoke about her loss. All Annie was left to remember Harry was an old golden locket that he had given her. In a poignant act, Annie gave the locket to her husband, Arthur, who always wore it, ensuring that while deprived of the life he perhaps dreamt of with Annie, Harry would always be close to her.

Like Annie, the people of Northamptonshire had been tested as never before over four years. Northamptonshire, like much of the country, had essentially

Figure 9.15: Annie Elizabeth Kinch (left), in her early twenties, with her friends during the war. Note Annie is proudly sporting a wristwatch, an accessory that came into mass popularity for men during WW1, suggesting Annie was an early adopter.

become a war machine. Its people, its output and its societies were all geared to support the war effort financially, materially and physically. Under the tutelage of its treasurer, the editor of *The Northampton Independent*, Mr W. Holloway, the Prisoners of War Fund raised millions of pounds, which went towards sending many tens of thousands of food parcels to prison camps. As an example of the efficiency achieved by the end of the war, 95% of parcels were sent in 1917 and 1918.

While a steady food supply is essential for sustaining war, 'boots on the ground' are needed to fight it. Again, the efficiency of the Northamptonshire factories is remarkable; Northamptonshire produced   more army boots than the rest of the country combined. These achievements are all the more illustrious when one considers the glaring shortage of working-age people available for this work. Factories were staffed with large numbers of women, men past their normal retirement age, those recovering from wounds, Belgian refugees, boys and girls out of school, and even prisoners, all producing footwear from Russian Cossack boots to African sandals, and, of course, the famous regulation B5 British army boot.

Behind all these phenomenal achievements lies a complex story. It is one first and foremost that resulted in the deaths of millions of young men across the world, including thousands who served and died for the Northamptonshire Regiment. It is also a story whose narrative is more complex and uncertain than is often portrayed. The idea of a nation erupting with great patriotic fervour to defeat a maligned enemy for the cause of justice is not wrong, at least in the early months of the war, but it betrays a more nuanced view of a society where a range of opinions existed across the societal spectrum. Social tensions grew as the war entered yet another year; the local press became outwardly hostile towards authorities for the lack of information regarding the reality on the war fronts; the introduction of tribunals was instantly unpopular and exposed the rawest of emotions people felt as they applied for military exemptions; and with each month that passed by and as food rations become tighter, Britain was a society ever more fatigued by war.

Although the exact moment in the war is not precisely identifiable, at some point it does appear that, while the enemy was Germany and the Central Powers, people were also fighting for a better future, one of opportunity and hope. Victory in the war would almost entitle those who won the victory, the people, to a better life. It was not enough for them just to defeat the enemy: public opinion now demanded that the old social conventions and living conditions no longer be tolerated. Drained of its youth by the war machine, long factory and agricultural hours were worked by millions of women who were previously thought unsuitable for such roles. They were also unwilling to go back to their old domestic roles. Change was forthcoming, too: the Representation of the People Act, enshrined into law in February 1918, enfranchised millions of men and women, almost trebling the eligible electorate overnight and dramatically changing party politics. The first experience of this new politics was immediately after the armistice, with a general election on 14th December 1918 producing a landslide victory for the coalition government and David Lloyd George continuing as prime minister.

In Northampton, Charles McCurdy, the Liberal candidate whose campaign produced a fourteen-point document to mimic US President Woodrow Wilson's famous peace speech, was elected. McCurdy's fourteen points dealt with the immediate aftermath of the war, including a commitment to secure a "righteous peace" and ensure punishment was dealt to the "authors of the war". Additionally, the list of promises focused heavily on the domestic situation, promising a restoration of civil liberties that were "patriotically suspended" during the war, enhanced pensions securing "a proper standard of living", and a range of commitments on jobs and new housing. Ending his fourteen-point list, McCurdy borrows the powerful, optimistic words of H. G. Wells as he asks not only for the vote of Northamptonians but also for them to dream of what the future could be like:

> *"Never have I been so sure that there is a divinity in man, and that a great order of human life, a reign of justice and world-wide happiness, of plenty, power, hope and gigantic creative effort, lies close at hand. Even now we have the science and the ability available for universal welfare; even now there exists all the knowledge that is needed to make human life sweet and noble. We need but the faith for it, and it is at hand; we need but the courage to lay our hands upon it and in a little space of years it can be ours."*

Figure 10.1: Remembrance Day 2017; Holy Cross Church, Daventry.

EPILOGUE

11TH NOVEMBER 2018

Carry Home

Born
At
Home. No
Time to roam our
Cobbles, our fields.
Greater odds await. One man's
Hobble. Solid as he shields. Another
As he charges forth. As he bends, as he yields.

You will be swallowed. No matter the country.
No matter the man. You will go on. Gripping
Each step the very best you can. You will bear rot.
No adust tan but dusty knot. You will forget
Such days, of shine, of polish, of fine fresh trot.

Your flooded sole. Your wrecked lining.
Weakened heels. For home pulls pining.
Back to the cobbles, back to the fields
You never knew. Come home.
To where you began.
Come home brave sole. Hitch,
Limp and carry   home
Each and every
Other brave
Soul.

'Carry Home' by Loz Anstey 2018; Kettering, Northamptonshire

It's a bright Sunday morning. The air is crisp, almost icy. The rising sun casts a sharp glow on the waking buildings. There's a crowd milling about, hands in their coat pockets, cheerfully talking among themselves as they wait. A boy, no older than six, can be seen wrestling with his scarf, the crimson garment touching the ground, much to the annoyance of his mother, who reaches over her son to fasten his clothing.

A single melodic strike of the bell on All Saints' Church rises above the general chatter, signalling the clock has reached 0915, a time when Northampton town centre on any other Sunday is almost silent, bar the occasional pedestrian or dog walker. This Sunday, however, is not like any other Sunday. It's Remembrance Sunday, and it's one hundred years since the bellowing guns across the battlefields , from the muddy fields of France and Belgium to the barren dunes of Gaza, all fell silent.

The crowd, growing in number with each passing minute, have risen early to witness the parade from the Market Square to All Saints'. Market Square is a hive of activity as the Northampton Pipe Band readies to lead the parade, and children from organisations such as the Air Cadets and Scouts quickly scurry to their positions, under the watch of beaming parents. Suddenly the air is filled with the sound of booming drums, soon followed by the piercing attack of the bagpipes. The Pipe Band descends The Drapery, followed by veterans and associated organisations as they head towards the church.

All Saints' Church is resplendent on these occasions; situated in the middle of Northampton town centre, its location has been a place of Christian worship since medieval times. A jewel of the town, the church seemingly hides in plain sight, always in the background of the hustle and bustle of the day. The parade ascends the stone steps and goes through the towering pillars into the narthex before entering the nave. For first-time visitors, and even returning ones, the intricate beauty of the church is a sight to behold. As the service begins people in coats cram every pew , while latecomers stand in the narthex, on tiptoes for a view inside. The second-floor gallery is also open, affording the public a special vantage point of the elliptical windows, vivid stained glass and finely detailed Georgian plasterwork.

Many members of the public and men in military uniform choose to remain outside, their gentle chatter merging with the hum from the loudspeakers the church has set up to broadcast the service. Inside, Father Oliver Cross stands tall at his pulpit, which has been beautifully decorated with a covering of poppies. His pure white vestment draping smoothly down his frame, he commands the attention of the gathered masses. In his closing remarks, Cross speaks about the ritual of silence those gathered will soon be observing.

"But regardless of the things that preoccupy us, we shall this day each stand in that same appalling, prevailing silence. It is not our silence,

though we have our own tears to shed, but the silence of souls so lost in the turbulence of war that they alone may tell us about peace."

Figure 10.2: The audience stands during the Remembrance Sunday service in All Saints' Church, Northampton.

After the church service, the crowd slowly emerge as the marching band and the thunderous drums once again take formation. While there was space to roam on the pavements surrounding All Saints' before the service started, the crowd has now swelled to such proportions that through traffic is a shoulder-to-shoulder affair. The skies that had been threatening to pour down earlier have now cleared up, revealing a composition of clear blue blended with placid dashes of white, sporadically allowing the warming sun to peek through. Politicians, clergy, veterans and other dignitaries congregate in the Remembrance Garden as the clock nears the eleventh hour of the day. The general conversation among attendees naturally quietens. For most in attendance, only a single voice is heard:

"They shall not grow old, as we that are left grow old."

The crowd falls silent.

"Age shall not weary them, nor the years condemn."

The sea of people surrounding the church now stands motionless.

"At the going down of the sun and in the morning
We will remember them."

The same church bells that joyfully rang to announce the end of war at this precise time one hundred years ago begin to chime once more. Everyone's attention is on a lone bugler who rises with a determined focus in his eyes, and the haunting notes of the Last Post radiate from his instrument, pushing the melodic bell ringing into the background.

And then silence.

But not any silence. The same silence heard to the very minute one hundred years ago on that momentous November morning; that same eerie silence that was heard louder than the thunderous bombs of war it suddenly replaced.

It's at this moment of silence that one is struck by a cold chill; in this silence your mind singularly focuses on the sacrifices those men went through, battling unimaginable conditions and suffering horrific pain. This is the point of remembrance. In modern life, for those born after the Second World War, the prospect of war seems so far removed from our daily lives that we are apt to forget we still live in the shadows cast by the Great War. Our modern day values and institutions, whether that is free speech, free elections, women's rights or employment laws, can all chart their emergence from this watershed moment in British and world history.

Of course, for many in that crowd, war is not a distant concept. Noticeable among the crowd are the numerous men in their thick, woollen trench coats, adorned with a colourful array of medals, each with their own complex histories. The Second World War, Korea, the Falklands, the Troubles, Iraq and Afghanistan: these conflicts too are remembered in the silence. Veterans of these more recent conflicts may be rightfully pondering if one hundred years later their sacrifices will still be remembered.

One hundred years is the traditional point when an event is thought to formally become 'history', as there are no persons with first-hand memory of the incident still living. As such, it is also the point when the strongest feelings of a war start to be forgotten too. The Napoleonic Wars, the Crimean War and the Boer Wars, for example, were all bloody with large casualties. Not only were they remembered but their victories were celebrated for years after their resolution. In the modern age, however, their stories and their folklore are no longer part of the national psyche. While monuments erected in the aftermath of these wars are found in every major city, and while they may stand tall and imposing in their masses of stone, they are relics left behind from another age that do not seem particularly relevant to modern society.

The Great War feels different. This war feels like in another century it will still be remembered with that same powerful silence. A silence where one's mind is cast back to the stark, depraved realities of that war; of millions of men decaying in a more punishing, cold environment than one can even dare to imagine; of the millions of once happy lives lost to the indiscriminate evil of war; and of the tears a million mothers shed for their departed sons. The reasons are numerous and complicated, but the core of the explanation must be that this war was fundamentally different to every war that came before it, regardless of the international dimension.

The suffering caused by the war was not confined to the terraced houses of blue-collar labourers, but everyone in society was exposed to the pain. No longer were social elites protected by their positions and rank from the harsh realities: Herbert Asquith, prime minister at the start of the war, lost his son while the future prime minister, Andrew Bonar Law, saw two of his sons killed. Law's second son, Charles John Law, was only twenty years old when he was killed in April 1917 during the Second Battle of Gaza, the same battle where the 4th Northamptonshire Battalion suffered gravely.

Yes, Britain had emerged victorious, but it was a victory paid for by the blood of its youth; young or old, rich or poor, working class or middle class – everyone paid. Not thousands, not tens of thousands, but hundreds of thousands of British men went to fight in foreign climes, never to return. Those who did return became a living legacy of the war: the common site of crippled soldiers with missing limbs and their daily pain was a constant reminder of the carnage suffered during those four tumultuous years. While the immediate end of the war might have been triumphant in nature, its subsequent anniversaries were not about celebrating. It was, and remains, about remembering. That's what this day is about. In the silence, in what is supposed to be the hour of triumph, we collectively remember the sacrifices made by those who came before us, we think about the stark reality of war, we feel for our common humanity and year after year we feel one final agony bequeathed to us by the Great War, one last remnant that does not seem to fade away.

This tradition of remembrance to commemorate, and crucially not to celebrate victory, began immediately on the anniversary of the armistice and has carried on every year since. For example, Delapre Primary School, on 11th November 1920, observed a two-minute silence, after which the headmaster gave a short talk on the meaning of the day. The following year, the children of Guilsborough Primary School gathered together in a room where they "reverently observed" the two-minute silence. After saluting the Union Jack, reciting the national anthem and singing hymns, the children received a talk from the headmaster on the significance of Remembrance Day. Every school, business and social group across Northamptonshire and indeed the entire country still commemorates this day in a similar manner.

Figure 10.3: (Right) A veteran lays a wreath at the Cenotaph in the gardens of the Church of St Peter, Raunds.

Figure 10.4: (Below) A large crowd fills the gardens of the Church of St Peter as the sun sets on a beautiful remembrance afternoon event in Raunds.

Figure 10.5: A choir performs in Holy Cross Church, Milton Malsor, during a special remembrance concert on Saturday, 10th November 2018.

Figure 10.6: St Lawrence's Church hosts the Towcester Choral Society and the Towcester Studio Band for a 100th anniversary remembrance concert on Saturday, 10th November 2018.

Figure 10.7: A remembrance concert at the unique Church of the Holy Sepulchre, Northampton, with the audience and performers circled around the towering pillars.

On the centenary of the armistice, dozens of ceremonies were held in villages and towns across Northamptonshire. There is nothing particularly unique about this. Each year, remembrance services are reliably held and well attended. What marked 2018 as particularly special was the number of extra events that took place in the run-up to the hundredth anniversary of the end of the war. Church services, concerts and readings too numerous to list here occurred all across the county.

Saturday night was a busy evening across the country. In Towcester, a collaboration of the Towcester Choral Society and Towcester Studio Band performed a concert in St Lawrence's Church in front of a sold-out crowd. Six miles away in Milton Malsor, an audience gathered at Holy Cross Church was serenaded with an array of popular wartime songs. In Northampton, tucked away just a stone's throw from the town centre, the Church of the Holy Sepulchre held a remembrance concert. With the audience circled around the band, the setting of the Holy Sepulchre made for a unique atmosphere. One of only four surviving medieval round churches in England, the Holy Sepulchre was also the regimental church for the Northamptonshire Regiment, and the military tradition carries on in the modern day. The link is clear as the Northamptonshire Regimental flag and motifs are proudly displayed inside the church.

This book is really only a beginning. The topics and stories contained in these pages barely scratch the surface of how the war dramatically changed Northamptonshire in four years. Nor does the book cover every experience, every defeat, every victory or every casualty of the Northamptonshire Regiment.

Part of the explanation for this book's limitations are the dates covered, 1914 to 1918. For both the men who fought in the war and the towns that were completely transformed by it, the impact of the war lasted far beyond 11th November 1918. No truer is this for the families of the 5,620 men from the regiment, 1,700 from Northampton alone, who were killed during the war; the pain caused by their deaths kept alive in the hearts of their grieving relatives.

Even the dates this book has covered contain insufficient detail on a range of issues. This book only touches upon the thousands of men and women who worked countless hours in boot factories, the nurses and doctors working to exhaustion attempting to heal broken men, and the experiences of the ordinary households in Northampton who took in 16,000 men from the Welsh battalion at the start of the war. Sadly it was not possible to cover the Northamptonshire men placed in other regiments who travelled as far as Iraq and India.

This book could certainly be improved, but it is unlikely to ever be perfect. The problem is intrinsic to the task. As Samuel Hynes has argued in his book *The Soldiers' Tale: Bearing Witness to Modern War*, the First World War was simply too vast for human minds to grasp: "Our imaginations simply can't encompass all those armies on all those battlefields." This war was fought by almost every country in the world. In each of those countries, almost every section of their society was affected. It is little wonder, then, that the war's legacy has been prone to gross

Figure 10.8: Father Oliver Cross delivering a speech during the Remembrance Service at All Saints' Church, Northampton.

simplification and vacuous myths, whether that be a 'just, moral war' fought for the good of civilisation, or a pointless war with 'lions led by donkeys'.

The truth is rarely so absolute. This book has strived to present detail not only accurately, but also objectively, providing the reader with a brief but sensible overview of the debates surrounding the legacy of the war. Where possible, common myths have been challenged with clear evidence, most notably in Chapter 5 regarding the tribunal system and conscription. The wider context that Northamptonshire and its regiment were living in has also been discussed on occasion, for example, the Shells Scandal in Chapter 3, in the attempt to give the reader a broader perspective on developments in the war and how they affected the county.

It is regrettable that Chapter 8, the Northamptonshire Regiment's actions in Gallipoli, Egypt and Palestine are recounted and treated, to a degree, separately from the main narrative. This might mislead the reader into thinking this theatre of war was of secondary importance, which was certainly not the case. The Palestine campaign featured prominently in the local press with the same fervour and calls for transparency from the authorities during key moments as any incident on the Western Front. In addition, the adventures of the 4th Northamptons were perhaps the most thrilling and dramatic of the regiment, involving marches across deserts and capturing historic cities in the Holy Land. Only to aid this book's structure and flow was a separate chapter devoted to the 4th Northamptons' actions.

This book has, above all, attempted to humanise the thousands of soldiers of the Northamptonshire Regiment and communicate their stories, whether that is through personal accounts, such as the diaries of Alexander Morley in Chapter 5 or Cyril Day in Chapter 7, or through stark descriptions of warfare, such as the Somme in Chapter 4 or the Dunes Disaster in Chapter 6. It is unfortunate so few primary sources exist from Northamptonshire soldiers that more could not be included. We must not forget what millions of young men with very real hopes and aspirations went through.

That is why certain chapters that are more 'battle heavy' may feel rather repetitive to some readers. A bombardment commences as soldiers get ready to charge. A battalion goes 'over the top'. The battalion suffers heavy casualties and retreats. The enemy then make a counter-attack, entering No Man's Land before they too get repelled and suffer casualties. And repeat. For days, weeks, months and years. If part of the narrative in this book seems repetitive, that is the point. The war, after the initial German march and retreat from Mons, was extremely repetitive. The soldiers who had to go 'over the top' knew, despite rallying calls from superior officers about an imminent breakthrough, the stark reality that awaited them. They lived and fought in conditions we cannot begin to fathom, and this book attempts to recount their experiences. Despite the conditions, despite the bleakest and most desperate situations imaginable, what has been striking throughout the research for this book is that simple values of kindness, decency and compassion have been a constant presence always shining through the darkness. This is perhaps best illustrated by the case of Johann Riesberg. This young German soldier, who passed away while a prisoner of war being treated at Duston War Hospital, was buried with full military honours at Billing Road, Northampton, at the height of the Somme battle.

If a personal opinion may be permitted in this book, and one that is best exemplified by the respectful funeral of Riesberg, it is that even in the worst excesses of mankind, humanity can emerge triumphant.

Figure 10.9: All Saints' Church gardens, Northampton.

EPILOGUE   255

Bibliography

Chapman, C.R. and S Richard Moss (2012). *Detained in England 1914-1920 : Eastcote POW Camp Pattishall, a brief, illustrated history*. Dursley: Lochin Publishing.

Crutchley, C. (1980). *Shilling a day soldier*. Bognor Regis: New Horizon.

Emsley, C. (2008). Violent crime in England in 1919: post-war anxieties and press narratives. *Continuity and Change*, 23(1), pp.173–195. doi:10.1017/s026841600800670x.

Goldstein, D.M. and Maihafer, H.J. (2004). *America in World War I : the story and photographs*. Washington, D.C.: Brassey's.

Greenall, R.L. (1976). *Old Northamptonshire in photographs*. Northampton: Northamptonshire Libraries.

Greenall, R.L. (1979). *Northamptonshire life, 1914-39 : a photographic survey*. Northampton: Northamptonshire Libraries.

Greenhalgh, E. (2008). *Victory through coalition : Britain and France during the First World War*. Cambridge: Cambridge University Press.

Hammerton, J.A. (1915). *The war illustrated album de luxe : the story of the great European War told by camera, pen and pencil* ; edited by J.A. Ha3mmerton. London: Amalgamated Press.

Holloway, W.H. (2008). *Northamptonshire and the Great War*. Uckfield, East Sussex: Naval & Military Press.

Hudson (2015). *The Northamptonshire Regiment, 1914-1918*. Uckfield, East Sussex: Naval & Military Press.

Jukes, G., Simkins, P. and Hickey, M. (2003). *The First World War*. Oxford: Osprey.

Kenyon, D. (2007). *British Cavalry on the Western Front 1916-1918*. Cranfield: University of Cranfield.

McDermott, J. (2011). *British military service tribunals, 1916-1918 : 'a very much abused body of men'*. Manchester: Manchester University Press.

Sawford, P. (2015). *Northampton : remembering 1914-18*. Stroud, Gloucestershire [UK]: The History Press.

The New York Times current history : the European war. Vols. 1-10. (1917). New York: New York Times Co.

The Northamptonshire Regiment (1914a). *War Diary, 1st Battalion*.

The Northamptonshire Regiment (1914b). *War Diary, 2nd Battalion*.

The Northamptonshire Regiment (1914c). *War diary, 4th Battalion.*

The Northamptonshire Regiment (1914d). *War Diary, 7th Battalion.*

The Northamptonshire Regiment (1914e). *War Diary, The Yeomanry.*

Turton, K. (2016). *Northampton in the Great War.* Barnsley, South Yorkshire: Pen & Sword Military.

Wyatt, J.D. (1933). *A short history of the Northamptonshire Regiment.* Aldershot: Gale & Polden.

NORTHAMPTONSHIRE RECORD OFFICE SOURCES

The following sources have been used in researching the book. The below contains sources that may not be directly referenced in the book. Abbreviated references are provided which should be sufficient to allow interested parties to locate the source.

Alice Robins, Hospital Poetry. ZB 1230 1+2

Anniversary of the Declaration of War, Programme of Public Meeting, 4th August 1915. ZB 1693-4.

Bonham Brother's Letters to Mother - ZB 556/27/1-22

'British Military Service Tribunals 1916-1918' by James McDermott

Bundle of Papers of the Northants Red Cross Committee - 1914 to 1920 - ZA 6686

Burghley House nurse album. ZB 359-25

Burial Records of Pattishall village. 254 P-11.

Butcher expense book, 45 Bridge Street, Northampton. ZB 1050

Cartwright diary, 1916. CE 346

Crutchley, Charles. *Shilling a Day Soldier*

Daily log of horse work for brewery, ZA 4072

Diary of Arthur Dyden, Canons Ashby. D(CA) 1122

Diary of Cyril Day, 2012/149/1/2

Diary of Private Alexander Morley – ZB 1234/1-4 IN V3130, 32 A-K

Diary of Private Alexander Morley - ZB1234/1-4 IN V3130, 32 A-K

Disinfectant adverts. ZA 7770

Ecton Soldier Pictures. WW1114p-230.

Instructions for the Civil Population in the event of a Landing by the Enemy in this Country, guidance issued to population. PZ 7156

Jackson, Peter. (1975). *The Glorious Sixth; A day to day history, recording the movements of the 6th Battalion Northamptonshire Regiment in the Great War, 1914-1918*. ROP 1431

L W Dickens news articles. ZB 667-10-60

Letter from Private Jarvis, 3rd Northamptonshire Battalion. ZB 1497

Local Food Control Minute Book 1917 - 1920 – NPL 3046

Midwife casebook from 1916. YZ 9619

Northamptonshire Casual Wards Hospital Network. Map 3594.

Northamptonshire Yeomanry Scrapbook. NY 2/4

Northamptonshire Yeomanry, 'In Action as Cavalry' by J A Townsend. NY 3/3

Northamptonshire Yeomanry, 8th Division Map, Feb 1915, Neuve Chapelle. NY 5/1.

Northamptonshire Yeomanry, Henry Simmons Scrapbook. NY 2/7.

Northamptonshire Yeomanry, Operation Order No. 30, NY 11/5

Northamptonshire Yeomanry, Regimental Scrapbook. NY 2/6

Northamptonshire Yeomanry, Soldiers' certificates. NY 11/7

Nursing Appeal Leaflet, Medicine. Box X266.

Official Programme of the Peace Celebrations, 19th July 1919. ZB 810/1

Pension certificate. ZA 7770

Provision of Meals for Land Workers - Sample Menus

Soldiers' letters home. Z9489

Thomas, Maurice. *The Women's Land Army (Translation by Tricia Holmes, Jan 1999)*. ROP 3007.

Tribunal papers. X204

War Agricultural Committee Tribunal. X4209.

Wellingborough Cottage Hospital, Annual Report 1918. ZB 1685.

Women in Agriculture. YZ 9619

NEWSPAPERS

The Northampton Chronicle

The Northampton Independent

The Northampton Mercury

SCHOOLS

Blatherwyckle Log Book - 1897 - 1926 - SLB/12

Blisworth - Northamptonshire County Council Education Committee Minute Book – ML 2317 (a)

Bugbrooke School Letters 1907-1914

Burton Latimer Infant School - 1898 - 1918 - Log Book - SLB/14

Burton Latimer Infant School - 1898 - 1918 - Log Book - SLB/15

Campbell Square School 1914-1921 - Log Book - ML 2670 - ZB 115/1

Campbell Square School Log Book 1914-1921 – ML 2670

Delapre Primary School, Far Cotton, Northampton, private archive

Guilsborough CEVA Primary School, Guilsborough, private archive

The Bliss Charity School, Nether Heyford, private archive

Wellingborough Winstanley Road Infants School - 1873 - 1917 - SLB/166

INDEX

NORTHAMPTONSHIRE IN THE FIRST WORLD WAR